This book is for people concerned with groups and with what can go wrong with organizations and groups. But it is intended to be a scientific work and not a kind of handy manual for leaders. The approach is that of the engineer who was called to repair a boiler. He found a stuck valve, rapped it sharply and restored service. He submitted a bill for $100. The owner said that was a lot for a single hammer blow; he requested an itemized statement. The engineer wrote back: "Hitting boiler with hammer, $1.00. Knowing where to hit, $99." That is to say that 99 per cent of the text is devoted to a practical understanding of how real organizations work, since knowing this is what makes the therapy of ailing groups possible.

—From the Introduction

Also by Eric Berne, M.D.
Published by Ballantine Books:

Transactional Analysis in Psychotherapy

A Layman's Guide to Psychotherapy and
    Psychoanalysis

Games People Play

Beyond Games and Scripts

THE STRUCTURE
AND DYNAMICS
OF ORGANIZATIONS
AND GROUPS

Eric Berne, M. D.

BALLANTINE BOOKS • NEW YORK

ISBN 0-345-28473-9

This edition published by arrangement with Grove Press, Inc.

Manufactured in the United States of America

First Ballantine Books Edition: September 1973
Fourth Printing: September 1979

TO MY ONLY SISTER GRACE

"Observations on my reading history, in Library, May Nineteenth, Seventeen Hundred Thirty-One

That the great affairs of this world, the wars, revolutions, etc., are carried on and effected by parties

That the view of these parties is their present general interest, or what they take to be such

That the different views of these different parties occasion all confusion

That while a party is carrying on a general design, each man has his particular private interest in view

That as soon as a party has gained its general point, each member becomes intent upon his particular interest; which, thwarting others, breaks that party into divisions, and occasions more confusion."

—BENJAMIN FRANKLIN

Preface

The object of the author in this book is to offer a systematic framework for the therapy of ailing groups and organizations. The use of the system in practice is demonstrated in Part I by the analysis in some detail of a single group meeting. In Part II a group model based on historical considerations and the observation of contemporary groups is set up, and its practical applications are illustrated. Part III is a consideration of the real individual as a member of groups and organizations and his anxieties and operations when faced with the emotional complexities of personal relationships. This section is based on the principles of transactional analysis, which are more fully discussed in my previous book, *Transactional Analysis in Psychotherapy* (New York, Grove Press, 1961). Part IV includes a chapter for group therapists and some examples of the direct application of the system to the therapy of ailing groups and organizations. There are two appendices, one devoted to the literature of group dynamics and the other to a classification of social aggregations. Finally, there is a glossary.

This study is based on a schedule of leading, observing and participating in groups over a period of 19 years, as well as teaching and supervising group therapists and acting as consultant to leaders of ailing groups and organizations of various kinds. This included experience with about 5000 shifting situations of different types with the Army, the Navy, the Veterans Administration, the California State Hospital and Correctional systems, municipal, county and private community service agencies, the University of California and Stanford University. The responsibilities and pleasures of everyday living have also offered learning opportunities in private psychiatric practice, politics, athletics, religion, education, science, the classroom, the courtroom, the theatre, at the buffet and around the campfire.

The ideas presented here have been under almost continuous critical review since their first presentation in 1953, mostly in San Francisco: at the Veterans Administration Mental Hygiene Clinic, Mount Zion Hospital, Langley-Porter Neuropsychiatric Clinic, Stanford Psychiatric Clinic and a section of the Human Research Unit from Fort Ord, and at the San Francisco Social Psychiatry Seminars, where the therapy of ailing groups has been pursued most systematically.

The ideal throughout has been to order the facts observed in a way that would be useful in the rough and tumble of practice where people play for keeps. Personal observations in many different countries have been compared with material in the literature and the experiences of others. Although the clinical view predominates, a wider audience, even beyond the social sciences, has been kept in mind, including undergraduates and laymen who have organizational responsibilities. The language has been kept as simple as possible, and technical terms are defined in the glossary. Notes have been appended where indicated for academic reasons and documentation, as much for the writer's pleasure as for the reader's edification, so that no one need feel obligated to read them unless he enjoys them.

SEMANTICS

"Is" and its cognates, in appropriate contexts, mean: "has been, in every case in my experience." "Seems to be" and "appears to be" mean: "has been, in the few cases seen so far." "He" in general statements refers to both sexes. The clinical vocabulary does not go beyond an introductory course in abnormal psychology.

One important reservation should be kept in mind. It is fashionable nowadays to speak of "the group" with unwarranted concreteness. Whether such an animal really exists is debatable. The expression is used here only as a concession to facilitate discussion and conceptual manipulation. As a reminder of this, "a group" (as a collective) is often substituted. The distinction is analogous to that between "the Allied troops" (with all their equipment, apparatus and potentialities) and "a party of friendly soldiers."

The writer prefers to use the word "however" like the Latin *autem,* never at the beginning of a clause; in this book, however, he has deferred to the editor's preferences in this and other matters of style.

ERIC BERNE

*Carmel-by-the-Sea, California
and Chichicastenango, Guatemala*

Acknowledgments

Thanks are due first of all to my parents, who bequeathed me the genes and the upbringing which sustain my curiosity about people and their problems and to my urge to do something about it. Hundreds of students and patients offered the stimulation and the material which enabled me to carry out this commitment as far as it has gone. Of the many teachers who influenced my thinking and feeling (and here I am name-dropping, getting considerable satisfaction from having had the privilege of knowing them), the most meaningful have been Professor Eugen Kahn, the late Dr. Paul Federn and Prof. Erik Erikson. In a more informal way I am indebted to Drs. Nathan Ackerman, Martin Grotjahn and Benjamin Weininger.

I am particularly grateful to those who provided special opportunities to present these ideas for discussion, especially Dr. Donald Shaskan of the Veterans Administration Mental Hygiene Clinic in San Francisco, Dr. Norman Reider of Mount Zion Hospital, San Francisco, Dr. Francis Palmer, formerly of the Human Research Unit at Fort Ord and now of the Social Science Research Council, Dr. M. Robert Harris of the Langley-Porter Clinic, and Drs. Seymour Kolko and others of the Stanford Psychiatric Clinic. All of these are men of outstanding generosity, who repeatedly invited me to speak whether or not they always agreed with me.

Dr. R. J. Starrels I thank for the interest he showed right from the beginning, Dr. Bruno Klopfer for his continued interest, Dr. Martin Steiner for having organized the first seminars at Mount Zion, Mrs. Gene Prescott, who started what later evolved into the San Francisco Social Psychiatry Seminars, and Miss Viola Litt, whose administrative abilities have kept the Seminars going.

Then there are the "nuclear" people, who came or continue to come to discuss and present week after week, year after year; besides Dr. Starrels and Miss Litt this group includes (in Carmel) Dr. David Kupfer, Dr. Herbert Wiesenfeld and Miss Anita Wiggins; and (in San Francisco) Mr. Melvin Boyce, Mr. William Collins, Mr. Joseph Concannon, Mr. Harold Dent, Dr. Franklin Ernst, Dr. Kenneth Everts, Miss Margaret Frings, Dr. Gordon Gritter, Mrs. Frances Matson, Mrs. Mary Michelson, Dr. Ray Poindexter, Miss Barbara Rosenfeld, Dr. John Ryan, Mrs. Myra Schapps, Dr. Claude Steiner and Dr. Robert Wald. Finally, there is Dr. Hubert Coffey, of the University of California in Berkeley, to whom I am most grateful for a careful review of an earlier draft. There are about 200 others who have discussed the material, so that I can only apologize for not naming everyone who has been helpful.

Those who helped in the preparation of the manuscript are my secretary, Mrs. Allen Williams, my son Peter and my daughter Ellen. But because people learn the practical aspects of group dynamics when they are very, very young, this book is dedicated to my only sibling.

ERIC BERNE

Contents

PART I
An Illustrative Analysis of a Group Meeting

PART II
The Group As A Whole

PART III
The Individual in the Group

PART IV
Applied Social Psychiatry

Part 1

An Illustrative Analysis of
a Group Meeting

INTRODUCTION

This book is for people concerned with groups and with what can go wrong with organizations and groups. But it is intended to be a scientific work and not a kind of handy manual for leaders. The approach is that of the engineer who was called to repair a boiler. He found a stuck valve, rapped it sharply and restored service. He submitted a bill for $100. The owner said that was a lot for a single hammer blow; he requested an itemized statement. The engineer wrote back: "Hitting boiler with hammer, $1.00. Knowing where to hit, $99." That is to say that 99 per cent of the text is devoted to a practical understanding of how real organizations work, since knowing this is what makes the therapy of ailing groups possible.

The application follows naturally for those who know how to use psychological tools when they are available or are willing to learn through practice. The plan is first to analyze an illustrative group (Part I); then to consider groups in general (Part II) and the situation of the individual (Part III); finally, some simple applications in consulting practice are demonstrated in Part IV. The language is kept as simple as clarity allows in a technical work of this kind (except in the notes). Words that are used in a special sense can be looked up in the glossary at the end of the book if their meanings are not clear or have been forgotten.

It will be shown later that social aggregations can be sorted into several different types according to their structures. The terms "group" and "organization" will be used here to refer only to aggregations which contain at least two classes of people, in general called "the leadership" and "the membership." An organization may be considered as merely a more complicated type of group. Since "groups" of only two people have characteristics all their own, it will be easier if they are not included in the discussion.

When anyone proposes to consider a particular organization or group, the first question should be: "What

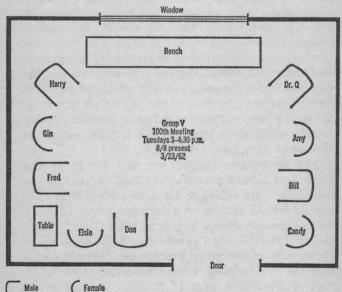

FIG. 1. A psychotherapy group—seating diagram.

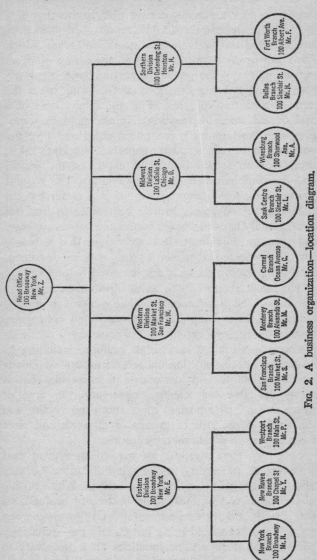

FIG. 2. A business organization—location diagram.

and whom does it actually consist of?" In the case of a small group, the answer may be represented most conveniently and instructively in a location diagram, which shows the position of the places in the group quarters and the names of the people occupying them. If an actual meeting is being described, the drawing takes the form of a seating diagram (Fig. 1). In the case of a large organization, the location diagram may look something like the familiar organization chart and give the locations of branches, posts, churches, stations, ships, aircraft or units; and again, the names of the people who are stationed at each place (Fig. 2). The request for such a diagram serves notice that it is preferable not to talk about imaginary groups but rather to find out what actually happened or is happening between certain real specific individuals. It is important that a blackboard be provided whenever a group is being discussed, even if, in addition, charts are prepared beforehand.

The small group chosen as an illustration here is a meeting which was attended some years ago by the writer and two group-minded professional colleagues. Its unusual interest lies first in its conciseness, since its life span was limited to a single evening, including its involuntary decomposition under external stress. This is an unpredictable and instructive phenomenon that is rarely available for scientific observation in time of peace and offers important hints about the vitality and the ability to survive of groups of all sorts and sizes from nations to psychotherapy groups.

Secondly, most meetings are carried on with at least a veneer of rationality, making it difficult to be sure about what is going on under the surface. While casting about for a meeting that would be free of professional artifacts found in experimental and psychotherapy groups and yet would bring out clearly the archaic aspects of the members' personalities (it is necessary to know about this if one is to understand what is happening in a group), the invitation to make a tape-recording of a spiritualist meeting was a welcome opportunity. The proceedings fulfilled the desired conditions: they were both spontaneous and archaic. In addition, because of the primitive character of the proceedings, the methods used by the leader in exploiting these archaic aspects were also more obvious than in any other situation we had encountered. Anyone can observe these characteristics for himself, since similar meetings are held almost every night in nearly every country in the Western world. It is important to add that the invitation was both extended and received with honor and good faith on both sides and without cynicism or subterfuge on either. Our position as skeptics and group dynamicists was declared and accepted from the beginning. Hence, we felt ethically free to present the tape-recording at several different group-dynamics seminars where it was thoroughly dissected and discussed.

Because the formulations are intended to apply to any group whatsoever (as defined), regardless of its size or purpose, examples will also be drawn from more familiar and conventional material such as history and politics, business and scientific organizations and psychotherapy groups.

Throughout the book aliases have been used when indicated. In his role as leader or member of a group, the writer is given the name of "Dr. Q" to avoid clumsy sentence constructions in the text.

1

Analysis of the Events in Sequence

ASSEMBLING THE GROUP

Before any group can come into being, it must first exist, however briefly, as an idea in the mind of its organizer. This picture of what kind of congeries is planned may be called the provisional group imago; if there is more than one organizer, this becomes a collective fantasy. In fact, anyone who wishes to become a member of any group has such a set of expectations. However, he may not be aware of their existence until he is confronted with the reality, which almost always differs in some way from his fantasy. From the resulting surprise, anxiety or disappointment he learns, if he did not know it before, that he did have specific expectations, which now must go through a process of adjustment to the actual situation in which he finds himself.

In connection with the relatively small group—the spiritualist meeting—whose proceedings form the subject of the first two chapters, the provisional group imago was shared by Mr. Pop Wood, at whose house it was held, Mr. Ken Mead, the medium, and Mrs. Mead, his wife. This imago was destined to be disconcerted several times during the evening. The first occasion was when Dr. Q unexpectedly brought two friends along with him. Since the imago included slots for exactly 10 invited guests, the living room had been arranged to ac-

commodate just that many. At first Mr. Wood seemed
chagrined and treated the friends like intruders. But after being reminded that Dr. Q had mentioned the possibility of bringing two skeptical colleagues, he soon adjusted himself to the situation and adapted the physical
arrangements by bringing in two more chairs.

The case was different in Dr. Q's therapy groups.
Since there he was studying the process of adjustment
itself, it was essential for him to keep his own provisional group imago as flexible as possible. He had
learned through experience to be prepared physically
and psychologically for all sorts of unusual occurrences.
Indeed, the unexpected was and had to be for him not a
contretemps, but a welcome opportunity for learning.

Mr. Wood's assignment in setting up the spiritualist
meeting (which will be called "Group S") was to deal
with the external environment. He selected the candidates for membership in the group from the general
mass of people on the outside. He also procured the
physical equipment, including quarters, utilities, seats
and other necessities and comforts, so that he had to
deal with people such as storekeepers, who were not
candidates or members of the group. It was also his
function to protect the group from intruders by
maintaining the integrity of the external group boundary, which in this case consisted of the walls of his
house. This boundary enclosed a special region into
which only members of the group could be admitted
legitimately. Such people, whose work it is to deal with
the external environment through procurement and recruitment, to see that authorized candidates meet the
admission requirements (in this case, the payment of a
fee), and to maintain the external group boundary
against intruders and disruptive forces, may be called
the external apparatus of the group.

Mr. Wood, like Dr. Q in his groups, performed all
these functions single-handed. In a large organization

the external apparatus may be very complex. In our country, for example, it includes among other things the Office of International Trade, the Consular Service, the Immigration Service, the Diplomatic Service and the Armed Forces. In a relatively small organization, such as a scientific society, it need only include the president, the secretary, the treasurer and a small staff for choosing candidates for membership.

In performing this last function, Mr. Wood first selected the people whom he considered eligible and then invited them to attend the meeting. Thus, membership in Group S was optional, being based on an invitation that could be declined. On the other hand, membership in a scientific society, while it may be optional, is also conditional, depending on the attainment of certain rigid standards. Membership in a nation is usually either accidental, as by birth, or conditional. Membership in a psychotherapy group is voluntary, since, generally speaking, such a group is open to anyone who applies. None of these memberships is obligatory, as is a prison sentence or a state hospital commitment, since in each case a member is free to resign or cross the external boundary outward into the external environment.

When membership is optional, conditional or voluntary, one of the attractions is that the candidates can expect their neighbors to be people of the same class: people who are interested in spiritualism, physics or opera. Dr. Q had two requirements in this respect. He wanted his neighbors to be interested in both spiritualism and psychiatry. Since he was not sure that he would find such people in Group S when he arrived, he brought along his own subgroup. Everyone in the room belonged to the class of people who were interested in spiritualism, but only he and his friends, Dr. Bell and Dr. Cuppy, belonged to the class who were professionally interested in psychiatry as well.

Thus, the assembling of any group, whatever its object or occasion, requires a provisional group imago. Because of the practical difficulties involved, the first raw fantasy undergoes some preliminary adjustment even before the group comes together. It is necessary to establish at least three items before the group can get under way: an external apparatus, a basis for membership (most poignantly, perhaps, whether it is voluntary or obligatory), and a statement indicating the class of people who will be found there. The last also implies or states the activity in which the group proposes to engage, but in practice this often is less important to prospective members than the statement of class.

THE PRELIMINARY PHASE

Already, it should be evident that a group consists of real people with active imaginations, and that the organizers must be capable of making decisions. After the group begins to assemble, there is an interval between the beginning of the assembly and what the members tend to call "the beginning of the meeting." During this phase, according to the present criteria, the group itself has not yet begun to function, since the distinctions between the leadership and the membership are not operative yet. The gathering now resembles a kind of party, an enclave from which unauthorized persons are excluded, but which lacks internal organization. The difference between this phase and "the beginning of the meeting" is often noted by patients in psychotherapy groups, who ask the therapist, "Why is it that we stop talking as soon as you come into the room?"

Usually, a party is characterized by social rituals and pastimes. At the spiritualist meeting, each new arrival was introduced to all the others present according to the accepted rituals of American (or Northern California) social etiquette. The rest of the time before the meeting began was then passed in various stereotyped conversations. People were getting acquainted—on the surface, by finding mutual interests in time, place, persons, materials, events and activities; underneath, by sizing each other up in the hope of finding someone interesting whom they might like to see again. There was a tendency for people with similar or complementary attitudes, interests or responses to seek each other out and stay together.

During this interval, the situation resembled in many ways an ordinary social gathering such as a tea party. But significant differences were already evident. These people had an agenda in mind, a set of more or less definite expectations, and some of them were comparing those expectations, trying to form some image of what was likely to happen after the meeting began. Their provisional group imagoes were based on fantasies or, in the case of "experts," on previous experiences with spiritualism, and these imagoes were undergoing a preliminary process of adjustment based on what they saw and heard around them. Because of the supernatural overtones, the imagoes were highly charged, and the attempts at adjustment were frequently accompanied by signs of tension, such as restlessness, talkativeness, giggling and withdrawal. These overt symptoms subsided when it became evident that their uncertainties were about to be confronted with realities. The bustling preparations of Mr. Wood and Mr. and Mrs. Mead, which had been carried on independently of the membership, were now directed toward the visitors.

THE ORGANIZATIONAL PHASE

Once the group membership and the physical equipment had been assembled within the external group boundary, Mr. Wood's mission had been accomplished. He now deferred to Mrs. Mead, who seemed to be in charge of the actual task of organization. There were four principal aspects of this work:

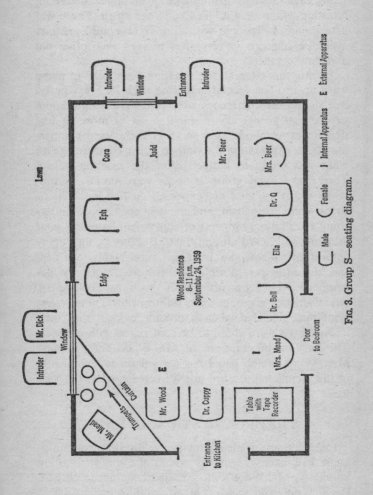

Fig. 3. Group S—seating diagram.

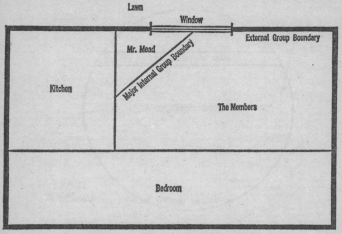

FIG. 4. The major group structure—location diagram.

1. The internal arrangement of physical equipment, such as chairs, lights and tape recorders

2. The separation of Mr. Mead and his insignia of office (his speaking trumpets) from the rest of the group

3. The assignment of regions to individual members (she requested one to sit near the door, another to move over a bit, and two others to trade seats)

4. The sanctioning of special departures from the etiquette of the community at large (she told them that gentlemen could remove their coats).

The seating diagram of the meeting after everyone was seated is shown in Figure 3. The most significant physical feature within the external group boundary was a curtain that separated Mr. Mead from the rest of the group, thus forming the major internal group boundary. The external group boundary (the walls of the house) and the major internal group boundary (the curtain), which separated the leader from the membership, together formed the major group structure (Fig. 4), shown schematically in Figure 5. The assignment of

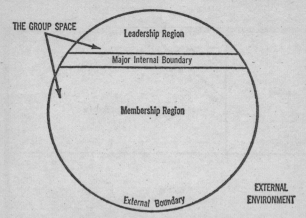

FIG. 5. The major group structure represented
diagramatically.

regions to the individual members was much less important for the outcome of the meeting than was the
major group structure. These assignments determined
the minor group structure, represented by the chairs.
The sanctioning of shirtsleeves was the first convention
of the group etiquette, i.e., those departures from social
etiquette which were permissible within that group.

All these items came within the province of Mrs.
Mead. Such people, who deal with the internal arrangement of physical equipment, the establishment and the
maintenance of internal group boundaries, group etiquette and other matters of internal regulation, may be
called the internal group apparatus. In a complicated
organization such as the United States the internal
group apparatus is very large, and the four functions
performed by Mrs. Mead are divided among a number
of agencies, typified by the General Services Administration, the White House Staff and the Secret Service,
the Department of the Interior and the law courts, respectively. In a business organization or scientific soci-

ety these duties devolve on various executives and committees. In his therapy groups, Dr. Q, like Mrs. Mead, performed them all single-handed.

During the phase of organization, it was noteworthy that Mr. Mead seemed to feel free to interrupt and give directions at any time, and that both Mr. Wood and Mrs. Mead seemed to defer to him. This gave the impression that neither the external nor the internal group apparatus was an independent influence and that both of them were agencies of the leadership. He also expected the general membership to follow his suggestions and to give up their individual seating preferences in favor of proper organization of the group. Indeed, it might be said that he could be picked out as the effective leader because he was the individual whose suggestions were most likely to be followed and whose questions were most likely to be answered.

ESTABLISHING THE LEADERSHIP

Leadership is attained by selection, as in our country; by accession, as in Great Britain; by pre-emption, as in revolutions; or by assumption, as in lecture halls and schoolrooms, where a certain person is assumed by most of the members to be the best qualified individual present. In any case, it is customary to inform the membership of the leader's qualifications. In a republic this is usually done before the election; in an accession, at the time of investiture; in a revolution, during the consolidation; in an assumption, before the proceedings begin, if at all. Such warrants may comprise a set of doctrines, a historical symbol, a show of force or a citation of titles. In most cases the warrants are presented by the morale branch of the internal apparatus, but, in Mr. Mead's case, he preferred to do it himself when he assumed the leadership.

When Mr. Mead began to speak, the public structure of the group had been completed. Any observer could note that the physical arrangements consisted of a room, divided into two regions by a curtain, and some chairs distributed in a certain way (see Fig. 3); that the organizational structure comprised a single leader with an external and an internal apparatus, and 10 more or less undifferentiated members. By proper enquiry he could get the name of the individual who filled each slot in the individual structure. It was not difficult for Mr. Mead to have these three aspects of the public structure (the physical arrangements, the organizational structure and the individual structure) set up according to his specifications. But it was a more delicate matter to try to influence the group imagoes of the members. The idiosyncratic group imago of each individual strongly influences his behavior and reactions in a group. Yet its more intimate aspects are not readily discussed, and, indeed, the individual himself may not be aware of all the characteristics of his own imago. The group imagoes of those present may be called collectively the private structure of the group.

Mr. Mead now took his place beside the trumpets (with the curtain open), and began to exert his efforts toward influencing the private structure of Group S. That is, he presented himself in a way calculated to encourage a certain attitude on the part of each member toward himself. After a few conversational preliminary enquiries, he took a deep breath and began to explain himself in a sonorous and evangelistic tone.

"Before we start out, I want to tell you something. . . . My name is Mead. I've been doing this kind of work since I was a child. Manifestations of various kinds happened to me from the time I was 6 years old, after my mother deserted me. The astral flight has been the most outstanding feature of my existence. I spend half of my time in the invisible world, whether I like it or not. I was told I was to do this work. I've learned many things in the visible and invisible world, many things the ordinary person does not have the opportunity to come in contact with. . . . It all depends on the individual how many planes of consciousness he evolves into. Don't look to me to give you any answers. What comes through will come from spirits, not from me. I am an inspirational speaker. My lectures are outstanding. With God, all things are possible. If people come into a meeting open-mindedly seeking for something worth while, they are going to get it. I can't do anything for you because I'm only furnishing the power. It's very tiring. I don't think there's anything in the world that will take more out of a man than this. But my spirits take care of me pretty well. I have no fear at any time. Please feel free to ask any questions whatsoever that come to your mind."

He went on in this strain for about 15 minutes. His self-description seemed well suited to appeal to certain needs of the members. It corresponded to the kind of leadership which many childlike people seem to want. Skillfully using a combination of drama and seductiveness to appeal to the archaic aspects of the personality, Mr. Mead characterized himself as a prodigy, from childhood on the instrument of supernatural forces that endowed him with magic powers, thus rendering him (he hinted) indefatigable, incorruptible, omnipotent, omniscient, immortal, fearless and invulnerable. He held out to the members the hope that they too could attain some measure of these qualities through him, if they put themselves at the disposal of the primal forces which he represented and adhered to a special canon of feeling and behavior. After he had finished outlining this self-presentation or persona, Mrs. Mead drew the curtain. This was the signal that the function of establishing the leadership was completed and that the group activity was about to begin.

THE GROUP WORK

As a first step in understanding what goes on in a group, it is helpful to categorize the proceedings in some useful way. Everything that happens involves some kind of work, and this group work may be classified according to its results. Whatever furthers or is concerned with furthering the stated purpose of the group is part of the group activity. Whatever changes or is concerned with changing the structure of the group itself is part of the group process. In many situations these two types of work are mutually exclusive. When native plantation workers in the South Pacific dropped their tools to engage in a factional fight, the time spent in fighting interfered with the stated purpose of the group, just as cultivating coconuts postponed the culmination of the quarrel.

After the fight was over, the physical, organizational and individual structure of the gang was the same; they had the same tools, assignments, foreman and co-workers. However, the private structure, i.e., each man's perception of his relationship with the others, was changed as part of the group process. The case is different after a successful revolution, when there is a new leadership, a reorganization of the government and a redistribution of the land; such a decisive event in the internal group process changes the public as well as the private structure of the group.

In a more peaceful situation it may not be so easy to distinguish the work done in the course of the group activity from that done as part of the group process, and a special kind of study is necessary for making this distinction. In Group S, the first spirit who appeared offered a nice blend of activity and process. She was a little girl named Ruby, and, since the stated purpose of the group was to summon spirits, her appearance was part of the group activity. On the other hand, she behaved very sociably and seemed to have the task of helping the members to get to know each other better. She asked them their names and drew out other information from each of them. At the same time she encouraged them to participate actively in what was going on. Meanwhile there were repeated offerings, declarations and reassurances of love between her and the visitors. This series of conjunctive transactions was part of the group process, changing the group by allowing the members to present themselves under favorable conditions and to observe each other in action. Ruby tried to make certain that everyone present became involved in this synthetic function.

THE GROUP CULTURE

During the Ruby phase, several aspects of the group culture began to emerge. This included various devices and procedures for managing (1) the physical world, (2) the social situation, and (3) individual anxieties.

1. The technical culture of a society may range from pottery to sputniks. Within the society, special groups have special equipment which is used in their activities—adding machines, chemicals, crucifixes, stethoscopes, etc. According to Mr. Mead, the technical aspect of the culture of Group S was based on the laws of physics and chemistry, the nature of the materials involved (such as ectoplasm) and their skillful handling. The trumpets, which were used to concentrate the spirit voices, were the most important item in the technical culture of this group.

2. The social situation was kept orderly by means of the group etiquette which, like all etiquette, was based on the social contract. Ruby presented herself as an innocent, sensitive, helpful, affectionate and well-behaved child, and the members respected this persona and treated her accordingly. The members presented them-

selves (or at any rate, Mrs. Mead, in introducing them to Ruby, presented them) as intelligent, serious, friendly students of spiritualism, and Ruby talked to them accordingly. Thus, both parties followed the social contract, which reads: "You scratch my back, and I'll scratch yours," or, more politely, "You respect my persona, and I'll respect yours." However, it was evident that for Group S this contract had its own special provisions. Certain ways of fulfilling it were encouraged, and certain ways of infringing it were permitted. It was proper to reinforce it by calling Ruby endearing names and permissible to infringe on it by questioning her origin, her method of operating and even her powers of divination. These departures from strict formality, which were legitimate there, made up the special etiquette of that particular group.

3. The character of a group arises from the psychological mechanisms which it favors for handling individual anxieties. Obscenity and sarcasm are permissible in criminal societies, for example, and are factors that give such groups their vulgar character. Sexual frankness is encouraged in many psychotherapy groups, provided that it is dealt with intellectually. It was evident that in Group S obscenity, sarcasm and sexual symposiums were all out of place, but it appeared that simple humor and a certain amount of teasing were encouraged. At one point Ruby was interrupted by the voice of a minstrel named Sambo, and Mrs. Mead remarked:

"If you hear someone moving, Sambo, it's just me closing the door because of the draft."

Sambo: "I thought you-all was too ole for de draft. Haw! Haw!" (Much laughter)

And as Ruby was about to depart, Mrs. Mead asked: "Don't you want to talk to Pop?"

Ruby: "No, I talk to him all the time." (Laughter)

Pop: "You don't need to come and make love to me in public, sweetheart." (Laughter)

The sources of these three aspects of the group culture—the technical, the social and the individual—are worth noting. The technical culture requires special skills, such as the manufacture and the use of adding machines, chemicals, stethoscopes and trumpets. The learning of such skills is a matter of objective adult intelligence. The group etiquette is a kind of ethical system, usually based on established traditions, the sort of thing that in families is passed on from parent to child in such matters as greeting rituals, hospitality customs and punctuality, varying from one society and social class to another. In special groups it includes canons or codes of behavior concerning business practices, private communication, scientific honesty and Hippocratic trustworthiness, some of which have been passed on from one generation to another with little basic change for hundreds or thousands of years. The group character allows some opportunity for archaic ways of individual self-expression within the limits of the group etiquette. Hence, the technical culture may be called the rational aspect, the group etiquette the traditional aspect, and the group character the emotional aspect of the group culture.

THE LEADER'S PERSONALITY

It was interesting to observe the series of personas presented by Mr. Mead. First there was the rational, sophisticated adult who gave a brief explanation of the principles of spiritualism; this was Mr. Mead himself. Then came the sensitive, obsequious, innocent child Ruby, followed by the clownish adolescent Sambo. These all paved the way for Dr. Murgatroyd, the principal figure of the evening, who was "materialized" by Mr. Mead in the fatherly role of a wise old teacher, whose pleasure it was to "enlighten those that are seeking for the truth." These components are illustrated in the diagram in Figure 6.

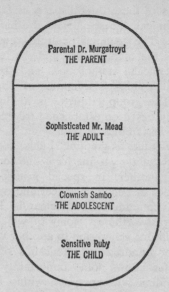

FIG. 6. The personality diagram of a medium.

This personality diagram is no different from that of any other leader. Shifts between rational, childlike, adolescent and fatherly behavior are frequently described in the biographies of heads of states. As parental figures, some were stern and some benevolent; in playful mood, some behaved amicably and some execrably. Some have been more notorious than others for shifting from one state of mind to another. To make acceptable personas out of such psychological realities is a work of art that is divided between the leader himself and the morale branch of his internal group apparatus.

The deepest qualities of leadership depend on certain irrational aspects of the relationship between the leader and the members. The effective leadership of a group may include a number of individuals, sometimes a very large number, who see that things get done. The psychological leader is the individual who, in the minds of the members, is most highly endowed with superior—usually superhuman—characteristics. The special qualities that are attributed to him explicitly or, in the case of a democracy, unconsciously, may be similar to the charisms mentioned in the Bible, such as wisdom, the working of miracles, prophecy and the discerning of spirits. These are the same qualities hinted at by Mr. Mead in his preliminary talk—omniscience, immortality, invulnerability, indefatigability and prodigality. Such attributes make up the *mystique* of leadership, which is preserved in the myths of classical heroes and the legends concerning medieval kings.

In any well-run group, an appearance of the psychological leader is preceded by a build-up. Thus, everything that preceded Dr. Murgatroyd's appearance in Group S is part of the build-up. One of these operations was a series of loud grunts that interrupted Ruby at one point. Mrs. Mead explained that these came from an Indian called Gray Bird, who was putting Mr. Mead in a trance, and Gray Bird himself then explained: "Me put um in trance!" (grunt). Strictly speaking, Ruby, Gray Bird and Sambo were all part of the morale branch of Dr. Murgatroyd's internal apparatus, which was responsible for the build-up. Ruby was his warm-up, Gray Bird was his warrant, and Sambo was his herald, announcing: "Hol' de phone. Heah come Doctuh Murgatroyd!" In show business, the master of ceremonies combines all these functions.

In Group S, Mr. Mead at first operated as the effective leader and presented himself as the psychological leader, but later the psychological leadership was shifted to Dr. Murgatroyd.

THE GROUP PROCESS

Although there was some activity during the build-up, this phase was mainly designed to influence the private structure of the group as represented by the group imagoes of the members. Hence, it was primarily part of the group process. When Dr. Murgatroyd appeared, the group began to work more directly on its official activity, which was to find out about the spiritual environment. Some of the members accepted the activity at face value and proceeded in a matter of fact way to ask questions of Dr. Murgatroyd. Others were more skeptical, and, in some cases, an attitude of hostility could be discerned behind the skepticism. On the surface, the hostile people were doing the same as everyone else—asking questions about the spirit world, but there were signs of stubbornness and slight sarcasm. The proceedings were carried on as an ordinary discussion, and any expressions of emotion were embedded in these factual exchanges. It could be said that in this group, activity and group process were not mutually exclusive; rather, the activity formed a matrix for the process. This dilution of the group process was one purpose of the group etiquette.

The fact that a certain amount of hostile display was allowed by the group culture, so long as it was expressed in the form of pertinent questions, attracted the scientific attention of Dr. Q. Having noted that the activity formed a matrix for hidden or ulterior transactions, he wondered what would happen if someone breached this etiquette by openly asking a question concerned not with the spirit world but with what was going on.

Any member who deliberately disrupts or tries to disrupt the activity of a group by breaching the etiquette may be called an agitator. In order to understand Dr. Q's experiment, it might be helpful to give an extract from the actual proceedings at this point.

Dr. Murgatroyd, who "materialized" after Sambo's announcement, presented the persona of a wordy, pompous sage with an authoritative and turgid voice. He began as follows:

"Good ee-vuhning, this is Dr. Murgatroyd speaking through the body of the mejum. I hope you will all get closer into his vibration and into your vibration . . . it is always a pleasure to enter into the earth vibration, and so I have set aside this tie-yum that we may ask what your questions are." After 15 minutes of such introductory matter, Mrs. Mead, with some difficulty, drew the first question from the audience.

Ella: "At the time of death, how long before one becomes conscious of the life afterwards?"

Dr. Murgatroyd: "It depends entirely upon the een-dee-vid-u-al. For some there is no period of unconsciousness. There are others who hover in the darkness of the afterworld for many years." (10 minutes of this)

Mr. Wood: "I would like to talk to Hermes Trismegistus. Ask him how much history there is to the Pentateuch."

Dr. Murgatroyd: "I cannot see that there would be anything of real value in finding out. Those history books you speak of have been changed so many times that the real and true meaning in the beginning has been lost."

Mr. Wood: "Doctor, if you don't mind, I was trying to get something from Hermes Trismegistus."

Dr. Murgatroyd: "He could not answer you much different."

Mr. Wood: "I would like to know what he says."

Dr. Murgatroyd: "I have given my answer."

Mrs. Mead: "Has someone else a question?"

After further questions, with Mrs. Mead acting as moderator, Dr. Q said: "May I ask a question?"

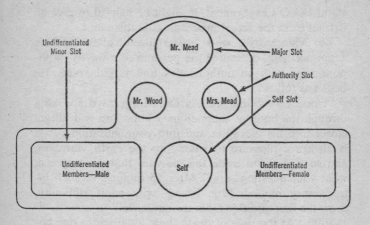

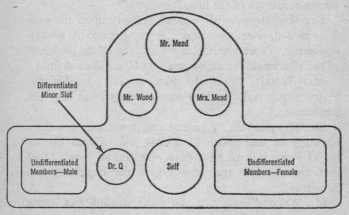

Fig. 7. A *(top)* An initial group imago (of any member). B *(bottom)* The group imago (of any member) following agitation.

Mrs. Mead: "Go ahead."

Dr. Q (blandly): "Is it necessary for us to like you in order for you to stay here?"

Dr. Murgatroyd (startled): "I beg your pardon?"

Dr. Q (blandly): "Is it necessary for us to like you in order for you to stay here?"

Dr. Murgatroyd: "It is not. I can stay here by my own will. I can come and go as I please, regardless of the vibrations which are created by any group of people, individually or collectively."

Dr. Q: "What I really wanted to ask is, why aren't you as nice as Ruby?"

Dr. Murgatroyd: "My dear sir, I am of a more forthright nature. There has to be a positive and negative force in all things of nature."

Dr. Cuppy (soothingly): "You mean that you're more aggressive than Ruby?"

Dr. Murgatroyd: "I do. She is working at a different rate of vibrations."

Up to this point, Dr. Q felt that his experiment confirmed three suppositions that he wanted to test.

1. That a breach of etiquette disturbs the efficiency of a group. That is, preserving the group culture takes precedence over the group activity.

2. That agitation arouses anxiety by threatening the effectiveness of the leadership. Even Dr. Cuppy, who was Dr. Q's guest, rallied to the defence of Dr. Murgatroyd. Experience shows that if this threat is too great, the group will attempt to extrude the agitator.

3. That agitation changes the private structure of the group. There was evidence that Dr. Q now occupied a special position in the group imagoes of the others present. The change is represented in Figure 7, which illustrates the group process at this point. All transactions that change the private structure of the group are part of the group process; conversely, the group process consists of all the transactions that change the private structure of the group, whether or not they also change the public structure.

It should be said that even before he started his "experiment," Dr. Q was already convinced, from hundreds of naturalistic observations, that his suppositions were correct. His action was a demonstration rather than an experiment. Indeed, if an experiment had thrown doubt on the supposition, he would have questioned the experiment rather than his hypothesis (just as a man who thought he had seen birds fly might question experiments that "proved" that they didn't).

But there was something more subtle that interested him. On the surface at least, he kept strictly to the group etiquette. His tone was bland and matter of fact, and his questions could be interpreted either as asking for information about the spirit world or as slighting Dr. Murgatroyd's persona. This introduced an element of suspense. Dr. Murgatroyd must have suspected that he might make a fool of himself if he jumped to conclusions and gave way to indignation which Dr. Q could claim to be unjustified.

Dr. Q allowed about 10 minutes to pass before he began the second phase of his investigation. Then he requested permission to ask another question.

Dr. Murgatroyd : "Yes, you may."

Dr. Q (blandly): "Why don't you go away and let Ruby come back?"

Mr. Wood (angrily): "Ruby is just a little girl. And he's trying hard to answer our questions."

Ella, Eph, Eddy and the others (indignantly): "That's rude! That's rude!"

Dr. Murgatroyd (in an injured tone): "I am doing my best to please you, but there is a lack of appreciation here. You feel I am not doing well enough!"

Mrs. Mead: "You're doing fine, doctor."

Dr. Cuppy and Dr. Bell (muttering to each other): "His feelings are hurt."

Mrs. Mead: "Yes, his feelings are hurt. Let's go ahead."

Dr. Q: "I'd like to have him answer the question."

There is a long silence. Then Dr. Murgatroyd says stiffly: "What is the question?"

Dr. Q: "Why don't you go away and let Ruby come back?"

Dr. Murgatroyd (righteously): "I am doing my best." (Pause) "I will say to all of you that I feel as though you are getting disturbed. I wonder why none of you have asked about flying saucers." (Here follows a long monologue about flying saucers.)

It is apparent from these proceedings that as Dr. Q became bolder, his suppositions were more dramatically verified than before. This second phase may be described as follows. A member breaks the social contract by challenging the persona of another member in a way which is not permitted by the etiquette of the particular group. Such an operation is called rudeness. Since in this case the rudeness was not merely personal but was deliberately intended to disrupt the activity of the group, the rude person must be called an agitator. The agitation was directed against the leadership in an attempt to disrupt the major group structure, and that kind of agitation is called revolutionary.

The consequences of this revolutionary agitation follow the principle that the need to preserve its own major structure takes precedence over all other work of the group. The major structure of a group, i.e., its external boundary and its major internal boundary, are threatened respectively by war and by civil war, both of which are intrusive operations. In war, an external force attempts to intrude through the external boundary, and in civil war an internal force attempts to intrude through the major internal boundary. These are the two most critical events in the life of any group. When Dr. Q went on with the second phase of his operation, the need of the group to preserve its own structure predominated over everything else, and the following things happened.

1. The efficiency of the group in regard to its activity dropped close to zero. Transactions were more direct and were no longer embedded in material. The intensity of the group process and the efficiency of the group activity had an inverse relationship. The more indignation there was, the less information came out about the spirit world.

2. Momentarily, Dr. Murgatroyd's leadership was not only threatened but suspended. That aroused some strong feelings as the members tried to cut short the agitation and restore the previous structure of the group. During this special mobilization of the group forces, many personas were thrown off, and the direct transactions that took place revealed to some extent the previously masked underlying personalities of those engaged and their psychological rather than their "official" relationships. Dr. Murgatroyd temporarily abandoned his role of leader in the organizational structure of the group and cast off his heroic persona to reveal a sensitive, injured personality. Some of the others abandoned their roles of disciples and cast off their personas of sincere truth-seekers to reveal indignant, defensive or "therapeutic" personalities. The relationships of these three aspects are illustrated in Table 1, where it will be noted that roles, as elements of the organizational structure, and personas, as elements of the individual structure, are both components of the public structure; while personalities belong to the private structure.

3. There could be little doubt that in the private structure Dr. Q was now sharply differentiated from everyone else. In most cases the slot that he occupied in the group imagoes of the other members became highly charged with hostility.

These events, which were all part of the internal group process, illustrate what can happen when an activity group is transformed into a process group.

TABLE 1. THE STRUCTURE OF A GROUP

NATURE	TYPE	REPRESENTATION	MATERIAL
Physical	Physical arrangement	Schedule	Space, time, volume, equipment
Public {	Organizational structure	Organization chart	Roles
	Individual structure	Location diagram	Personas
Private	Psychodynamic structure	Group imago	Personalities

THE MINOR GROUP PROCESS

It has been said already that when he attacked the leadership, Dr. Q was threatening the major group structure and, hence, the very existence of the group. Such a conflict is part of the major group process, as illustrated in Figure 8. The next episode did not directly involve the leadership but represented a localized struggle between two members.

Mrs. Beer wanted to make certain that Mr. Mead was in a trance. She asked Mrs. Mead for permission to

FIG. 8. The major internal group process.

see him, and it was granted. Mr. Wood turned on a
faint glimmer of light, and Mrs. Beer went over and
peered at the medium. She stood a long time looking at
this manifestation of leadership until both Mrs. Mead
and Mr. Wood began to get impatient, whereupon Mr.
Wood said irritably:

"You can see him from there, for heaven's sake.
You can see him, can't you? He looks like a man sitting there."

Mrs. Beer glared her displeasure at this interference
but said nothing. Dr. Murgatroyd let the contention go
on without making any attempt to stop it, for it did not
threaten the major structure of the group. This type of
conflict was part of the minor group process, since it affected only the minor structure of the group, as shown
in Figure 9. The major group process is like a civil
war, while the minor process is like a local dispute between two states or provinces, in which the Central
Government need not intervene. In this case the conflict centered around the fact that Mr. Wood wanted to

continue with the talking, while Mrs. Beer preferred looking.

THE EXTERNAL GROUP PROCESS

After Dr. Murgatroyd had been on the scene for about an hour, he said farewell and departed. Mrs. Mead then led the group in singing "Let Me Call You Sweetheart!" This brought Ruby back on the scene. Ruby was in contact with various spirits and offered to exchange messages between them and the members of the group.

"I'm talking to your grandma, Cora. There's also a young man in uniform here who was killed. His name is Jimmy."

She paused for someone to claim Jimmy, and Ella finally said, "I know the young man you're talking about. What does he say?"

About this time, there was some disturbance on the lawn outside the house. No one seemed to pay much attention except Ruby and Dr. Q. Ruby asked who was

Fig. 9. The minor internal group process.

there, and Mrs. Mead reassured her that it was just the door rattling. Ruby proceeded to offer a message from Professor Freud to Dr. Bell. In the midst of this, there was a knock on the front door, and a new voice said: "Open the door. It's the police."

At this point, Mr. Wood left the meeting to find out what was going on. Rather unexpectedly, Judd, who was a reporter on the local newspaper, followed him. The rest of the group acted as if nothing were amiss. Ruby proceeded to ask if anyone knew a woman called Yvette. While they were discussing the problem of whom Yvette belonged to, the lights were turned on in the kitchen and loud voices could be heard, so loud that they could no longer be ignored.

Ruby: "I'm afraid I'll have to go. I'll have to bring daddy out of the trance."

Many voices: "Good-by, Ruby! Good night, honey! God bless you, sweetheart!"

These farewells were followed by groans and creaks from Mr. Mead's corner. There were thumps and heavy boots in the kitchen. Mr. Wood could be heard asking someone to go slowly. "It's bad to bring him out so fast." A few minutes later the lights went on in the living room and the kitchen door opened, revealing three strangers who were looking at the names in the Guest Book, which each visitor had signed on entering. Some of the members walked in to confront them.

Cora (indignantly): "I'll stand on my constitutional rights!"

Mr. Wood: "Who turned us in? Look at that man with the flashlight camera. They came prepared for bear." (To Cora): "Did he get your name?"

Cora: "I don't care if he got *my* name, I'm going to get *his* name!"

1st Plain-clothes man: "I'm Officer Dick. Somebody might be required to have a licence to conduct this. Is Mr. Mead an ordained minister?"

Mrs. Mead: "You can look in the county register. It's recorded."

Dr. Q (to second policeman): "What are you people trying to do here?"

While the organizers, Dr. Q and his friends and a few others stayed to talk to the policemen, the rest had fled. They did not get far, since they were picked up by two police officers who had been stationed outside the house for just that purpose.

It will be noted that the police represented an unpredictable, autonomous, powerful force from the external environment. Such influences, which threaten the structure of a group from without, represent a special class of forces which are of decisive significance in the history of any group. An invading army, a hurricane or an order from higher authority are all representatives of this class. Since again the first task of a group is to ensure its own survival, all other work tends to be suspended in the face of an external threat, and the group mobilizes its energies to engage in the external group process, as represented in Figure 10. A group in this state may be called a combat group. In dire straits, if the will of the group to survive is strong, the whole membership is drawn into the external apparatus and devotes its energies directly or indirectly to fighting the threatening external environment.

Group S first tried to deal with the threat by ignoring it. But such an active force cannot be ignored. Sooner or later it has to be met. Mr. Wood, as the external apparatus, initially tried to meet it on the lawn outside the external group boundary. When the police penetrated this, he then tried to hold them off from Mr. Mead's curtain, the major internal group boundary and so long as he succeeded in doing that, the group activity proceeded, albeit with some loss of efficiency. It was not until the leadership was seriously threatened that the group broke up. The will to survive of this particular group was not very great, and the members never rallied effectively into a combat group. When Mr. Mead resigned his leadership, the structure of the group disintegrated. Such a sequence of events, resulting from the application of external force, may be called disruption. Here the leadership and its apparatus, which had withstood internal attacks from individual operations, gave way before the assault of external necessity. With the group structure destroyed, there was no longer any effective boundary between the group and the invaders, so that the intruding party mingled freely with the members and even with the leadership. The group had decomposed into an unstructured enclave within which it was every man for himself, since there was no organized resistance. In this case the external disruptive force was represented by the internal apparatus or police force of the community at large.

It was discovered later that the situation arose from a clash of principles or canons. According to the rumor, it was Judd, the reporter, who was alleged to have arranged the raid, after having himself included as

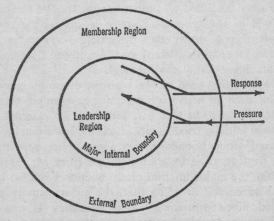

FIG. 10. The external group process.

a member so that he could get a good story. He acted as an agent who had been delegated by another kind of group to penetrate the external boundary of Group S for ulterior purposes. It is noteworthy that everyone concerned acted correctly according to the canon of his own group, but none of the groups showed much respect for each other. Judd and his editor were justified in their behavior, according to the principles of journalism. The Chief of Police, as the executive of the legal canon, was justified in the eyes of his group in sending his men to see that that canon was obeyed. The Meads and Mr. Wood, on religious principles, were justified in the eyes of their own group in holding the meeting. But the police, who later said that they had been exploited by the journalists, did not see eye to eye with the spiritualists, and from the point of view of Cora and Mr. Wood, the conduct of both the other groups was "unethical and lousy." The interest of this lies in the rare opportunity that arose to obtain a complete record of what happens when two or more group cultures clash while each is behaving "correctly."

2

A Systematic Analysis

INTRODUCTION

There were a number of aspects of Group S that were of some scientific import. The psychological origins of spiritualism, the nature of Mr. Mead's trance, the personalities of the members, Dr. Q's experiments and the raid were among the items of professional interest.

However, it was the last two that were of greatest concern to those who had attended. For example, when Mr. Wood met Dr. Q subsequently, he scolded him for his behavior. On the other hand, Cora complimented him for his courage in asking his questions but remained incensed for a long time afterward at the intrusion of the police. Such events, which arouse uncomfortable feelings in the members of social aggregations, constitute the field of social psychiatry.

It has already been noted that Dr. Q's experiments were a part of the internal group process and the raid a part of the external group process. The following systematic analysis will be oriented toward a clearer understanding of these two events. Experience has shown that the most revealing aspects which can be considered in the course of such an analysis are:

1. The public structure, represented by the Seating Diagram.

2. The group authority, represented by an Authority Diagram.
3. The private structure, represented by the Group Imagoes.
4. The group dynamics, represented by Dynamic Diagrams.
5. The details of the group process, represented by Transactional Diagrams.

These five features are the minimum necessary for a workable understanding of what goes on in the mental life of any group, and their accompanying diagrams may be called the five basic diagrams of social psychiatry. In order to discuss any particular aspect of the proceedings of a group, it is helpful, and sometimes indispensable, to have the basic diagrams available for reference. The time and effort required to gather the pertinent information usually is found to be a good investment, while the diagrams themselves can be roughly drawn on the blackboard in 2 or 3 minutes. If the structure of the group is not as simple as that of Group S or a psychotherapy group or small organization, a sixth basic figure, the Structural Diagram, should be added. Consideration of more complex groups will be deferred until the later sections of this book.

THE PUBLIC STRUCTURE

Some knowledge of the public structure is necessary if one is to understand almost anything that goes on in a group. It would be meaningless to ask out of context: "What do you think of this—one man said to another: 'Why don't you go away and let Ruby come back?' " A seating diagram supplies much of the context and answers many of the questions which would immediately come to the mind of anyone presented with this problem.

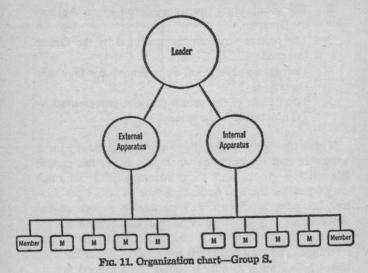

FIG. 11. Organization chart—Group S.

Such a diagram (see Fig. 3) gives in a conveniently condensed form nearly all the information that might be contained in a more formal analysis of the public structure, and a great deal besides. A formal analysis would require a number of separate diagrams: for example, a manning table and an organization chart for the organizational structure, and a roster of members and a personnel chart for the individual structure. The Manning Table (Table 2) for the spiritualist group calls for: Leaders, 1; External Apparatus, 1; Internal Apparatus, 1; Members, 10. Each of these special designations may be called a role. Thus, there are four roles in the Manning Table. The Organization Chart (Fig. 11) shows the arrangement of these roles in the public structure. The roster of members, most of whom the reader has become familiar with as the proceedings were described, is given in Table 3; their arrangement as they fitted into the individual structure of the group is shown in the Personnel Chart (Table 4). Each person

TABLE 2. A MANNING TABLE

ROLES	SLOTS
Leaders	1
External Apparatus	1
Internal Apparatus	1
Members	10
Complement	13
Roles	4

TABLE 3. A ROSTER

PEOPLE		SPIRITS
Mr. Beer	Mrs. Ella·	Gray Bird
Mrs. Beer	Mr. Eph	Dr. Murgatroyd
Dr. Bell	Mr. Judd	Ruby
Miss Cora	Mr. Mead	Sambo
Dr. Cuppy	Mrs. Mead	
Mr. Eddy	Dr. Q	
Mr. Wood		

TABLE 4. A PERSONNEL CHART

SLOT	INCUMBENT
Leader	Mr. Mead
External apparatus	Mr. Wood
Internal apparatus	Mrs. Mead
Member	Mr. Beer
Member	Mrs. Beer
Etc.	

on the roster presented himself in a certain way when filling his role: as an authoritative person, a humble person, a superior person, an objective person, and so forth. This typical behavior of each individual constituted his persona, which he exerted considerable effort to maintain.

The seating diagram also gives useful information concerning the physical structure of the group, which might otherwise be more fully presented in a schedule. The schedule for Group S outlines the particulars of space, time, equipment and number (volume) of people that formed the matrix for the group activity. It was relatively simple (Table 5) and may be contrasted with

Table 5. A Schedule ·

Place............................	Mr. Wood's house
Time.............................	8 p.m. to 11 p.m. September 24, 1959.
Volume (Number).................	13 people. Ten regular members and three others
Equipment.......................	Room, electric lights, 13 chairs, curtain, 5 trumpets 2 tape recorders

the schedule of a large organization such as a railroad, which is a relatively bulky document and generally includes maps to show the group space, timetables to show the time structure, and equipment tables to show how large a volume of traffic can be carried on each train. One of the most significant items in the physical structure of Group S was the tape recorder. The fact that the proceedings were being recorded may well have had some sort of influence on almost everything that was said. Some experiments with other groups indicated this possibility.

In addition to conveying in a single diagram much of the significant information contained in the manning table, the organization chart, the roster, the personnel chart and the schedule, the seating diagram shows several other important features of the meeting. It gives information regarding physical situation and proximity; it shows which individuals are sitting where and next to whom, and the relative positions of men and women in the group. It makes it clear that the leader was set off in one corner with his equipment and that the members sat in a rough circle with an empty space in the middle of the otherwise crowded room. All of these factors may have had some bearing on Dr. Q's experiments, and certainly it seems desirable that all the information contained in Figure 3 should be shown to anyone undertaking an analysis of the situation.

THE GROUP AUTHORITY

One of the most effective ways of understanding what happens at a group meeting is to have the clearest possible idea of what the group stands for. This is studied best by investigating that set of influences which may be conveniently (and, from the psychological point of view, rightly) called the group authority. This authority is rarely as simple or as obvious as it might seem. It includes psychological factors that can be ferreted out only by careful investigation.

There appeared to be at least four interwoven influences that constituted the authority in Group S. These may be called personal, organizational, cultural and historical influences.

1. The personal influence came from Mr. Mead himself. There were many evidences of his power as a personal leader, such as the vigor with which his disciples defended him and their readiness to obey him.

2. The organizational influence was based on the fact that Mr. Mead was an ordained minister. This meant that he had a place in the organizational structure of a mother group. His ordination papers constituted a warrant that his authority as a group leader was backed by the authority of the mother church. Therefore, anyone who recognized the authority of this mother church felt bound to recognize Mr. Mead's authority; conversely, recognition of Mr. Mead's authority meant acceptance of the authority of the mother group. It happened that at this particular meeting the mother group was not mentioned until Mr. Dick arrived. Then the members seemed to be reassured and impressed by the fact that Mr. Mead had taken out ordination papers, which also represented his warrant from the legal authorities.

3. The cultural influences comprised a set of tradi-

tional beliefs, recognized as orthodox by the mother group and, hence, binding on Mr. Mead as the representative of the mother group, and constituting the group canon. Those who belonged to the group accepted Mr. Mead not only as their personal leader and as the agent or delegate of the mother group, but also as the executive of this canon.

It was evident that Mr. Mead derived some of his authority from the canon, just as kings and presidents derive some of their authority from the fact that they are the executives of their national constitutions; their people's loyalty to these constitutions is a strong influence in keeping them in office. Mr. Mead recognized this when he claimed to be the executive of two canonical authorities, "science" and the Bible, both parts of the orthodox canon of spiritualism. Some of the more important items in the canon were set forth in a pamphlet that Mr. Wood handed out before the meeting began. This pamphlet may be called the manual of Group S.

4. The historical influences are intimately connected with the canon and comprise the individuals who made it, the canon-makers. Every canon requires interpretations, amendments and elaborations, and canonical authorities are held in high esteem, especially after they are dead. Thus, Mr. Wood wanted to know what Hermes Trismegistus and Moses thought about the Pentateuch, and in general he had a high opinion of old-time departed leaders and a much lower opinion of the present living ones, as he said in the discussion that preceded the meeting. In his pamphlet entitled "The True Basis of Spiritualism," he mentioned, to begin with, some of the canon-makers who especially impressed him. His argument (paraphrased) runs as follows:

The traditions have come down to us through Hermes Tris Magistos, the Egyptian Hierophant who arrived from Atlantis under the name of Troth . . . Madame Blavatski, founder of the Theosophical Society, described these lost civilizations in her Secret Doctrine ... Ezra performed a similar tremendous task for the Bible about 700 B.C. . . . These accounts make it clear that communication with superphysical planes was common in those days, and it still is, according to a man named Newbrough who wrote the Oasphe Bible, which is said to come from one of the order of gods. . . .

The canon may be defined as the traditional influences, written and unwritten, which regulate the attitude and workings of the group, including the group culture, and give authority to the leader. Mr. Wood gave the impression that he felt much more intimate with the canon-makers than he did with the canon itself. He spoke familiarly of Hermes, for example, but the three visiting investigators would have been surprised to learn that he had actually read very many of "The 42 Sacred Hermetic Writings." Dr. Bell and Dr. Cuppy were in a similar position; they thought of themselves as "Freudians," but neither of them felt that he had a complete understanding of "The Collected Works of Sigmund Freud."

The tendency for groups to venerate their dead canon-makers even to the point of giving them godlike attributes was noted by Euhemerus, an ancient African philosopher whose views are defined in dictionaries as "euhemerism." In honor of this long-departed student of group psychology, a dead canon-maker who occupies a special position in the esteem of a group may be called a euhemerus. Mr. Wood seemed to feel that it was important for those who attended the meeting to know something about the euhemeri of the spiritualistic movement, and he put this information at the beginning of his pamphlet.

Figure 12 gives the authority diagram for Group S, and shows all four of the influences that have been described above. Figure 12A shows the personal and the

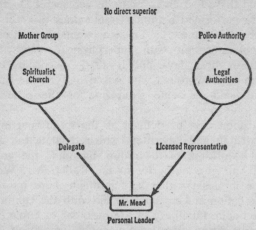

Fig. 12A. An authority diagram—personal and organizational aspects.

organizational aspects. It is worth noting first, that Mr.
Mead, the personal leader, has no immediate personal
superior and, secondly, that he derives his administrative authority as a clergyman from two sources. The
mother group, the spiritualist church, authorizes him to
hold meetings; the legal authorities authorize him to
perform marriages and other civil duties but do not
necessarily permit him to hold meetings without a special license.

Figure 12B shows the cultural and historical influences, represented by the canon and the euhemeri
(using Mr. Wood's spelling of proper names). The first
figure is that of Hermes Tris Magistos. If Mr. Wood's
indications are taken at face value, Hermes was the
founder or primal leader of the spiritualist movement
and, hence, the maker of its first, or primal canon—in
this case "The 42 Sacred Hermetic Writings." Some-
where along the line, Hermes was given the attributes
of a god under the name of Thoth or, as Mr. Wood has
it, Troth. This is one of many cases in which a man

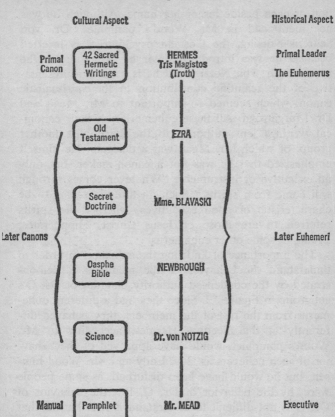

FIG. 12B. An authority diagram—cultural and historical aspects.

who was a primal leader during his lifetime is given a different name after his death, when he becomes a euhemerus.

Then follow in chronological order the later euhemeri mentioned by Mr. Wood: Ezra, Madame Blavaski, and Newbrough,* with the canonical contribu-

* The "Oasphe Bible" referred to by Mr. Wood is most likely "Oahspe, A Sacred History of . . . the past 24000 years" by

tion of each beside his or her name. Although he was not mentioned in Mr. Wood's pamphlet, Dr. von Schrenk-Notzing, the German psychiatrist, is inserted because he was introduced later by Ruby under the name of Dr. von Notzig, and he is a good representative of the scientific contribution to the spiritualistic canon, which seemed so important to Mr. Mead and Dr. Murgatroyd. All these euhemeri with their canonical writings lent authority to the spiritualist mother group, of which Mr. Mead was a delegate. He himself emphasized that he was not a canon-maker, but only an executive or instrument: "Whatever comes through will come from spirits." Such an attitude seems to be characteristic of good executives, whether the spirits referred to are those of Jesus Christ, Hippocrates, Freud, or some other euhemerus.

The importance of knowing the euhemeri in order to understand the behavior of the members is demonstrated by the condensed authority diagram of Dr. Q's subgroup in Figure 13. Since they had a different euhemerus from the rest of the members, they behaved differently at the meeting. Hermes, according to Mr. Wood's pamphlet, would have approved of the behavior of such believers as Ella, Eddy and Mr. Wood himself, but he would have been disturbed, as some people were, by the behavior of Dr. Q. But the behavior of Dr. Q is not difficult to understand if it is known that his euhemerus here was not Hermes, with his occult canon, but Hippocrates, with his canon of scientific observation. In fact, Dr. Q's experiments may be usefully

John Ballou (Newbrough), 1882, republished by Essenes of Kosman, Montrose, Colorado, in 1950. It was probably the canonical Bible of *O as pe,* an ascetic theosophical sect founded by a California medium at the end of the 1870's, which was active for several decades as a community in South Texas. They practiced dietary, alcoholic and sexual abstinence and tried to perpetuate themselves by adopting abandoned newborn babies from the city. (von Racowitza, Princess Helene: Autobiography, p. 310 ff. New York, Macmillan, 1910.)

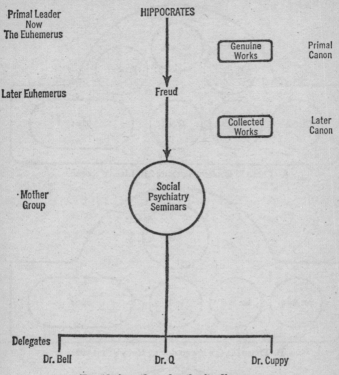

FIG. 13. A condensed authority diagram.

regarded as a conflict between Dr. Murgatroyd, representing Hermes and all that he stood for, and Dr. Q, representing Hippocrates and the objective attitude he personified.

THE PRIVATE STRUCTURE

The organizational structure prescribes for each person a role—the way in which he is supposed to be seen; the individual structure allows him to exhibit his persona—the way in which he wants to be seen; the

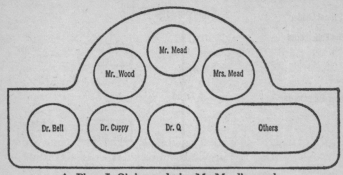

A. Phase I. Q's imago during Mr. Mead's speech.

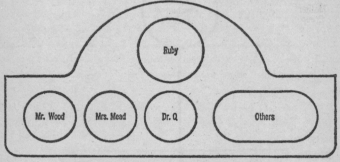

B. Phase II. Q's imago during Ruby's first visit.

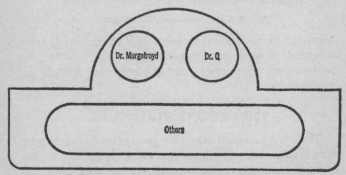

C. Phase III. Q's imago during his experiments.
FIG. 14. An unstable group imago.

private structure puts him into a slot—the way in which he is seen.

The private structure, as represented in the group imagoes of the members, was different for different people and varied with the same person from time to time according to his emotional attitude of the moment (Fig. 14). With certain people or at certain times it corresponded very closely to the public structure; for other people or at other times it was quite different. The group imago is formed as follows. The members are distributed among previously prepared slots according to their "real" personalities; that is, according to the way the individual actually perceives them at the moment, regardless of how he is supposed to see them (roles) or how they want him to see them (personas). These slots are emotionally charged in accordance with the past experiences of the individual; such charges of psychic energy are well known in other connections under the name of cathexis.

Figure 14 represents Dr. Q's group imago during three different phases of the proceedings. Mr. Mead occupied the major slot while he had the floor because Dr. Q accepted his experienced leadership at that point; he was also prepared to accept the authority which Mr. Mead delegated to Mr. Wood and Mrs. Mead. His imago at that time (Figure 14A) corresponded very closely to the public structure, except for certain personal features in the minor structure of his imago. He regarded Dr. Bell and Dr. Cuppy with equal amiability; yet his relationship with each of them was different enough so that each occupied a separate slot. As for the remaining members, he did not know much about any of them, and his relationship with all of them was superficial; therefore, he unconsciously lumped them together in one undifferentiated slot.

In Figure 14B. his imago was again adapted to the public structure. But at that time he was so interested in what Ruby did that he was no longer aware of Dr. Bell and Dr. Cuppy as people with a special relationship to himself, and he lumped them with the undifferentiated members. However, he did have a special awareness of Mr. Wood and Mrs. Mead—no longer as authority figures, but as interesting, well-differentiated people who sat in the group on the same level as himself. Others may have felt differently about Mrs. Mead's role at that time, but Figure 14B represents the way Dr. Q felt about it.

In Figure 14C, his feelings had changed. Now he saw himself as up in the major slot on the same level as Dr. Murgatroyd; the other members were all lumped together in his mind as Dr. Murgatroyd's supporters, whom he had to contend with.

Dr. Q's slots, like those of the others present, already were charged with feelings before he came to the meeting. Like a casting director, he had only to find the most likely candidate among the members to fill each slot. Figure 14 is intended to illustrate that in his case past experience had prepared slots charged with respect, curiosity and skepticism. He was accustomed to respecting legitimate authority, being curious about children and confronting people whom he thought presumptuous. These three slots were filled by Mr. Mead, Ruby and Dr. Murgatroyd, respectively, each slot being activated at a different stage of proceedings.

On the other hand, it was evident that his own position in the imagoes of some of the others changed from time to time. For example, at first he was accepted by Mr. Wood as an interested visitor; then he was resented as a rude agitator; and, at the end, when he took the group's side against the police, Mr. Wood seemed to have a friendly feeling for him as an equal. Dr. Bell and Dr. Cuppy had already established Dr. Q in their "big brother" slots, and he occupied the same position

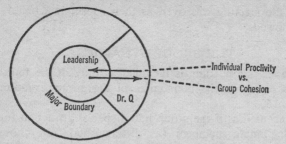

A. The major internal group process

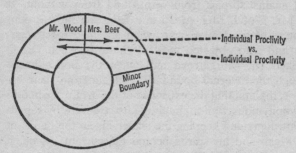

B. The minor internal group process.

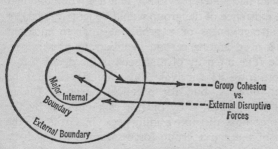

C. The external group process.

Fig. 15. The group forces.

after the meettng was over, as their subsequent behavior showed.

THE GROUP DYNAMICS

Under this heading is included a study of the influences acting on the boundaries of the group structure (Fig. 15).

It seemed as if the group had a special attraction for the legitimate members (as distinguished from those who were there from extraneous motives, such as Judd and Dr. Q), and they were willing to fight for its survival against threats from within and from without. It was Mr. Wood, Mrs. Mead and Ella, the most ardent devotees of the leader, who when attended most regularly and who objected most strenuously when Dr. Q attacked Dr. Murgatroyd and when the police broke through the external boundary. Judging from their behavior, maintaining the existence of the group seemed to be synonymous with maintaining its structure by repelling intruders and keeping the leadership in the hands of Mr. Mead and his spirits behind the curtain. Again, it was Mr. Wood and Mrs. Mead who expressed the most uneasiness when Mrs. Beer went to look at Mr. Mead (Mr. Mead had stated previously that if anyone touched him, the existence of the group would be jeopardized).

The attractiveness of a group at a given moment arouses a need among certain members to preserve its existence. The intensity of that need is the decisive factor in ensuring its survival. This intensity cannot be measured directly, but, for practical purposes (as in war), it is represented by the forces mobilized by the group to combat disruptive influences. In Group S, the strength of the active group forces seemed to reach its peak during Dr. Q's second experiment; the forces mobilized against the intrusion of the police were not strong enough to save the group.

Dr. Q's attack on Dr. Murgatroyd was an internal

threat. He evidently felt a need to express his individuality even at the risk of, or perhaps with the purpose of, disrupting the major internal boundary. The need of an individual to express himself in a characteristic way may be called his individual proclivity. The individual proclivities in Group S were manifested by attempts to structure the group according to the members' individual needs. Thus, Mr. Mead's proclivity was strongly active during his preliminary talk and, at that period, tended to strengthen the group forces. Dr. Q's proclivity was strongly active during his experiments, and it was opposed to the group forces. An individual proclivity that is in harmony with the group forces and tends to strengthen them may be called syntonic; one that is opposed to them and tends to weaken them may be called dystonic. Thus, Mr. Mead's proclivity was syntonic during the organizational phase, while Dr. Q's was dystonic during his experiments. All the dystonic proclivities added together comprise the internal disorganizing forces of any group or organization.

Mr. Dick and his men were clearly disruptive forces from outside the group. All such forces that threaten the external boundary at any given moment collectively make up the external disruptive forces acting on a group. Mr. Dick and his men were there for quite a long time before they became active, and at first their activity was weak. When the external disruptive forces became strongly active, the group structure gave way, and the leadership resigned.

The dynamic relationships of these three forces (group, internal disorganizing and external disruptive) as they act on the boundaries of the group structure are shown in Figure 15. Figure 15A illustrates the situation during Dr. Q's first experiment. Here the fraction of the group forces contributed by the leadership is shown maintaining the major internal boundary against the opposition of Dr. Q's individual proclivity. In the second experiment, several of the members joined the leader in a special mobilization of the group forces for the same purpose. This situation, in which the leadership, with or without help from the membership, fights internal disorganizing forces in order to maintain the major internal boundary, may be called the major internal group process.

Figure 15B illustrates the conflict between Mr. Wood and Mrs. Beer during her inspection of the medium. Each of them had a different idea as to how the group should proceed at this point, so that there was a struggle between Mr. Wood's "talking" proclivity and Mrs. Beer's "looking" proclivity. Since the leader did not engage himself on either side, the conflict concerned only the minor structure of the group. Such a situation, involving only two or more individual proclivities of the membership, without the engagement of the leadership, may be called the minor internal group process.

Figure 15C illustrates the situation during the raid when the group forces (in this case ineffectively) opposed the external disruptive forces at the external boundary. Such conflicts are part of the external group process.

Dynamics diagrams like these provide a convenient way in which to analyze the interplay between the three sets of forces in the major, minor and external aspects of the group process.

THE GROUP PROCESS

The group performed two different kinds of work. One was the work performed on the external environment—in this case the spirit world—in accordance with the agenda of the meeting. This work constituted the group activity. The other, here termed the group process, was the work required in order to maintain or promote the orderly existence of the group. Therefore, the group process consisted of the work done by the dynamic forces engaged at the major and the minor boundaries of the group structure. For convenience, a group may be regarded as existing in a certain state at any given moment, according to the kind of work to which its energies are chiefly devoted. When the boundaries are in a state of well-established equilibrium, so that most of the group's energies can be devoted to its activity, it may be called simply a work group. When it is chiefly involved in internal conflicts and concerts between forces, that is, in the internal group process, it may be called simply a process group. When it is engaged in a conflict between the group forces and the external disruptive forces, that is, in the external group process, it may be called a combat group. These relationships are shown in Table 6.

TABLE 6. THE GROUP WORK

CLASS	NATURE	STATE OF ENVIRONMENT	GROUP STATE	CONVENIENT NAME	GOAL
External	Group works on environment	Not threatening	Activity	Work group	Work on material
		Threatening	External process	Combat group	Conquest of external disruptive forces
Internal	Group works on itself	Either	Internal process	Process group	Promotion of order

The group process is carried on by means of more or less diluted transactions between personalities. Since schematically, people in groups are either filling roles, exhibiting personas or expressing their personalities, it is evident that there are three proper types of transactions: (1) Those proper to roles are concerned mainly with the group activity and are "business" or work transactions. (2) Those proper to personas reveal facets of the individual structure and may be called structural transactions. (3) Those between "real" personalities establish the private structure of the group and may be called interpersonal transactions. These are typified by (1) the constitutional activities of "The President" ("That's his job"); (2) the revealing but carefully thought out statements of "Mr. President" ("That's the kind of President he is"); and (3) the spontaneous social and family remarks of "JFK" ("That's the kind of person he is"). But in practice nearly all transactions have some interpersonal aspects, and it is with these elements that we are concerned here.

Pure interpersonal transaction may be consummated most dramatically as physical assaults. Diluted interpersonal transactions may be so embedded in the group activity that they are barely perceptible. In Group S many of these were heavily disguised as business transactions and were carried on in the course of the discussion by means of superficially innocent questions and answers relating to spiritualism. But others were hardly diluted at all, as when some of the regular members expressed their resentment quite frankly by calling Dr. Q rude. There were also some pure interpersonal transactions between the members and Mr. Dick, but they occurred after the group had been disrupted.

The group culture is directly concerned with the group work. Physical equipment, part of the "rational" aspect of a group's culture, is largely designed to deal with the external environment and thus is most frequently used in the work group (heavy machinery in our culture, for example) and the combat group (submarines in our culture, for example). The group etiquette and the group character are designed to regulate the internal group process. In Group S, the technical equipment consisted of the trumpets that were used in the group activity. This group had no physical equipment for combat with external disruptive forces. The

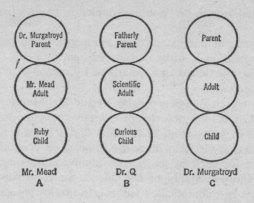

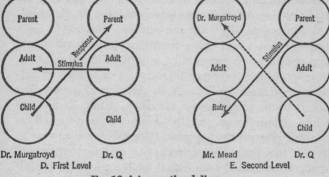

FIG. 16. A transactional diagram.

group etiquette, the "traditional" aspect of the culture, was the regulating instrument of the group forces. It required standard ways of behaving and standard sets of transactions. These reinforced the group structure and gave form to the internal group process. The group character, the "emotional" aspect of the culture, allowed exceptions for the expression of individual proclivities. This gave substance to the internal process. In short, the group culture gives the rules for how to be "acceptable" and how to be "not acceptable" in any particular group.

In order to understand the group process in detail, the proceedings must be considered item by item. Individual transactions can be clarified by means of transactional analysis.

The interchange between Dr. Q and Dr. Murgatroyd in Dr. Q's second experiment is analyzed in the transactional diagram (Fig. 16D). The first step in making such an analysis is to draw a structural or personality diagram for each of the parties involved. Figure 16A shows the personality of Mr. Mead. Since personality structure is a complicated subject, the following explanation must be followed closely.

From the evidence at hand, the culture of this group was described as having three aspects: the rational, the traditional and the emotional, represented by the physical equipment, the etiquette and the character. Each member had a rational, a traditional and an emotional component in his personality, and these found their expression in the corresponding aspects of the group culture. In transactional analysis, these three personality components, or ego states, are called Adult, Parent and Child, respectively, and these are the terms used in drawing personality diagrams. (Capitals are used only to denote that the terms are meant to describe personality components rather than actual adults, parents and children. A more extensive discussion of personality structure will be found in Part III).

In the case of Mr. Mead, it was noted that the spirits he summoned were Ruby, Gray Bird, Sambo and Dr. Murgatroyd. Gray Bird and Sambo appeared only briefly and may be ignored here. This leaves three main characters: Ruby, Dr. Murgatroyd and Mr. Mead himself. For illustrative purposes, Mr. Mead himself may be regarded as an Adult. He talked to the members in a reasonable, factual way. Ruby exemplified the

Child—compliant, rather timid and a little mischievous. Dr. Murgatroyd behaved like a Parent—authoritative, somewhat dogmatic, rather dominating and stern. But it seemed probable that Ruby and Dr. Murgatroyd were closely related to aspects of Mr. Mead's own personality. Therefore, his personality diagram is drawn with Dr. Murgatroyd as the Parent, Mr. Mead himself as the Adult and Ruby as the child.

Figure 16B shows a personality diagram for Dr. Q. Here the Parent is represented by the traditional fatherliness of the medical profession; the Adult aspect is represented by the objective scientist; and the Child by the naïvely curious explorer. At the meeting, his questions were asked not with a fatherly or a naïve attitude, but in the sophisticated, matter-of-fact tone of the rational Adult.

Since the questions were not asked of Mr. Mead, but of Dr. Murgatroyd, it is necessary to draw a personality diagram for the latter. Here the three aspects are labelled simply Parent, Adult and Child (Fig. 16C).

The transaction itself, Dr. Q's last experimental question, "Why don't you go away and let Ruby come back?," and Dr. Murgatroyd's response, is represented in Figure 16D. Dr. Q's question, the transactional stimulus, came from Adult Q and was asked of Adult Murgatroyd, as represented by the stimulus arrow S. However, the transactional response, as shown by the arrow R, came from Child Murgatroyd and was aimed at Parent Q. The analysis of this transaction is as follows:

Asked objectively, the question "Why don't you go away?" is a rational question. It may be translated in either of two ways. (1) "As a rational person with a scientific interest in spiritualist meetings, which, after all, is my official position here, I should like to know why you are here rather than Ruby at this particular point in the proceedings; what are the advantages of having you and the disadvantages of having Ruby from a spiritualistic point of view? Can you give me a rational explanation?" (2) "As a person with a scientific interest in group dynamics, which after all is my official position here, I should like to know what happens when the leader of this particular group is asked an unsanctioned question. Perhaps you will understand that this is what I am testing and give me a rational response, such as: 'When someone in a spiritualist group asks such a question of the leader, the usual procedure is as follows . . .' "

The question may be interpreted as a query from one Adult to another. Dr. Q made it possible for Dr. Murgatroyd to interpret it as such; indeed, as noted above, he offered him two different ways to answer it objectively.

However, Dr. Murgatroyd did not avail himself of either of these opportunities. He did not say either: (1) "The advantages of having me here instead of Ruby at this point are as follows . . . ," or (2) "The usual procedure after such an unsanctioned question is as follows . . ." Instead, he said: "I am doing my best to please you . . . but you feel I am not doing well enough." And later: "I am doing my best." He made it clear that Dr. Q's question was not taken as a question but as a rebuke. He acted as would an injured child who was in exactly the situation he stated: doing his best but not appreciated. He talked to Dr. Q not as if Dr. Q were an inquiring scientist, but as if he were a critical, demanding parent. The others went along with him and comforted him, just as they might a hurt child; no one pointed out that as a rational adult he might give a rational answer to this question. Dr. Q tried to force him to behave like an adult by repeating the question but only succeeded in making him run away from the situation completely; following this episode, Dr. Murgatroyd did not permit any more questions from the membership, as though he were saying: "You're mean, so I shan't play with you any more; I'll just recite my lesson about flying saucers and go home." Which is just what he did. For this reason, his response is regarded as coming from Child Murgatroyd to Parent Q.

This transaction, as later events showed, was an important item in the group process, since it changed the imagoes of many of those present. This became clear when Dr. Q met Cora and other regular members from time to time on the street; it was evident that they had a special attitude toward him because of his questions. Dr. Bell and Dr. Cuppy reported that their picture of Dr. Murgatroyd changed because his childlike response weakened his position as the group leader.

It is possible through transactional analysis to understand many of the details of the group process. Such an analysis can go to any psychological depth, according to the information available. For example, Mr. Mead mentioned at one point that his mother had deserted him by the time he was 6 years old. This provided some understanding of Child Mead, represented by Ruby, who was described as an "unwanted child"; of Adult Mead's tender feelings for the "unwanted" Ruby; and of Ruby's craving for affection from the members. On the surface, both of Dr. Q's experiments could be interpreted as hostile to Dr. Murgatroyd, but it can be seen that they also implied affection for Ruby. This level is illustrated by the thick line in Figure 16E, where the transactional stimulus from Dr. Q is interpreted as: "I, Parent Q, love Ruby, Child Mead." Ruby did not make any manifest response to this. For a still deeper analysis of why Dr. Q might have wanted the group structured so as to exclude Dr. Murgatroyd and include Ruby, Dr. Q's personality would have to be studied in more detail. At this level, the contribution of Dr. Q's Child to the stimulus would have to be considered, perhaps as represented by the dotted line in Figure 16E.

SUMMARY

The authority diagram, which gives the "descent" of the group, is useful in the same way that the scientific name of a specimen is useful to a zoologist. Animals may be classified as large or small, black or white, or in any other way that seems convenient. But a large black dog may resemble a small white dog in more ways than it resembles a large black horse. A "scientific" classification gives more useful information than an "impressionistic" one because it is based on biologically important factors. Therefore, it is helpful to look for a system of classification that will distinguish dogs from horses rather than large black animals from small white ones. In the same way it is useful to look for psychologically important factors in classifying groups. Many such factors can be found in the basic diagrams.

The present group may be usefully classified by beginning with the authority diagram (as in Fig. 12). Thence it may be noted that the group is descended from the euhemerus Hermes Tris Magistos, or Troth, with the Sacred Hermetic Writings as its primal canon. Thus, it belongs to the large Class of Occult groups, along with such groups as the Theosophists and the Swedenborgians. But since the mother group is the Spiritualist Church, it is evidently a member of the Spiritualist Family of the Occult Class. This Family includes a number of different Genera, such as prayer meetings, table tappings and ouija readings. Turning now to the seating diagram (Fig. 3), it is seen readily that the present group belongs to the Genus Trumpet Séance. Such séances might be conducted in a variety of ways, and the seating diagram shows that this particular séance will be conducted according to the method of Mr. Mead, so that it may be said to belong to the

Meadian Species of this Genus. Since theoretically Mr. Mead might conduct an almost infinite number of trumpet séances with different groups of people, it is also useful to know the individuality of the present group. This, too, is shown in Figure 3.

The seating diagram gives some descriptive information which is probably important. It shows that the group is "medium" sized and overcrowded; that it has two organs, an external and an internal apparatus; and that communication is face to face between all the members, including the personal leader.

Group imagoes may be useful in predicting what is likely to happen in the course of the group process. A study of Dr. Q's group imagoes (Figure 14) is worth-while, since they show where he is headed and how he perceives the situation. They show him passing from a state of acceptance of the group structure, or involve-ment, to another state in which the leadership is to be questioned. His transformation from a member into an agitator gives warning that something is likely to occur that the group will find disturbing.

The dynamics diagram is a reminder that the effec-tiveness of the group activity can be influenced by forces that act in various ways on the group structure. Fig-ure 15A shows that Dr. Q's agitation, which caused the group to suspend its activity for the moment, was en-gaged in the major process. setting his individual pro-clivity in conflict with the group forces in a dystonic way.

The fifth diagram, the transactional (Fig. 16), illustrates a way in which to begin analysing any indi-vidual item in the proceedings. It is useful because it may indicate what has to be done in order to lessen the interference with the group activity caused by the group process. The diagram of Dr. Q's second experi-ment (Figure 16D) shows that the stimulus is Adult to Adult, while the response is Child to Parent. This gives some information to an alert observer about a weak spot in Dr. Murgatroyd's leadership abilities.

Table 7 summarizes what can be learned from the five basic diagrams, with particular reference to Dr. Q's experiments.

Experience has shown that this type of analysis is fruitful not only for understanding what is going on but also for indicating what might be done to remedy unsatisfactory conditions. It can be helpfully applied to practical problems in groups of different Classes and Families. Such experiences have offered encouragement for developing these ideas in more detail, and that is the task that takes up the remainder of this book.

TABLE 7. SYSTEMATIC ANALYSIS OF A GROUP AND A TRANSACTION

INFORMATION		DIAGRAM
1. *The Group*		
A. Classification		
Class:	Occult	Authority (Fig. 12)
Family:	Spirtualist	Authority
Genus:	Trumpet Séance	Seating (Fig. 3)
Species:	Meadian	Seating
Individuality:	As noted	Seating
B. Description		
Size:	Medium	Seating
Condition:	Overcrowded	Seating
Organs:	Internal	
	Apparatus, 1	Seating
	External	
	Apparatus, 1	Seating
Communication:	Universally·face to	
	face	Seating
2. *The Experiments*		
C. Imago:	Agitation	Imago (Fig. 14)
D. Dynamics		
Process:	Major Internal	Dynamics (Fig. 15)
Forces:	Internal Disorgan-	Dynamics
	izing vs. Group	
Orientation:	Dystonic	Dynamics
E. Transaction		
Stimulus:	Adult to Adult	Transactional (Fig. 16 D)
Response:	Child to Parent	Transactional

Part 2

The Group as a Whole

3

Group Structure

INTRODUCTION

The first task here will be to construct a model, something like a skeleton or an armature, and then to apply flesh and blood and spirit to make it come to life. First there should be a model of the group as a whole and then one of the individual human personality. This makes it possible to consider the interplay between them: What such an ideal group does to the personality, and what such ideal personalities do in and to the group. As soon as life is breathed into the situation by talking about real people in real groups, the models become alive.

Of course, this reverses the process of observation and discovery. There the vibrating psyche and the pregnant situation are investigated first. After many observations of the living tissue, common factors begin to emerge. Soon it is possible to speak of principles or generalizations. Further observations modify these principles, increase their accuracy and usefulness, and reduce their number in accordance with the demands of scientific thrift. If this phase is successful and the observations are clear, some of the principles begin to fit in with each other. Then the model starts to take shape like some mastodon whose bones are only partly unearthed. But the greater the number of the elements at hand, the clearer it becomes where elements are missing and where to look for them. Finally, except perhaps for a few missing digits, the whole structure becomes clear. Then it can be put under glass, as it were, like the standard meter, and used as a criterion, perhaps with occasional changes on the basis of new observations, until some major discovery makes it necessary to restudy the whole situation.

The requirement of a general theory is that it should be applicable to any example whatsoever in its field. For example, the atomic theory of matter is only tested if it applies to every case that can be brought to it and if paradoxical cases can be explained without damaging the theory. In reference to groups, such a theory helps to avoid errors in organization and in administrative procedures, to increase the effectiveness of group activities and to treat ailing groups and organizations. It makes it possible to predict to some extent what will happen to certain people in certain groups and what will happen to a group as a whole. For instance, it offers a formula for predicting which patients will withdraw from psychotherapy groups. It is also useful in considering historical events and current political situations. However, for many people the chief attraction of a general theory is the intellectual interest that it offers as a basis for thinking and research and the esthetic satisfaction that can be obtained from its consistency.

SOCIAL AGGREGATIONS

A group may be defined as any social aggregation that has an external boundary and at least one internal boundary.

Group S was a small informal "one-shot" group of simple structure. This is illustrated in Figure 5, which may be called the chordal form of structural diagram. At the opposite end of the scale are large, formal, relatively permanent groups such as nations. The major structure of such enormous organizations is about the same as that of Group S, except that they are better represented by the ameboid form of structural diagram (Fig. 17). The larger circle, the external boundary, means that the group distinguishes between members and nonmembers, and the smaller circle—the major internal boundary—signifies that there are at least two classes of people in the group, the leadership and the membership.

From the diagram, it may be seen that there are at least two other types of social aggregations: those with an external boundary but no internal boundaries (parties) and those with neither external nor internal boundaries (crowds and masses). A more detailed explanation of this means of classifying social aggregations will be found in Appendix II.

Although parties, crowds and masses are each interesting in their own way, their dynamics are different from those of organized groups. This book will be confined to a discussion of structured enclaves, i.e., groups

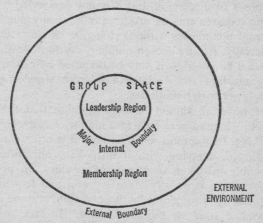

FIG. 17. The major group structure—ameboid form.

and organizations. These include most of the collections of people that are of academic, practical or scientific interest: historically important organizations such as nations, cities, parliaments, armies, navies and religious bodies; aggregations that are important in everyday life, such as schools, universities, business organizations, labor unions, professional societies, athletic leagues and social clubs; and most of the aggregations that are currently of interest to students of group dynamics, such as hospitals, psychotherapy groups, military and industrial units, families and experimental groups. All of these have the two essential features in common: they distinguish between members and nonmembers, and they contain at least two classes of people generally distinguished as the leadership and the membership. Thus it can be seen at the outset that relatively little is lost and a great deal gained in clarity by separating this type of aggregation from all others.

In this system of classification, it is not necessary to draw a strict line between a group and an organization. Such a distinction may occasionally be convenient for purposes of discussion, but it is not demanded by theoretic requirements. A group may have any number of internal boundaries without changing its characteristics materially. At any chosen number, say four, five, or six internal boundaries, it may be dignified by calling it an "organization" to distinguish it from simpler groups with fewer such boundaries.

However, it should be kept in mind that the word "group" is used here only as a matter of convenience in thinking. In common scientific talk, it is often carelessly employed, carrying with it unspoken, unjustified and probably mistaken overtones of mystery. In practical situations, it is usually more graceful and less forward to speak of "you people," "those people," "some of us," "some of you," or "some of them." In fact, to speak offhandedly of "this group" and "that group" may be evidence of some hidden arrogance toward the individual members as well as of a certain lack of sophistication.

But then, it is just this attitude of detachment which is desirable for objective thinking. It makes it possible to speak of "a group" as if it were some kind of animal and of observed happenings as though they were caused by this animal—something that may be necessary in certain situations for leaders on the inside, and for friends and opponents on the outside. A general has to think of "our forces" or "the enemy forces" rather than of "some people from our country" or "some people from the other country." It is with this caution in mind that we shall now attempt to answer simultaneously (in grown-up language, unfortunately) all the little boys who have ever asked: "Mommy, why is daddy wearing that uniform?"—whether the uniform is gray flannel, blue denim or olive-green.

THE STRUCTURE OF A GROUP

The external boundary and the major internal boundary form the major boundaries of a group, and together they represent the major group structure. It is evident from Figure 17 that there are three regions to be considered. The external boundary, or boundary zone, separates the external environment from the group space, and the major internal boundary divides the group space into a membership region and a leadership region.

In the case of a nation, and many other groups, a map may be substituted for the diagram. The external boundary, coast or frontier, separates the country from the rest of the world, while the central authority is situated within a special region inside the state. The country as a whole—the United States, Great Britain, the Soviet Union—is represented by the region inside the larger circle, but official pronouncements come from

Washington, London or Moscow, represented by the region within the smaller circle.

It would be very convenient if the structure of all groups could be represented geographically, since there is a natural tendency to think of groups in spatial terms, using such expressions as "entrance requirements" and being "discharged." Whole books have been written from this point of view. Unfortunately, in many cases serious problems arise. It would be very difficult to enclose the whole British Empire in a single curve on a map and almost impossible to distinguish Roman Catholics from other people in this way, even if a circle could be used to represent the Vatican. Evidently, therefore, a map is not the best way to represent all situations, and it is necessary to describe more carefully the meaning of the major boundaries.

An even more important consideration is the fact that a map of a group is not a group. One can learn a lot from a map, in some respects more than one can by actually visiting the country, but it gives only the most general hints of what might be going on in the minds of the people. In order to begin to understand that, it is necessary to know the psychological significance of the lines on the map.

For these two reasons, it is more satisfactory to describe the meaning of the structural diagram in other than geographic terms. The external boundary is defined as representing those factors which meaningfully distinguish members from nonmembers, and the major internal boundary is defined as representing the factors which meaningfully distinguish the membership from the leadership. These definitions are sufficient to take care of the many different situations that arise. At the same time, they do not interfere with the use of spatial terms in the discussion; this is unavoidable because the everyday language of organizations is replete with spatial words.

In this natural way of speaking, membership "in" the group is determined by the position of the individual in relation to the external boundary. In some cases he finds himself involuntarily and automatically included at birth, as in citizenship and kinship. In other cases it must be crossed inward by such processes as immigration, baptism, initiation, employment, admission or matriculation. Withdrawal across the external boundary is known variously by such terms as emigration, resignation or graduation; extrusion across it is called expulsion, excommunication, or discharge; and exclusion is known by such terms as failure or rejection. The major internal boundary is crossed inward by election, succession or appointment and similar processes. Withdrawal from the leadership region occurs through abdication, resignation, retirement or expiration of term; extrusion from it is called variously deposition, demotion, recall, expulsion or removal. Curiously enough, there are more terms for the outward crossing of the major internal boundary than for the inward crossing.

While it is helpful to try to understand what a structural diagram might represent, it must always be remembered that this is only a preparation for meeting real people participating in real transactions. Such a diagram is like a menu in that it gives some idea of what the possibilities are. The test of the pudding is in the eating.

A homosexual woman said that she had met on the street the owner of a bar where she used to go to meet her friends. She said that this barmaid treated her as if she were no longer a member of the group. Dr. Q asked her what the criteria of membership were, and she answered: "To go where they meet, to speak their language, to be seen with them, to consent to pairing off."

It was evident that this group, whose leader was the barmaid, distinguished between members and nonmembers. A member is one who not only goes where they meet, but also speaks their language, is willing to be seen with them and to pair off. A nonmember is one who doesn't do those things. The group has a map, too; the external boundary is the saloon, and the major internal boundary is the bar. The woman who is legitimately behind the bar is the leader, and the people in front of the bar are members on the map. However, they are not actually members unless they meet the other criteria for membership. Anyone can go up to the bar, but this alone, this process of locomotion, does not make the person a real member of the group. That requires feeling the guilt, the anxiety and the pleasure.

Many groups distinguish not only between members and nonmembers (in this instance, homosexuals and heterosexuals) and between leadership and membership (barmaid and customers) but also between various categories of leaders and members. These additional distinctions make up the minor structure of the group. A minor structure that distinguishes between such vertical (hierarchical) classes as voting and nonvoting members or senior and junior officers is called a compound group and may be represented by a concentric diagram (Fig. 18A); while one that distinguishes between horizontal (homologous) classes such as Californians and New Yorkers, Uzbeks and Ukranians or monks and nuns is called a complex group and may be represented by a segmented diagram (Fig. 18B).

A group that has a single leader and whose members are all on an equal footing organizationally is called a simple group. Such a group has no organizational minor structure, since the major structure (Fig. 17) is sufficient to distinguish the sole member of the leadership class from the single membership class. A psychotherapy group is a typical example.

The distinction between a map and a structural diagram is emphasized by the fact that a structural diagram may be valid only for a particular viewpoint.

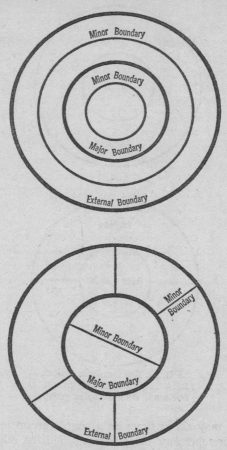

Fig. 18. The minor group structure. A
(top). A compound group. B *(bottom).*
A complex group.

(This is true of a map also, but with a different order of
specifications.) In one respect the Roman Catholic
Church may be regarded as a compound hierarchy,
while in another it may be treated as a complex organization with male and female segments. In everyday life,

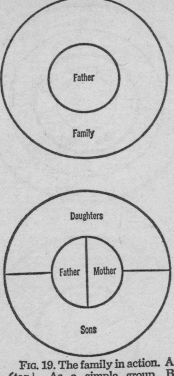

FIG. 19. The family in action. A
(top). As a simple group. B
(bottom). As a complex group.

a family may act at times as a simple group in which
the father represents the leadership and the others the
undifferentiated membership, and on other occasions as
a compound or complex group in which the leadership
is split between the father and the mother, and the sons
and daughters or older and younger children must be
differentiated in the membership (Fig. 19).*

* A family that acts like a true complex group with organized splits in the membership is probably in trouble.

There are some organizations, such as hospitals, whose structure can be looked at from so many different points of view that they are put in a special class called complicated groups.

ORGANIZATIONAL, INDIVIDUAL AND PRIVATE STRUCTURE

The formal or organizational structure of a group is found in its constitution. For a large group, such as a nation, the constitution may give only the main outlines of the leadership and the departmental structure, leaving the lesser aspects of the minor structure to be set forth in manuals issued by the leadership of each department. The Constitution of the United States indicates the tasks and the limitations of the House of Representatives, the Senate, the states, the President and the Supreme Court, all branches of the leadership or its apparatus or semi-independent divisions of the mother group. Within this structure, the government of each subdivision—state, county, city or borough—then can set up its own organizational structure and its own manuals, including local constitutions, charters, laws and ordinances. However, it is easily recognized that the constitution of a group does not have to be a written one. For instance, the constitution of a psychotherapy group is usually understood by all its members without any of its articles being written down.

An organizational structure has two important features. The relationships between the various organs are usually shown by an organization chart, and the strength of each organ is set forth in a manning table. Typical organization charts and manning tables may be found in military manuals and books on management and political science.

The relationships between the organs are defined in the constitution according to their duties, seniority, responsibilities, accountability, privileges and limitations. According to the American Constitution, the main task of the President is an executive one (to see that things are done properly). He has seniority over all military officers and is responsible for the Armed Forces. He has the privilege of veto, but this also has its limitations. Finally, he is accountable to the Senate through impeachment. In legal matters, the distinctions between various organs are clear cut: only the Senate can try an impeachment; only the Supreme Court can try a lawsuit; only the President can grant reprieves and pardons for certain offences; and the House can do none of these things.

In practice, these functional differences are represented by geographic ones. Not only do Senators, Representatives and Supreme Court justices assemble in different places, but the meeting places themselves are often used in referring to these organs. This is particularly true in the case of the President, many of whose acts are described as coming "from the White House." This is also true of smaller organizations when statements are described as issuing from "the News Desk," "the boss's office," "the New York office" or "the Chair." In fact it is fashionable to send memos "From the Desk of . . ." as well as over a personal signature. Hence, in most cases an organization chart may be regarded as either functional or spatial. This is important because in operation the relationships between the departments of an organization are carried on through channels of communication, which are determined by both functional and spatial factors.

Manning tables, like organization charts, can be divided into primary and secondary components. The primary components are those that are defined numerically in the constitution and whose absolute or relative strength cannot be changed without a constitutional amendment. The secondary components are those whose strength can be changed at the discretion of the leadership.

The organizational structure is one factor that gives a group its organizational identity. Identity depends on historical continuity, so that, even if there are some changes, it can be recognized that the group is the same from one epoch to another. If the structure is radically altered, then the group's identity is blurred, and it may not be immediately recognizable. Diplomats are confronted with the problem of "recognition" after a drastic change in the major organizational structure of a state or nation, as when the historical evolution is interrupted by a revolution.

Nearly every constitution provides for evolution in the organizational structure by due process. This provision, which is customarily placed toward the end, may be called the autotelic provision of the constitution. One function of the autotelic provision is to allow changes in the constitution itself and in the organizational structure without weakening the identity of the group. The autotelic provision of the Constitution of the United States is found near the end in Article V. The United States has the same organizational identity now that it had 50 years ago, partly because all the structural changes have been by due process. But Russia, i.e., the Soviet Union, has a different identity, partly because its organizational structure was radically changed by unconstitutional means. It was this change in identity that brought up the question of "recognition" after the Bolshevik revolution. The deciding factor as far as structure is concerned is a change in the primary organs of the organization chart.

The manning table gives the number of slots in each organ, and this provides a bridge between the organizational structure and the individual structure. The organizational structure itself is only a skeleton. A group does not come to life until it is activated by filling some or all of the slots in the manning table with specific individuals. These people form the individual structure of the group. So the press might ask "What does Washington (or London or Moscow) say?" or else "What does Roosevelt (or Churchill or Stalin) say?" according to whether it saw the leadership as part of the organizational structure or as part of the individual structure. The individual structure at a given moment is shown in the personnel chart (derived from the roster), which lists the names of individuals who occupy the slots in the manning table.

It is evident that the constitutional structure of a group is independent of its individual structure; in fact, the purpose of the constitution is to keep it so. The United States retains its organizational structure even after the most extensive changes in the personnel chart following a national election.

The fact that a group retains its organizational identity even when there is a complete turnover in its individual structure is simliar to the process found in living organisms. Normally, about 95 per cent of the atoms in the human body are said to be replaced in the course of a year, but this turnover in the atomic structure, which would correspond to the individual structure of a group, has little effect on the recognizable identity of the person. This is because the relationships between the new atoms are approximately the same as were the relationships between the old ones. This corresponds to the historical continuity of the organizational structure of a group. In both cases, a relatively small change in the major organizational (central) structure may produce much more profound effects than a complete turnover in the individual (atomic) structure.

Conversely, it is possible to make fundamental changes in the organizational structure of a group without necessarily altering the individual structure. Such a process is called reorganization (without "restaffing") and is most clearly illustrated in the reorganization of railroad corporations that are in financial distress, every step being subjected to detailed scrutiny under the laws regulating these situations, while the unions keep a watchful eye on the preservation of the individual structure. The cession of the Fiji Islands to the British Empire in 1871 is another carefully studied situation in which the roster of a group was little changed, while the major structure and the identity (as well as the character) were radically altered. Thus, the relatively permanent organizational structure and the transitory individual structure of a group are largely independent of one another.

The organizational structure and the individual structure together constitute the public structure, since they are both open to public observation. But each member has his own personal way of viewing the group. These private structures are based on personal needs, experience, wishes and emotions. For example, the Constitution of the United States gives each member of the United States Senate a slot of equal importance, but a constituent may see the Senate structure differently. He may regard his own senator as occupying the most important slot, with the rest of the Senate left in a single, undifferentiated slot for "other senators." "Common citizen" slots each have the same relationship to the Presidential slot in the organizational structure, but a man who has received a personal letter from the President may see himself, rightly or wrongly, as much more important than his neighbors in his private group structure.

A convenient and psychologically apt way of representing such a private structure is represented in Figure 7. This is the way an experienced person is likely to visualize his private way of seeing the group. (1) The leader is commonly felt to be on a "higher" level than the members; this is revealed in such expressions as

"What will they say upstairs?" or "It depends on the higher-ups." (2) The individual tends to think of his own relationship with the leader as being the central problem of the group, the other members being pushed slightly off to the side. This applies even when the member feels himself to be a very peripheral person. If he is concerned about the group at all, his chief concern is likely to be the problem of his relationship with the leader.

Thus, the organizational structure of a group is based on its constitution; the individual structure is made up of the personnel who occupy the organizational slots at a given moment; and the private structure is based on the personal feelings of each member. These three aspects can be seen readily in a family group. The organizational structure is the official relationship between husband and wife and parents and children, as set forth legally. The individual structure remains the same, except for any additions, so long as the family endures. The private structure determines the outcome; for example, a psychological separation precedes a legal divorce or an elopement. It is interesting to note that the organizational structure of colonies of bees and ants is set up biologically rather than "constitutionally." The question of whether individuals recognize each other in this structure is still to be answered, and whether or not such organisms react as "private persons" toward each other, differently from what the organizational structure calls for, is still farther from a solution.

SUMMARY

In this chapter, one kind of social aggregation is distinguished from others and is called a group.

There is one major hypothesis to be validated: that each member has a different mental picture of the group, based on his personal feelings.

SPECIAL WORDS INTRODUCED
IN THIS CHAPTER

Group | Organizational structure
External boundary | Organization chart
Major internal boundary | Primary component
Major group structure | Secondary component
External environment | Individual structure
Group space | Manning table
Structural diagram | Roster
Minor structure | Public Structure
Simple group | Private structure
Compound group | Organizational identity
Complex group | Autotelic provision
Complicated group | Reorganization

TECHNICAL NOTES

INTRODUCTION

It is difficult even for specialists in scientific methodology to make a rigorous distinction between models, conceptual vocabularies, hypotheses and theories. One might be willing to settle for something like P. W. Bridgman's statement:

"We use a concept in all possible situations and if we never run into trouble with it, we begin to feel safe with it, and grant it the status of 'existence.'" (*The Nature of Physical Theory*, p. 52, New York, Dover Publications, n.d., reprint from 1936). Einstein gives some of his views on this problem in *The World As I See It* (New York, Covici Friede, 1934), and Henri Poincaré does so in *Science and Method* (New York, Dover Publications, 1952). Cf. Max Planck, Science *110*:319, 1949; H. Cantril, *et al., Ibid.*, pp. 461, 491 and 517. An elementary exposition may be found in *An Introduction to Logic and Scientific Method* by M. R. Cohen and E. Nagel (New York, Harcourt Brace & Company, 1934).

SOCIAL AGGREGATIONS

The difference between crowds and masses, parties and groups is analogous to the differences between schools, colonies and organisms as discussed in Clifford Grobstein's review of

J. T. Bonner's *Cells and Structures* in *Scientific American* (January, 1956, p. 109.)

The derivation of the word "group" is given in standard dictionaries as Italian *gruppo, groppo*. Pulford's Italian-English Dictionary gives for *gruppo*: group, knot, roll of money, group of notes. Wessley's much older dictionary gives *gruppo*, see *groppo*: knot, knob, group, difficulty. Other romance languages have cognates, such as Romanian *grupa, grup*; Portuguese, *grupo*; French, *groupe*; etc. The closest cognate in Latin is *globus* for crowd, troop, mass of people. Cognates occur in the modern Germanic, Slavic and Finno-Ugric (?) families; cf. Dutch *groep*, Polish *grupa*, Russian *gruppa*, and Turkish *grup*. A linguist friend informs me that the original root was probably the proto-Germanic *kroppo*, swollen protuberance, bunch; cf. Old English *crop* (of a bird).

In two of Norbert Wiener's books, *Cybernetics*, Chap. 8, (New York, John Wiley & Sons, 1948) and *The Human Use of Human Beings* (Garden City, New York, Doubleday & Company, 1954), he discusses the connection between information and organization from the point of view of the mathematical theory of communication. Here the same problem is studied empirically, stating the kind of information that seems to determine the properties of human social aggregations: namely, information concerning the classes to which one's neighbors belong. (See Appendix II.) In everyday terms this could be stated as follows: the structure of a mass can be telegraphed as one item of information, either as a density, or simply whether or not it exists ("Paris streets full, or empty, tonight"); the structure of a crowd requires the transmission of a probability that one's neighbors belong to the same class as oneself ("90% of refugees French"); the structure of a party requires differentiation of the class of members from the rest of the world ("Party exclusively of Zouaves approaching"); the structure of a group requires in addition information concerning the internal structure ("One Zouave regiment moving up").

The individual structure of a mass or crowd is indeterminate; that of a party requires only that the members be named; that of a group requires in addition the assignment of each individual to a slot in the organizational structure. The private structure of any member of any of these congeries contains an enormous amount of information, since the psychology of each individual is partly determined by the previous history of the universe. If this amount were infinite, no private structure could ever be fully known or fully communicated. It could only be communicated as nearly completely as one chose.

The concept of "Class" is relevantly discussed in Schumpeter's essay on "Social Classes in an Ethnically Homogeneous Environment" (*Two Essays by Joseph Schumpeter*, p. 107, New York, Meridian Books, 1955).

THE STRUCTURE OF A GROUP

Defining "boundaries" here presents similar problems to defining the "boundaries of words" in connection with translating machines. (See W. N. Locke's discussion of N. Wiener's approach in *Scientific American*, January, 1956, p. 29). Etymologically, "boundary" is related to roots meaning "bind" and "limit."

Further extension of the discussion of maps and meanings leads into the Topological Psychology of Kurt Lewin, the General Semantics of Alfred Korzybski, and Aristotle's doctrine of Forms, among other areas.

ORGANIZATIONAL, INDIVIDUAL AND PRIVATE STRUCTURE

Among personnel workers and army officers job positions are colloquially known as "slots."

P. C. Aebersold is quoted (*Time,* October 11, 1954, p. 77) as saying that 98 per cent of the atoms in the human body are renewed each year, so that it should not be considered permanent in a material sense.

Article I, Section III, of the U.S. Constitution deals with impeachments.

E. H. Erikson is one of the most active students of the problem of "identity." See his *Young Man Luther* (New York, W. W. Norton & Company, 1958).

Regarding the structure of beehives and ant colonies, see the well-known works of Maeterlinck, Fabre and Lubbock.

Regarding the reorganization of railroads under Section 77 of the Bankruptcy Act, see W. H. Moore, *The Reorganization of Railroad Corporations* (Washington, D.C., American Council on Public Affairs, 1941).

For the Fiji Islands, see R. A. Derrick, *A History of Fiji* (ed. 2, revised, Suva, Printing & Stationery Department, 1950) and G. K. Roth, *Fijian Way of Life* (London, Oxford University Press, 1953). Also see Margaret Mead, *New Lives for Old* (New York, William Morrow & Company, 1956).

4

Group Dynamics

THE SURVIVAL OF A GROUP

The most important thing about any group is the very fact of its existence. A group that ceases to exist becomes a mere historical curiosity, like ancient Egypt or Assyria. Hence, the overriding concern of every healthy group is to survive as long as possible or at least until its task is done. The standards of health for a group, as for an organism, are durability, effectiveness and capacity for full growth. And it is clear that the first requirement for all these is survival.

There are two sets of influences which can threaten the existence of a group: disruptive forces from without and disorganizing forces from within. Dealing with such threats must take precedence over everything else to ensure survival. In time of external or internal danger, other work has to be given up in order to deal with the emergency. The vigor with which these threats are met depends on how strongly the members wish to maintain the existence of the group. Even in quiet times most groups have to divert some of their energies into maintaining an orderly existence. This is something that cannot be neglected for long, as the police strike in Boston showed many years ago. Thus, there are three forces that must be taken into account in a group's struggle for survival: external assaults, internal agitation and the opposing strength of the group.

The essence of a group, the "existence" which must be preserved, is the group structure. In some cases, a member will fight for the sake of his own private structure, his real or imaginary personal relationship with the leader and the ideals that he thinks the leader represents; a good leader will see to it that this motive is strengthened as much as possible. Others fight to preserve the individual structure: to save their families and friends or to save the queen. However, if the group is to survive as an effective force, what must be preserved is not the changeable private structure nor the expendable (within limits) individual structure, but the organizational structure.

In fact, there are three different kinds of survival that the therapist of ailing groups is interested in: ideologic, physical and effective. Ideologically, a group may survive in the minds of its members or their descendants long after it has ceased to exist as an organized force in the community. The land of Israel was such an ideologic remnant for many centuries, and the Austro-Hungarian Empire still survives in this form. This is a survival of the private structure. The potentialities of such ideologic survivals is demonstrated in cases of resurgence.

The physical survival of a group is necessary if it is to carry on. Thus, the village of Lidice may survive as an ideologic remnant for many people, but when its individual structure was wiped out, it could no longer do any work. Nevertheless, the individual structure is expendable to a large degree. Even a nation that is deeply concerned with the welfare of its individual citizens is willing to sacrifice some of them in time of danger, and they in turn are willing to make the sacrifice. Similarly, a nation will sacrifice enormous quantities of physical equipment in order to survive as an organized force in the face of a threat from the environment, and also when the threat is an internal one, as in civil war.

The effective survival of a group is measured by its ability to do organized work. Of course, this depends to some degree on its ideologic and physical strength, but the deciding factor is its organizational structure. Its effective strength can be reduced almost to zero if that can be disrupted or if it is weak to begin with. The Jews of Eastern Europe had a strong, deeply-rooted ideology and an enormous manpower, but they were overwhelmed by superior organization.

Hence, there are three ways in which a group's existence is terminated. If the private structure is weak, it cannot survive ideologically. The members feel so little need to keep it going that it simply falls apart from lack of love as they drift away. The group disintegrates physically and becomes ineffective. This is called decay. If the individual structure is wiped out, regardless of how strong the ideology may have been, the organizational structure cannot work. This is called destruction. But even if there are enough people ready and anxious to keep the group going, so that it survives both physically and ideologically, it can be destroyed as an effective force by violating its major group structure. This is called disruption. Therefore, in attempting to destroy a group as an effective force, the usual procedure is to attack it ideologically to induce decay (erosion), to attack it physically to bring about partial destruction (attrition), and finally to penetrate the major group boundaries in order to disrupt it (infiltration). If the disruption is sudden, it may lead to panic.

In practice, the chief concern of the leadership and the apparatus is the effective survival of the group, even at the expense of its ideologic and physical strength. The most dramatic threat to effective survival is war. The strategic goal of a war is violation of the major group structure: on the map in Figure 17, penetration of the frontier and conquest of the capital. The object is either to seize power—i.e., to penetrate the major internal boundary and set up a new leadership by simple intrusion and reorganization—or to annihilate the group structure, "to leave nothing to the vanquished but their eyes to weep with," as one warlike writer put it. The first policy was employed by the United States in Japan after World War II. After a brief period of reorganization, "Japan" emerged again as an effective entity. The Germans and the Russians, on the other hand, followed the second policy in Poland; the effect of this was the same as that of the raid on Group S. In both Poland and Group S there resulted a mere unorganized crowd, so that the group could do no organized work. It was destroyed as an effective force by the disruption of its boundaries and the disorganization of its structure. It was only a long time later that "Poland" came to life again, but with a different ideology, a seriously damaged physical structure and reduced effectiveness.

Ideologic wars and physical wars, cold and hot wars as they are called nowadays, are only means to an end. Hitler "finished" Czecho-Slovakia, destroyed it as an effective force, by penetrating the major group structure even though there was little erosion of its ideology and little attrition of its physical strength. Austria he first eroded and then "finished" with almost no attrition. In the case of Poland, he had to cause intolerable attrition before he could penetrate the major internal boundary.

In the case of a nation, the physical map and the organizational structure are more closely related than in many other instances. The frontier is a constitutional as well as a geographic boundary that separates members from nonmembers. An attack on the frontier is regarded as the first step in attacking the major internal boundary, i.e., the government. Such attacks are met by a force whose strength is derived from the need of the leadership and the membership to preserve the existence of the group, its organizational structure together with as much of the individual structure as can be saved. The apparatus that deals with such threats to the survival of the group is the external apparatus which first meets the invading force at the external boundary. Such a situation is represented in Figure 20A.

An assault on the leadership from the membership may be represented as an attack on the major internal boundary without involvement of the external boundary. Again, as in civil war, this is met by a force whose strength is derived from the need of the leadership and the loyal membership to preserve the organizational structure of the group. The apparatus that deals with such threats is the internal apparatus. This simple revolutionary situation is represented in Figure 20B.

A third type of threat arises from conflicts between individual members, individual components or individual categories of members which do not directly involve the leadership (Fig. 20C). Such an intrigue interferes with orderly work and if allowed to go unchecked may eventually disorganize the whole group. Gang warfare is an everyday example of dangerous intrigue which the group forces deal with by means of the internal apparatus.

Wars, revolutions and internal intrigues, then, are the three types of conflict that endanger the organizational structure and threaten the effective survival of the group. Each of them at first involves a different boundary. Wars start at the external boundary, revolutions at the major internal boundary, and intrigues at the minor internal boundaries. They all have analogues in Group S: the police raid, Dr. Q's experiments and the conflict between Mr. Wood and Mrs. Beer, respectively.

Things are not always as clear cut as in the case of armed conflict, but more subtle situations can be un-

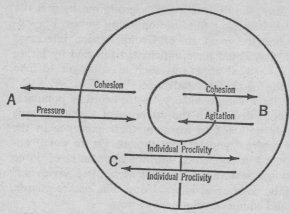

FIG. 20. The group forces. (A) External group process; (B) major internal group process; (C) minor internal group process.

derstood by studying the nature of the group apparatus. The group apparatus is the instrument which attempts to maintain the organizational structure of the group. In time of emergency the whole membership may be mobilized into the apparatus. If the external threat is very great, all other work may be suspended so that every able-bodied citizen can fight with the army. A similar mobilization takes place when an internal threat is grave, as in time of civil war. The external apparatus of a nation consists principally of the army and the diplomatic corps. The internal apparatus consists of the police apparatus and the morale apparatus.

Every failure of a group to maintain its existence indefinitely, or at least long enough to accomplish its task, is due to a failure of the group apparatus. Either the threatening forces are capable of overwhelming even the most intense efforts of the loyal members, as in the conquest of Poland or the Spanish Civil War, or the apparatus is relatively weak because of lack of love, as in the Russian or Turkish revolutions or in Group S.

At any rate, the destruction of a group means that the apparatus is weaker than the opposing forces. For example, had the members of Group S been interested enough, they could have anticipated the raid by hiring a public external apparatus such as a lawyer to take care of the formalities in advance.

To a large extent, history, as the word is popularly understood, deals with the attempts of various groups (not only nations) to maintain their existence in the face of external and internal threats. Or, to put it another way, it is concerned with the adventures of group apparatuses: external ones such as armies, navies and diplomatic corps, and internal ones like palace guards, police and counterrevolutionary forces.

The problems involved in the survival of a group are as well illustrated in small groups as in nations. In a psychotherapy group the leader functions as his own apparatus in ensuring the orderly survival of the group. Similarly, a housewife has to deal with the outside world and also keep her children in order if she wants her household to run smoothly.

THE FORCES OF THE GROUP

If one is to be able to discuss intelligently the art and the science which deals with the treatment of ailing groups, it is advisable to give names to the three forces that are concerned in the effective survival of a group.

The external forces that threaten to disrupt a group at any given moment make up the external pressure. This may include any force whatsoever that does not come from the members themselves and that threatens to intrude or has intruded into the group space. Typhoons, termites, torpedoes, typhus, troops and orders from higher authority all may be treated alike from the point of view of group dynamics, since they are all dealt with by the external group apparatus. In this conflict, a success of the external pressure results in fatal erosion, attrition or infiltration. A notable success of the external apparatus becomes part of the victorious history of the group.

Internal agitation arises from the actions of the members who tend to disorganize the group according to their individual proclivities. The success of internal agitation brings about a change in the group structure, and the concerted efforts of many individual proclivities may result in a complete revolution. A determined gang of people with criminal proclivities may take over the government of a whole nation or city and structure it to fit their own desires, and a party with revolutionary proclivities may start a civil war. Internal agitation is dealt with by the police branch of the internal apparatus.

The force that opposes both pressure and agitation comes from the need of the loyal members to maintain the orderly existence of the group and is called the group cohesion. This term is used here in a more specialized (operational) sense than is usual. The real test of a group's cohesion is its ability to do a measurable amount of work against opposition, i.e., to overcome external pressure and internal agitation. A successful outcome strengthens the group ideologically; a failure may terminate the life of the group. It is the task of the morale branch of the internal group apparatus to strengthen the cohesion and to mobilize it in time of need.

These three forces, as they meet at the boundaries of the major group structure, are shown in Figure 20.

THE GROUP WORK

In Greene's preface to his *Short History of the English People* he remarks that he devotes "more space to Chaucer than to Creçy, to Caxton than to the petty strife" of the Wars of the Roses. He reproaches historians for turning history into a mere record of butchery, and says *he* does not shrink from telling the triumphs of peace.

With these remarks Greene seems to divide the work of a nation into three catagories: the triumphs of peace, Chaucer and Caxton; wars abroad, Creçy and Agincourt; and wars at home, the Wars of the Roses. These had their parallels in Group S: the spirit talk which went along well when the group was peaceful; the struggle with the outside world, represented by the raid; and the civil strife between Dr. Q and Dr. Murgatroyd. These three kinds of work interfered with each other. The raid put an end to the experiments, and both crossed up the spirit talk. In the same way, England's war with France and the Wars of the Roses both interfered with the productivity of the country, and in fact almost bankrupted her. Peaceful activity, internal strife and resistance to external dangers do not go along well together, and to some extent each impairs the effectiveness of the other two.

A great many history books deal with one or another of these aspects in almost pure form. Schwegler's *History of Philosophy* and Long's *History of English Literature* deal almost exclusively with peaceful productivity. Sallust's *Conspiracy of Catiline* deals with an internal revolutionary intrigue concerning the major group structure, and his *Jugurthine Wars* deals with a similar intrigue involving the minor group structure. It is interesting to note that the fight in Africa between Jugurtha and his cousins at first did not directly affect Rome but later threatened to get out of hand. This is a good example of how difficulties in the minor structure may threaten to disorganize the whole group if they are allowed to go unchecked. Thucydides' *History of the Peloponnesian Wars* is a classic example of the history of an external struggle. Herodotus, the Father of History, seems to deal with all three aspects at once: productivity, internal strife and external strife.

The work of a group (the energy expended by the members) can be devoted either to productivity or to maintaining its own structure. When the group is engaged principally in working on or enjoying an environment which is not regarded as threatening, it may be called an activity or work group. When it is engaged in maintaining its own structure against external pressure, it is called a combat group. When it is dealing with internal agitation, it may be called a process group.

The constitution of a group usually states its purpose, and this purpose is the group's activity. Anything in the environment that serves as an object of physical or mental work or enjoyment may be called the material of the group activity. However, some groups are principally concerned with the bodies or the souls of their own members. For example, muscles, voices, manners and symptoms are the material of gymnasiums, speech classes, charm schools and psychotherapy groups. Most work groups are interested in making the environment more orderly, manageable and rewarding in such activities as farming, studying, praying, training, manufacturing, selling or performing. These are constructive activities. Others, such as juvenile delinquent gangs, are most interested in spreading disorder. This is a destructive activity.

One of the main concerns of the morale apparatus is to keep the effectiveness of the group, i.e., the amount of work done on the environment or the amount of enjoyment obtained from it, at a maximum, and this depends in many cases on the available strength of the group cohesion. If the cohesive forces are diverted by pressure or agitation, less peaceful work is done or less enjoyment is obtained from the activity. Hence, it is considered good policy to conceal internal conflicts from the members or the audience; in this way the diversion of forces and the interference with the group activity are kept at a minimum.

This may sound like a roundabout way of saying that when a group is engaged otherwise it has less time for peaceful activities, which may seem rather obvious. However, in the long run, the advantages of saying it in the roundabout way may be greater than the disadvantages. Perhaps all that the theory of relativity says is that it is harder to read a clock that is far away than it is to read one that is nearby, but there are certain advantages in studying the problem further and expressing it in a formal statement.

When the environment becomes threatening or is perceived as threatening, the group tries to meet the threat at its external boundary. Such a group, which opposes its cohesion to the external pressure and fights in time of danger, is illustrated in Figure 20A. This kind of work constitutes the external group process. Under ordinary conditions it is the task of the external group apparatus to carry on the external group process, but, as the pressure increases, more and more of the group's energies are diverted from the activity to be thrown into the fight. As this happens, the group passes from the working state into the combat state, like a nation going to war.

In special cases, such as epidemics, earthquakes and fires, the danger may not be met until it has already intruded itself into the group structure because it takes the apparatus unawares. However, once the apparatus swings into action, such disasters are treated much like any other invasion. Large fires and infected rats or mosquitoes are handled very much as an invading army would be.

One thing that should be made clear is that the external environment is seen by the group members not as it might appear to an outside observer but as the morale apparatus tells them to see it. If they are told that it is not threatening, they are expected to carry on their activities as usual. If they are told that it is threatening, they are supposed to act accordingly. Anyone who disagrees with the apparatus is likely to find himself in trouble and may be treated as an agitator. Therefore, whether a group continues in the working state or swings over to the combat state is usually decided not by the actual condition of the environment but by how the leadership chooses to interpret the environment to the membership. For example, he may grossly exaggerate or distort external conditions in order to mobilize them for offensive combat.

The group activity and the external group process together make up the external group work—the total work done by the members on the external environment or its equivalents. The internal group work includes all aspects of the internal group process, the work done by the members on the internal group structure itself—organizational, individual and private. If this work directly involves the leadership with the members so that the major internal boundary is affected, as in the case of elections, conspiracies, rebellions, constitutional changes or agitation, it is part of the major internal process. If it involves only the minor group structure, as in the case of quarrels and operations confined to the membership, or intrigues or palace revolutions confined to the leadership, it is part of the minor internal group process. A group which is engaged principally in this type of work at a certain moment may be called a process group. As represented in Figure 20B, the major group process involves a conflict between individual agitation and the cohesive forces under the management of the leadership; the minor group process involves a conflict between individual proclivities only, as illustrated in Figure 20C. As already noted, the internal group process is supervised by the police apparatus.

Both the combat group and the process group as described so far deal with conflicts between the dynamic forces. But the group's effectiveness will increase if the forces work together instead of conflicting. Promoting such co-operation, particularly between individual proclivities and the group cohesion, is a job for the morale apparatus. An individual proclivity that conflicts with the cohesion may be called dystonic, and one that reinforces the cohesion may be called syntonic. The difference is readily apparent in attitudes toward finances. It is one task of the internal apparatus to obtain funds from the members in the form of taxes, assessments, loans or contributions. Paying taxes or contributing money shows a syntonic proclivity, and withholding taxes or contributions shows a dystonic proclivity.

So far nothing has been said about external contributions to the psychological and material strength of a group. Such supplies often come from the mother group, if there is one, or are obtained through the efforts of the external apparatus. If there is competition between groups, procuring external supplies is part of the external group process and belongs to the combat group; if such procurement is routine, or is itself the activity of the group (as on a fishing boat), it belongs to the work group.

The most important features of the external and the internal group work are summarized in Table 6. These characteristics apply equally well to a large group such as a nation, a medium-sized group such as a professional association or trade union, and a small group such as Group S. One advantage of being systematic is that it helps to say useful things in a shorter way. For example, the earlier discussion about history can now be summarized as follows: Greene claims to devote more space to the group activities than to the group process; Schwegler and Long deal with the group activity (the work group); Sallust with the major and the minor group processes (the process group); Thucydides with the external group process (the combat group); and Herodotus with all three.

Returning now to the housewife, the work of a family can be analyzed as follows: typically, the group activity consists of such things as getting the housework done and watching TV; the external group process is concerned with such matters as earning a competitive living and fighting illnesses; the minor internal group process is illustrated by a fight between two children or between the mother and the father; and the major internal group process is concerned with bringing up the children, the parent asserting his authority over a rebellious child.

The first objective of any group is to maintain its orderly existence. That is mainly the concern of the process group. Once this existence is assured, the group is free to turn its attention to its activity. Thus the effectiveness of the work group depends on the success of the process group. This can be said in another way which may be of interest to people who like theories. It is very similar to the theory of surplus goods which economists talk about. If an isolated society can produce no more during the year than is absolutely necessary for its own subsistence, then it is impossible for the members to take time off to build the machines that would enable them to produce more. If some of the men took a year off to build a tractor, they would starve to death long before it was finished because there would be no extra food to give them while they were working. Such improvements are only possible if there is something left over to begin with. Let us call such a limited society a Turgot society, in honor of one of the economists who reflected on this idea.

A Turgot group would work similarly in regard to its only dynamic resource, its cohesion. If a group used all its cohesion in combat, there would be none left over for activity or process. It could produce nothing but armaments and fortifications, would be in continual danger of revolution, and would have to be sure of conquests in order to makes its living.* If it used all its cohesion in an activity, such as agriculture, it would have none left over for external combat and would also be in continual danger of revolution. Without any weapons it would be an easy prey for any warlike group that came along. Worst off would be a group that used all its cohesion in keeping internal order; it would be fit for neither combat nor activity and would fall under the first external pressure or starve to death. All three types of Turgot groups, or something very close to them, have actually existed in the course of human history: predatory tribes, helpless herdsmen and disputing nomads, each more or less vulnerable in its own way.

Just as a Turgot society has to produce a surplus of goods in order to make economic progress, so a Turgot group has to produce a surplus of cohesion in order to ensure its survival. The predatory combat group needs extra cohesion to prevent internal strife during or between wars and to produce enough goods to be self-supporting in case its conquests fail. The sedate activity group needs it to fight off enemies and deal with internal agitation. The agitated process group needs it to fight off enemies and make its own living.

In investigating an ailing group, it is sometimes helpful to regard it as a Turgot group: primarily either a combat, activity or process group, devoting most of its cohesive forces to one kind of work and doing the other kinds or work only with the surplus cohesiveness at its disposal. Group S, for example, can be seen that way, as a Turgot activity group. The activity went smoothly enough so long as it was not disturbed by agi-

---

* A fallout shelter is after all nothing but a fortification and can be so treated in theory.

tation or pressure, but there was not enough surplus cohesion to deal effectively with either Dr. Q or the police, and either of them could have destroyed it. If the members' syntonic proclivities had been stronger, they might have contributed enough money to hire either a bouncer or a lawyer; best of all, with maximum cohesion, financially supported, they could have hired one of each, and the group would have been safe from both internal and external threats. Therefore, the most important use of surplus cohesion (as of surplus economic wealth) is to support a group apparatus that will be effective both internally and externally.

SUMMARY

In this chapter, the "health" of a group is discussed, and several major hypotheses are stated.

1. The principal concern of every healthy group is to survive as long as possible, or at least until its task is done.

2. There are two sets of influences that can threaten the existence of a group: external pressures and internal agitation.

3. The continued existence of a group as an effective force depends on maintaining its organizational structure.

4. Every failure of a group to maintain its effective existence is due to a failure of the group apparatus.

5. All the work of any group falls into three categories: the group activity, the external group process and the internal group process.

6. The existence of a group is continually in jeopardy if it cannot mobilize enough cohesive force to support all three kinds of work.

SPECIAL WORDS INTRODUCED
IN THIS CHAPTER

Ideologic survival	Activity group
Physical survival	Combat group
Effective survival	Process group
Decay	Group activity
Destruction	Material
Disruption	Constructive activity
Erosion	Destructive activity
Attrition	Effectiveness
Infiltration	External group process
External apparatus	External group work
Internal apparatus	Internal group work
Intrigue	Major internal group process
External pressure	Minor internal group process
Internal agitation	Syntonic proclivity
Individual proclivity	Dystonic proclivity
Group cohesion	Turgot group

TECHNICAL NOTES

THE SURVIVAL OF A GROUP

That the predominant concern of a group should of necessity be to provide for its own survival has long been known to practical men such as Machiavelli—"Princes and republics who fail to have national armies are much to be blamed" (Discourses I, xxi)—and Justinian who said that the highest law was the safety of the state. The views of Napoleon and Frederick the Great may be found in *Roots of Strategy* (T. R. Phillips [ed.], Harrisburg, Pa., Military Service Publishing Company, 1940). A. H. Leighton brings the question up in his article on "Psychiatric Disorder and Social Environment" (*Psychiatry 18*:367-383, November, 1955). Any group that does not have this as an overriding consideration may be regarded from a dynamic point of view as trivial and certainly unreliable as a paradigm. Even so transitory an outfit as Group S fought as hard as it was able to.

The information about the conquest of Poland was obtained from the *Britannica Book of the Year*, 1946.

of Organizations & Groups 107

The term "ideologic survival" may sound ambiguous when used to refer to the private structure, since much ideology is contained in the constitution of a group and in its official publications. Such "official" ideology, it is true, belongs more properly to the organizational than to the private aspect of the group structure. However, the nostalgia of ex-members of extinct organizations and empires is usually highly selective and personal and refers more to what they think they could get out of a revival than to what the official ideology tells them they are supposed to get. Hence, it is justifiable to speak of ideologic survival as a personal rather than an organizational matter.

The Forces of the Group

Because the terminology of group dynamics has rarely been precise and has become more and more vulgarized, the temptation to coin new words is almost irresistible. I myself would prefer to call the three forces mentioned in the text "anancasms" after the word *anagkasma* (a compulsion) attributed to Josephus, the Jewish historian of the first century A.D. (H. G. Liddell and R. Scott: *Greek-English Lexicon,* Oxford, Clarendon Press, 1883). Its cognate "anancastic" was made psychiatrically respectable by Eugene Kahn (*Psychopathic Personalities,* p. 360, New Haven, Yale University Press, 1931) who borrowed it from Kurt Schneider and Donath. Ananke, the Greek Goddess of Necessity, had precisely the three connotations desirable to emphasize the ineluctibility of the forces involved in group dynamics. Freud was fond of her and in one place even refers to her as "the sublime Ananke" (*Beyond the Pleasure Principle,* p. 55, London, Hogarth Press, 1922). With her, the external disruptive forces would become the external anancasm, the fateful dangers that must be met; the cohesive forces would become the group anancasm, the intimate ties of blood and friendship; and what is here called mildly an individual proclivity would become an individual anancasm, the character which is man's destiny and which drives him inexorably to his fate at the hands of his fellows.

With this terminology, the whole theory of group dynamics could be considered on the basis of an interplay between the three anancasms: external, group and individual. Plato considered that "the true creator" of the state is necessity (*Republic,* B. Jowett [ed.], Book II, p. 369, New York, Modern Library, 1941), but in this connection he uses *chreia* rather than Ananke, although it is interesting to note that *chreia* also has the two connotations of necessity and intimacy (Liddell & Scott, *loc. cit.*).

Be that as it may, the introduction of new terms in our conservative nonclassical society is risky, and "anancasm" might meet no better fate than similar attempts, such as the "syntality" of R. B. Cattell (D. Cartwright & A. Zander [eds.], *Group Dynamics*, p. 14, Evanston, Ill., Row, Peterson & Company, 1953) or the "tele" of J. L. Moreno ("Foundations of Sociometry," *Sociometry 4:*15-35, 1941).

Therefore, I have elected to stay with established terminology, but some clarification is in order. The word "cohesion" is defective in the first instance because it is often used to describe a phenomenon rather than a force, and that often with some smugness. "Cohesiveness" describes a property rather than a force. "Coherence" might do, but its novelty is against it. Therefore, "cohesion" is selected, with the reservation noted in the text that it is meant to denote an emergent measurable force even more than to name a phenomenon.

The term "individual proclivity" may be acceptable to "objective" students, but it is really much too bland for the historical realities it is meant to describe. To call Hitler's murderous viciousness, Napoleon's driving ambition, Mussolini's tragic pomposity and Stalin's appalling tenacity "individual proclivities" is certainly an understatement. Nevertheless, for the sake of avoiding polemics, "proclivity" is retained.

The three forces of the group, as described in the text, are reminiscent of the "factors" discussed by Schumpeter (*loc. cit.*, pp. 107, 114, and 160 ff). He mentions: (1) behavior and events that are independent of the position of the members, corresponding to external pressure; (2) the adaptation of the individual to new situations, corresponding to individual proclivities; and (3) cohesion, which prevents the group "from scattering like a heap of billiard balls." Evidently he regards cohesion as a kind of glue, whereas it is used here to denote something much more chemically active. H. Ezriel also sees a triad of forces in conflict in the group, although he approaches and formulates them differently, nor does he stress the anancastic aspects. (Notes on psychoanalytic group therapy, *Psychiatry 15:*119, 1932).

See also the following works:

L. du Noüy: *Human Destiny* (New York, Signet Books, 1949). (External disruptive forces from the point of view of a religious scientist)

R. Allendy: *Le Problème de la destinée, étude sur la fatalité intérieure* (Paris, Librairie Gallimard, 1927). A discussion of the accidental—or non-accidental—nature of human destiny. ("Individual proclivities" from a psychoanalytic point of view)

W. C. Allee: *Animal Life and Social Growth* (Baltimore, Williams & Wilkins, 1932). ("Cohesive forces" from a biologist's point of view)

A most interesting discussion of the origin of societies among primates and primitive men—in our language, the formation of groups by integrating the syntonic components of individual proclivities into cohesive forces—is given by Marshall D. Sahlins ("The origin of society," *Scientific American 203:*76-87, September, 1960). Some of his ideas are questioned by S. L. Washburn and I. DeVore ("The social life of baboons," *Ibid., 204:*62-71, June 1961).

THE GROUP WORK

The exact quotation from Greene is as follows: "I have devoted more space to Chaucer than to Creçy, to Caxton than to the petty strife of Yorkist and Lancastrian . . . It is the reproach of historians that they have too often turned history into a mere record of the butchery of men by their fellow-men . . . I have never shrunk from telling at length the triumphs of peace." J. R. Greene: *A Short History of the English People* (New York, Colonial Press, 1900).

The other references are as follows: A. Schwegler: *History of Philosophy* (Edinburgh, Oliver & Boyd, 1871); W. J. Long: *English Literature* (New York, Ginn & Company, 1909); Sallust: (New York, Arthur Hinds & Company, n.d.). Herodotus and Thucydides can be found in *The Greek Historians,* translated by G. Rawlinson (New York, Random House, 1942).

In regard to the minor group process, special problems arise in compound and complex groups which go beyond an elementary treatment. Let us imagine a nation, within which are states, within which are counties; or a village, within which are families, within which are parents and children; or a marital therapy group, within which are couples, within which are individual spouses. Then the major internal boundary separates the capital, the town hall or the therapist from the subgroups and the individuals within them. But there are two kinds of minor boundaries: those between subgroups, separating states, families or couples from each other, which may be denoted as the $Minor_1$ boundaries; and those separating counties, individuals or spouses from each other within the subgroups themselves, which may be denoted as the $Minor_2$ boundaries.

The proceedings of such a group may then be sorted into three types of transactions instead of the two (major and minor) found in simple groups. Transactions between the leadership and any of the subgroups or individuals in the membership form the major group process; transactions between subgroups (states, families or couples) may be denoted as the $Minor_1$ group process; and transactions between individuals within their subgroups (counties, individuals or spouses) may be denoted as the $Minor_2$ group process. An even further refinement would subdivide the major group process into $Major_1$ (between the leadership and state, families or couple) and $Major_2$ (between the leadership and individual counties, people or spouses). This type of second-order analysis offers a useful and fairly rigorous framework for discussing problems which often must be dealt with in complex groups. A similar analysis may be applied to the proceedings of compound groups.

ADDENDUM

Further study of agitators and their leaders reveals that there are two types. A revolutionary agitator is one who attempts to change the constitution of a group. A constitutional agitator is one who accepts the constitution but attempts to change the way it is implemented. Thus a Communist leader in a non-Communist country is a revolutionary agitator, while the leader of a protest march in a democratic country is a constitutional agitator. A "palace intrigue" may partake of the nature of both: it may be revolutionary in that the leader is replaced by violence, thus violating the structural provision of the constitution, but the remainder of the constitution may be respected, although perhaps implemented differently. A stable leadership will tolerate constitutional agitators, while an unstable, apprehensive, or selfish leadership will suppress both revolutionary and constitutional agitators.

5

Some Quantitative Considerations

STRUCTURAL CLASSIFICATION

Social aggregations may be divided into two types—those that do not have an external boundary and those that do. Those that do not have an external boundary may be called open congeries, and those that do may be called enclaves.

According to the classification given in Appendix II, there are two kinds of open congeries—masses and crowds. In a mass no member can predict with any degree of certainty to what class of people his neighbors at any given moment will belong. Although a crowd has no external boundary and anyone is eligible to join, nevertheless it can be predicted with a certain degree of confidence to what class of people one's neighbors at any given moment will belong.

Whether an open congeries is classed as a mass or a crowd depends on the observer. The people walking down 42nd Street during the rush hour are to most observers a mass. For example, a baseball fan cannot predict with any degree of certainty whether or not the next person he encounters will be able to tell him the score of yesterday's game. However, a demographer can state with considerable confidence the odds that the next man he meets will be an American citizen, so that to him the people form a crowd.

111

There are also two types of enclaves—those without and those with internal boundaries. Those without any may be called parties, and those with internal boundaries are called groups or organizations. Here the distinction is more objective. At a staff picnic it cannot be predicted where anyone will sit, but it can be predicted that everyone present will be a staff member or can be accounted for by the staff, and these are the special characteristics of a party. At the office, it can be predicted not only that everyone working there will be a staff member or can be accounted for by the staff, but it can also be predicted which people will be sitting near each other, with exceptions accounted for; these are the special characteristics of a group.

Therefore, this system of classification is based on an axis with randomness, ignorance or unpredictability at one end, and order, information or predictability at the other. Such an approach not only has the advantage of being open to numerical studies, but it is also psychologically natural. Where there is a free choice between memberships, the possibility of predicting to what class one's neighbors will belong has an important influence on the decision, as in choosing a college, fraternity or country club. In fact, in these examples, the word "class" has not only its general meaning of "distinction by any common significant factor" but also includes the popular meaning of "social class."

Therefore, this classification of social aggregations, in theory at least, is based on degrees of probability or certainty. Concerning the classes of people in it, a mass has a predictive possibility of zero, and a crowd has a predictive probability greater than zero but less than 1, offering an opportunity to compare crowds of different probabilities. An enclave has a predictive value of 1, concerning the class of people included. However, the internal distribution of the members has a predictive possibility of zero in a party, and a predictive probability greater than zero in a group or organization, offering an opportunity to compare groups of different probabilities.

A group with an "internal" probability of 1 may be called a completely organized group. In such a group there are as many roles in the organizational structure as there are slots in the manning table. In practice this means that each member has a special position different from the positions of all other members, with no doubts about responsibilities or privileges. Ideally, it means that each member can state with complete certainty the roles and the duties of each of his neighbors in the organizational structure, as in a completely organized football team, and also the organizational distance of every other individual in the group.

The predictive probability of a group, represented in a more practical way, may be called its degree of organization, which is expressed as a percentage. This may be illustrated as follows. In a class of 99 students and 1 professor, there are 2 roles in the organizational structure: "professors" and "students." The degree of organization is 2 per cent (2 roles, 100 slots), and two things can be predicted: that the professor and none of the students will be regularly on the platform, and that the person sitting regularly next to a student will be another student and not the professor. If a university has 24 undergraduate students, 24 graduate students, a full professor and an associate professor, there are 4 roles and the degree of organization is 8 per cent (4 roles, 50 slots). A graduate student can state (if a certain curriculum is adhered to): that all his neighbors in class are graduate students and none are undergraduates; that the man on the platform is an associate professor; that all other students are undergraduates; and that all other teachers are full professors. In an operating room with a surgeon, an assistant surgeon, an anesthetist, a scrub nurse and a roving nurse, there are 6 people, including the patient, and 6 roles, so that the degree of organization is 100 per cent (6 roles, 6 slots). Each member has a special duty different from that of all the other members, with no overlapping of responsibilities or privileges. The assistant surgeon knows that he will be standing across from the surgeon, and the surgeon knows who is standing across from him, who is beside the instrument tray, who is lying on the table, who is at the head of the table, and who is walking across the room, so that his predictive probability is 1.

In a sales organization with a sales manager, 39 salesmen with allotted territories and a stenographic pool of 10 persons, there are 41 roles and 50 slots, a degree of organization of 82 per cent. In this situation, each salesman knows who his neighbors are in adjoining territories and who will read his reports, but no salesman knows which stenographer will type his reports. Stenographic pools are a means of employing time and equipment most economically, usually when there are more reporters than stenographers. However, it is evident that if each salesman had enough work to keep one stenographer busy full-time, it would be more efficient for him to have a specific secretary assigned to him, since her familiarity with his individual problems and correspondents would be helpful. He could then predict whom he would be dictating to, and she could predict every day whom she would be working for. This is an example of the relationship between efficiency and organization, which may be expressed according to the following principle: other things being equal, the efficiency of a group varies directly with the degree of organization. This is well illustrated by the surgical team, whose efficiency, as measured by recovery and death rates, is likely to be greater if the responsibilities of each member are clearly stated and if they do not try to do each others' jobs during the course of an operation.

Conversely, since the degree of organization of a classroom is low, it would be expected that its efficiency would be low. This is recognized in the efforts to reduce the size of classes, which naturally increases their degree of organization. Hence, public schools with large classes are thought to teach less efficiently than private schools with smaller classes (the same number of roles with fewer slots). Students with special learning problems may be assigned a tutor, which represents complete organization (2 roles and 2 members). (However, it should be emphasized again that all applications of statements and conclusions regarding groups to "groups of two" must be treated with caution).

The degree of organization of a group, that is, the ratio of roles to slots, deals with the organizational structure. It compares the organization chart to the manning table. The manning ratio (members/slots) concerns the individual structure. It compares the roster to the manning table. It tells what percentage of available slots are filled, so that one can speak of over-manned, fully manned and undermanned groups. The degree of organization determines a group's efficiency. If it is efficient, then the manning ratio determines its effectiveness. Taking these two ratios together, the relationship between the group activity and the public structure as a whole can then be stated as follows: other things being equal, the greater the degree of organization, the more efficient the group; given efficiency, the closer the manning ratio approaches 100 per cent, the more effective the group. In order to make this clearer, it should be understood that efficiency refers to potentiality for working economically; effectiveness refers to the actual amount of work done.

In some groups there are more roles than slots, so that a single individual has to fill two or more roles in the organizational structure, popularly referred to as wearing two or three hats. Strictly speaking, the degree of organization (roles/slots) in such a group is greater than 100 per cent. But it is simpler to think of such groups as undermanned rather than overorganized, although a mathematically trained "operations analyst" might find it more useful in some situations to do it the other way.

The corresponding ratio in the private structure is the degree of differentiation. So long as one or more other members have little psychological significance for Member X and are lumped together in his mind as "bystanders," then for Member X the group is not completely differentiated. On the other hand, if some other member has to fill more than one slot in the imago of Member X, then for Member X the group is overdifferentiated. The simplest situation from the point of view of arithmetic would be one in which the number of members equalled the number of active slots in Member X's group imago; then it might be said that for Member X the group was fully differentiated. Since the degree of differentiation varies from time to time and from member to member, it is a psychological rather than an organizational problem.

QUANTITATIVE GROUP DYNAMICS

The group cohesion is an organizing force, while, from the group's point of view, pressure and agitation are disorganizing forces. Cohesion represents the forces of order, and the other two the forces of disorder. Every time a group is formed, the amount of order in the world is increased, and every time a group breaks up through disruption, destruction or decay, the amount of order in the world is decreased. When a group forms, individuals begin to push in the same direction, and when it breaks up, individuals who were pushing in the same direction begin to push in different directions. This may also be illustrated by the standard of predictability. When a section gang arrives for work, it can be predicted with a certain degree of confidence that most of them will be working most of the time on the railroad. After they finish work for the day, it cannot be predicted what they will be doing unless organization is introduced from without, as by a theatrical company or a sports contest.

The activity of a group may be concerned with increasing either order or disorder in the external environment. A constructive group is one whose object is to increase order, while a destructive group aims to promote disorder. In either case, it is usually possible to devise methods for measuring the group's effectiveness during a given period: the number of houses built or windows put in or the number of houses bombed or windows broken.

Generally speaking, a family is a constructive group in which each member contributes to the group cohesion and promotes internal order. However, by expressing their individual proclivities, the children also may cause internal disorder. A mistress might represent an external disruptive force threatening the survival of the group. The purpose of marriage is to combat this type of external threat.

If there were some way to measure the strengths of the three dynamic forces and also the effectiveness of the group activity during the same period, it might be possible to show that there was some regularity in the connections between them. The full study of such possibilities is again the province of mathematically trained "operations analysts." The most difficult part is the first problem, that of measuring accurately the comparative strengths of the dynamic forces, but there is a simple way to make at least a rough estimate in dealing with an ailing group.

It is curious but true that organization introduces order even in spheres beyond the declared purpose of the organization. This is something like the appearance of side-effects in pharmacology. A drug which is taken with the intent of reducing fever may also induce labor, whether it is intended to or not. On the other hand, the same drug taken with the intent of inducing labor may reduce fever and cause buzzing in the ears, whether it is intended to or not. Nature is not necessarily influenced by intent but produces her effects regardless of the expressed wishes of those who try to control her.

A series of open-house parties was held every Sunday evening in Carmel, California, for about 2 years. No special invitations were issued, but it was generally understood in the area that anyone who cared to come would be welcome. The weekly attendance at these unorganized parties was very much like an appropriate series of random numbers. One week there might be 2 guests, the next 58, the next 23, and so on. This unpredictability created serious difficulties in buying the refreshments.

The same individual who conducted the open-house parties was the leader of 5 organized psychotherapy groups which met under a variety of conditions. The attendance records showed that all members of these groups were present at about half the meetings. The chances were even that everybody would be present at any given meeting. This predictability was convenient for such matters as arranging the furniture. The important point was that in these groups no stress was placed on attendance. Thus, one effect of organization was regularity even in an area with which the groups were not purposefully concerned, and this regularity distinguished these groups from the unorganized parties. This distinction could not be attributed to the personality of the therapist, since that same personality did not stimulate people to come to the parties regularly. It was attributed to the influence of organization in creating cohesion in the therapy groups, a force that did not manifest itself in the series of unorganized parties.

Furthermore, in spite of the many differences between the various therapy groups, attendance in each of the five groups over a long period was just about the same, ranging from 83 to 89 per cent in groups that met weekly during periods ranging from 6 months to 3 years. That is, these groups were all about equally attractive to the patient members, or, in the present language, the cohesive forces had about the same strength in each of them.

This interpretation was confirmed by another regularity. The proportion of patients who withdrew from each group was exactly 50 per cent in three of the groups, and a little less in the other two. This was another indication that all the groups were about equally attractive, or had about the same strength of cohesion.

Interestingly enough, the same regularity was noted in comparing the series of psychotherapy groups to other group series, at least on the basis of published attendance records. The total attendance for all five therapy groups was 88 per cent. The average daily attendance in the whole school system of the same town for 1 year during the same period was 89.6 per cent. The aggregate attendance records for all Rotary Clubs in the United States for 1 month selected by chance during that period was 87.8 per cent; and for several hundred Kiwanis Clubs, covering California, Nevada and Hawaii for 3 randomly selected months during the same period, 89.7 per cent. According to these figures, the attendance in such different categories as therapy groups, schools and service clubs was about the same at that time, being within 1 per cent of 88.8 per cent. If gross attendance is taken to indicate the attraction of the group, these almost incredibly small differences would mean that at the present time the cohesive forces have about the same strength in different kinds of group series in this country.

One of the most important things about this regularity is that it occurred in spite of differences in the attitudes toward attendance. Attendance at school is a legal compulsion. There is no legal compulsion with service clubs, but strong social pressure is used to encourage attendance. In the therapy groups there was neither legal nor social pressure; on the contrary, a member could save money by missing a session, since absences were not charged for. These variations in attitude made no practical difference in the actual results.

The strength of the cohesion, measured in this way, which was about the same for these four group series during the years under consideration, seems to change from decade to decade. The average daily attendance at all public elementary and secondary schools in the United States was 87.3 per cent in 1948, which is about the same as in the other four series. But in 1870, the average daily attendance was only 59.3 per cent. Presumably in the old days absences from school were more frequent, partly because of poor motivation and partly because of transportation difficulties, high disease rates, inadequate police forces, labor shortages, financial stress and other pressures due to defective control over the environment. As the apparatus of the country (transportation, health, police and labor branches, for example) became more effective, the external difficulties in the way of attendance became easier to overcome.

From the point of view of the school authorities, any influences that keep pupils away are treated as part of the external pressure. Not only does irregular attendance have an undesirable effect on the classroom, but if it is not opposed, it may result in a budget cut. Such opposition to irregularity appears to be a regular procedure with most groups the world over. Whenever external forces threaten the survival or the growth of a group by keeping people away, those forces are treated as part of the external pressure; if not, the group may die of attrition.

The relative strength of the external pressure during a given period is represented by the proportion of members who are absent from the meetings due to external necessities. Thus, the relative strength of the external pressure on the educational system was greater in 1870 than it was in 1948. In the psychotherapy groups, over the whole period, such absences due to external necessities were 2.6 per cent of the total possible attendance.

There was evidence that the remaining absences from the psychotherapy groups, which amounted to 9.4 per cent of the possible attendance, were due to some sort of reluctance on the part of the members to attend. Since these absences in each case were determined by internal psychological factors, they were manifestations of individual proclivities. In this series, therefore, the total attendance was 88 per cent, which may be taken to indicate the strength of the cohesion; the absences due to external necessities (the external pressure) were 2.6 per cent; those due to internal resistances (individual proclivities) were 9.4 per cent. Hence, the strengths of the three dynamic forces in that situation may be taken as roughly in the ratios 88/3/9. This shows that it is sometimes possible to measure these forces, at least against each other.

Unfortunately, at present this approach is limited to certain types of psychotherapy groups, since only a well-qualified psychotherapist is competent to distinguish reliably between the two types of absences, those due to external pressure and those due to individual proclivities. The actual information is usually clear cut once it has been obtained. For example, a student stayed away the night before his final examinations. It

was easy to classify this as an external necessity interfering with his desire for the therapy group to survive
(accidental absence). Another man put sugar in his car-
buretor so that he could truthfully say that he could not
get to the meeting because his car had broken down.
This was evidently a manifestation of his own inner
problems, i.e., his individual proclivity (resistance absence). The difficulty was that it took more than a year
of careful psychiatric treatment before this man felt
free to confess what he had done, and there was no
way for anyone to learn the facts until he himself was
ready to reveal them. The usual research methods, such
as questionnaires, are useless in such situations.

Since the results of psychotherapy are difficult to
measure, it is not possible to compare with any exactness the ratios of the dynamic forces with the therapeutic effectiveness of these groups. Nevertheless, it can
be said that as the therapeutic technic was changed
from time to time, there were accompanying rises and
falls in the total attendance, the proportion of resistance
absences and the therapeutic results. (The proportion of
accidental absences remained about the same.)
Roughly, at certain periods attendance rose and patients improved more quickly, and with other technics
attendance fell and the patients improved more slowly.
These and other experiences indicate that it is worth-
while in the treatment of ailing groups, as far as it is
possible, to try to estimate the relative strengths of the
dynamic forces and their relationship to the effectiveness of the group activity. The simplest way to estimate the forces is through the careful study of attendance records. At the very least, the percentage of total
attendance during the life of the group (or for a reason-
ably long period) should be available to indicate the
strength of the cohesion. If this figure is below 75 per
cent, something is probably wrong, and the leader
should, as it were, "retire to his tent for meditation."

SUMMARY

The hypotheses stated in this chapter are as follows:

1. Structural: Other things being equal, the greater the degree of organization, the more efficient the group; given efficiency, the closer the manning ratio approaches 100 per cent, the more effective the group.

2. Dynamic: The strengths of the dynamic forces are measurable, and their ratios may determine the effectiveness of the group over a given period.

SPECIAL TERMS INTRODUCED
IN THIS CHAPTER

Open congeries	Degree of organization
Mass	Efficiency
Crowd	Manning ratio
Enclave	Effectiveness
Parties	Degree of differentiation
Groups	Constructive group
Class	Destructive group
Roles	Accidental absence
Slots	Resistance absence

TECHNICAL NOTES

STRUCTURAL CLASSIFICATION

For more precise formulations of order-disorder, see: C. E. Shannon & W. Weaver: *The Mathematical Theory of Communication* (Urbana, University of Illinois Press, 1949); L. Brillouin: "Life, thermodynamics, and cybernetics," *American Scientist* 37:554-568, 1949, and "Thermodynamics and information theory," *Ibid.,* 38:594-599, 1950; M. Ostow: "The entropy concept and psychic function," *Ibid., 39*:140-144, 1951. An interesting psychiatric discussion by Eugene Kahn of the antinomy "Order/Disorder" may be found in the *American Journal of Psychiatry 110*:427, 1953.

QUANTITATIVE GROUP DYNAMICS

The discussion on attendance is formally presented in the author's paper on "Group Attendance: Clinical and Theoretical Considerations," *International Journal of Group Psychotherapy* 5:392-403, 1955. The figures given tend to show that different types of groups in this country during the present decade have each exerted the same degree of attraction; that is, the strength of the cohesive forces does not vary significantly from one type of group to another for a given time and place.

Within each type of group series, however, it does vary with time and place. The figures for the average daily attendance at all reporting public and elementary schools in the United States may be found tabulated for almost a hundred years back in the annual *Statistical Abstract of the United States* (Washington, D.C., Government Printing Office). These figures show that the average daily attendance has increased steadily since 1870; this is a variation of the cohesion of public schools with time. Figures kindly sent me by Mr. Russell A. Perry of Rotary International show the geographic variations in the cohesion of this organization. Some attendance averages for 1954 to 1959 are as follows:

United States, Canada and
    Bermuda ....87.16%   ("American" areas)
Australia, New Zealand,
    South Africa and others ..81.78%   (South Temperate Zone)
Asia 76.32%
South and Central America,
    Mexico, the Antilles .....65.79%   ("Mañana" areas)

What remains to be done by some interested sociologist is to see if there are correlations between different groups over long periods of time and between different groups in the same places. Thus, the influence of historical and cultural factors on the strength of group cohesion could be studied.

6

Growth and History

THE BIRTH OF A NATION

Every group starts out as an idea before it becomes a reality. This idea may undergo years of preliminary discussion, as in the case of the United Nations; or at the other extreme, in the emergency of a rescue, for example, it may occur as a flash in the mind of one energetic individual. The preliminary idea or mental picture of what the group is going to be like is only provisional. Things usually turn out differently by the time the group is under way.

Any mental picture of what a group should be or is like may be called a group imago. The difference between what a member anticipated or hoped for, his provisional group imago, and the way he sees the actual group at any given moment, his actual group imago, gives rise to dissatisfaction and psychological tension, which results in attempts to reduce the discrepancies. This can be done in two ways: by changing the provisional imago or by changing the group itself. The imago is changed through the process of adjustment, in which the member gives up, at least temporarily, some of his requirements. This is made easier if at the same time he finds that some of his fears and apprehensions were unnecessary. The process of adjustment usually begins even before a member enters a group and is based on whatever information is made available to him.

On the other hand, a member who is not willing or able to adjust in some respect will either go off by himself or try to change the structure of the group to conform to his provisional imago. His efforts become part of the internal group process, in which he takes the initiative.

When a new group is being organized, the object of each organizer is to reduce the discrepancies between his provisional imago and the planned reality as much as possible. This is done through the process of negotiation. Individual proclivities clash and compromise until the activities, the physical structure, the external boundary and perhaps also the major and the minor internal boundaries are defined. If the organizers cannot adjust to each other, or to the ones with the most initiative, the negotiations will be unsuccessful, and the group will not be activated. Success requires that parts of the individual proclivities be resigned in favor of cohesion. If the resignations are only temporary or pretended, the differences will be settled later in the course of the group process.

These principles are illustrated in the history of the founding of our country. The Declaration of Independence resulted from the provisional group imagoes of some of the signers. This particular organization began, as many do, by a revolutionary process in which the original group authority was challenged. What were previously minor internal boundaries of the British Empire became the external boundary of the new group. The territory and the rights of the new group were distinguished from those of the mother group. The minor internal boundaries of the interior, which had existed before the new external boundary was established, were kept much as they were.

The first plan for the Government of the United

States, embodied in the Articles of Confederation, had the structure of a party rather than of a group. The Congress under this form of government had no internal apparatus for exacting taxes and regulating interstate relations. And it had no effective external apparatus to protect the country from invasion, from attacks by Indians or from interference on the high seas. The peaceful activity of the country was disturbed by eruptions of individual proclivities in rivalry and by external threats. Finally, the faults in structure became so obvious that something had to be done about them.

The Constitution was drawn up as a remedy. At the Constitutional Convention, each member (state) had to resign some of its individual proclivities in favor of the group cohesion. When the boundaries were more clearly defined, especially the major internal boundary represented by an effective Federal Government, each state was gratified that the Constitution met the expectations of its provisional group imago in some respects and disappointed because it did not meet those expectations in other areas. The discrepancies have resulted in continual agitation, reinforced as new circumstances arise. This internal group process was and is carried on by due process through referral to the organs of the internal apparatus, such as the Supreme Court, except when the tension between the North and the South broke through in a revolutionary attempt to overthrow the group authority. This revolution required an enormous enlargement of the internal apparatus, which finally resulted in a victory for the cohesion and the preservation of the group structure.

At various times in our history the external pressure became active, and in each case it was successfully opposed by an emergency mobilization of cohesion, represented by the strength of a tremendously enlarged external apparatus, the United States Armed Forces. The success of the cohesion in overcoming the external threat in these situations was due partly to the effectiveness of the police apparatus (such as the F.B.I.) in dealing with internal agitation, and of the morale apparatus (such as the O.W.I.) in reinforcing the cohesion. In these cases, the forces contributing to the cohesion were officially called patriotism.

It should be noted again that the group process always interferes to some extent with the ordinary activities of the members. Due process interferes least of all, requiring merely that certain members stop work long enough to vote, appear in court or serve on juries. But the external process and the revolutionary process, wars and civil wars, have a more profound effect on the peaceful pursuit of happiness in work or play.

One reason the country found itself in difficulties at the beginning, under the Articles of Confederation, was because the provisional group imagoes of the founders did not include an effective group apparatus; it survived later under severe external pressures and internal agitation because the group apparatus did the job that it was designed for. Good intentions, enthusiasm and patriotism are not enough to ensure the survival of a group or a nation; they must be backed up by efficient and effective organization as well as by hardware if that is also necessary. In a showdown, none of the three can be neglected. That is why the practical measure of cohesion is not its input but its output. The input—the brave words, the cohesive attitudes, the answers to the psychological questionnaires and polls—cannot save the group. The output—the effective use of hardware or its equivalent—is its only salvation. Napoleon preferred "Infantry, Cavalry and Artillery" to "Liberty, Equality and Fraternity" for a barracks motto, and he was a great loser whose precepts are studied seriously all over the world. The therapist of ailing groups should have inscribed over his doorway "Morale, Organization and Equipment."

Many other newly organized groups run into trouble because they neglect the details of the internal structure, especially the group apparatus. If they survive in this condition, it is more by luck than by skill. They may be able to do some work, but they cannot cope effectively with external threats or internal conflicts. They must learn by harsh experience to increase their degree of organization. Machiavelli attested to this in some of his political precepts, stressing the need for strong leadership and a well-organized group apparatus.

However, even with the most careful planning, the organizers of a group nearly always encounter difficulties because the provisional group imago is never quite appropriate for the actual conditions. The plans themselves, the paperwork, may be faultless, but they can never anticipate completely all the behavior of the members, which is based on the more personal motives to be found in the private structuring of their group imagoes. A large number of business failures are due to impractical private structuring. A man who fancies himself, rightly perhaps, as a salesman, may provide on paper for financing, purchasing and production, but in practice he runs the business according to his group imago and stresses selling at the expense of the procurement branch of his external apparatus, so that he fails due to poor credit or bad purchasing. Or he may be a good financier but a poor salesman or production supervisor. His company fails from poor morale, poor organization or poor equipment. The morale and the organization are useless without the equipment, the morale and the equipment are useless without the organization, and the organization and the equipment are useless without the morale. There are exceptions to these rules in business as in war, and there are straight flushes in poker, too, but they do not have much to do with good poker playing.

The party type of provisional group imago, in which

the leadership and the group apparatus are poorly defined, is perhaps the commonest source of trouble in newly organized groups, but there are other peculiarities that may have serious consequences. Hitler's provisional group imago had a very clear major internal boundary and a very effective group apparatus. Nevertheless, a universal tragedy resulted from irregularities in the rest of the structure; particularly from the discrepancy between the external boundary of the map in his provisional imago and the actual German frontiers. It was his efforts to correct this discrepancy and to create a Greater Germany that brought about World War II. Other tragedies resulted from abnormalities in the minor structure, which required the extermination of Jews and gypsies. A similar pathology in Ataturk's provisional imago led him to try to get rid of all the Armenians in Turkey.

The purpose of this discussion is to emphasize that a group starts off as a mental concept, and that efforts to make the reality correspond to this concept are likely to make trouble for all sorts of people, including innocent bystanders.

HISTORY AND TRADITION

After the negotiations have reached a certain point, the group can be activated. The stated purpose of the group, its external boundary, and the time and the place where the membership or the leadership will come together are ratified. Each of the members resigns part of his individual proclivities in favor of cohesion, so that the group can become an effective force. The group work, including the activity, and the major, the minor and the external group processes, are regulated by the group canon, which consists of (A) the Constitution, (B) the laws, and (C) the culture.

(A) The constitution regularly includes several important features, not all of which may be written down; but they are always well established in the minds of the members and cannot be changed easily.

1. The name of the group, which gives it formal existence and, in this country, often involves certain legal privileges and responsibilities, such as the right to own property and engage in litigation.

2. A statement of the purpose or activity, which may be very brief, adaptable and subject to different interpretations. In the American Constitution this is stated in a single sentence.

3. The major group structure, which is usually stated or understood clearly: the external boundary, i.e., who is eligible for membership, and the major internal boundary, i.e., who is eligible for leadership and how leadership is attained. Often the minor structure is included: the leadership slots, the membership slots and the minor internal boundaries.

4. The official regulations concerning the internal group process: the major process, and the rules governing the members in the minor process. The American Constitution is typical in that most of it is concerned with this aspect.

5. Provision for adding to or altering the constitution by due process.

In the American Constitution these provisions were set down in the beginning. In others, such as the British Constitution, they evolved and are evolving gradually during the life of the group. In unlettered cultures, where nothing is written down, the same provisions can be found. The model of an unwritten constitution may read something like this:

(1) We are called The Men. (2) Our job is fishing. (3) We have a Paramount Chief and subchiefs, and all who are born in the tribe are subject to their hereditary authority. (4) The chiefs can take taxes and sentence murderers and adulterers. We have special marriage

customs. (5) No chief may change any custom without the consent of the medicine men.

And whether the group is large or small, the same provisions can be found: in an empire, an international scientific society, a juvenile street gang or a psychotherapy group. The first, the existential provision, gives the group a name (even if it is only "This Group"), with rights, privileges and responsibilities. The second, the teleologic provision, indicates the purpose or activity. The third, the structural provision, sets forth the requirements for membership and leadership. The fourth, the regulatory provision, provides means for enforcing discipline and order. The fifth, the autotelic provision, provides machinery for changing the constitution itself (although in empires, street gangs and therapy groups the leader may sometimes have the power to do this autocratically).

(B) It is only a formality to separate the constitution from the laws, since the laws are simply details concerning the group process and, for the most part, are elaborations of the constitutional regulations.

(C) There are three sides to the culture: the technical side, which supplies implements for the group activity; the group etiquette, which tells people how to go about being polite to each other; and the group character, which guides them in expressing their feelings forthrightly without being rude.

In a group without any experience of serious internal or external conflicts, the canon is not taken seriously except by fussy members. However, in a group of long duration which has experienced serious difficulties, it becomes more meaningful. Such a group is said to have a history, and that kind of history is made by the group apparatus.

The canon becomes particularly important if it has had existential reinforcement. Existential reinforcement means that a group, its members and especially its leaders have had to make decisions which, once carried out, cannot be revoked, such as those involving blood and death. Such decisions, even if they are bad ones, often reinforce the group's cohesion by the evolution of traditions. History is simply old newspapers; it becomes literature only when it is embroidered into traditions. These become more and more meaningful in any group of long duration, and the psychological history of a group is found in its traditions rather than in the mere account of events. As a small example, most members of a fraternity remember an exaggerated story of a graduation party held 10 years previously better than they do the minutes of last month's business meeting.

The most important traditions center around heroes, i.e., people who performed extraordinary feats in the history of a group, especially those who founded them, enlarged them or saved them from destruction in the face of strong opposition by killing or by being killed. A typical hero is one who slays or defies the old leader and sets up a new order. From the psychological point of view the history of a group begins, not always when the group began, but often with the deeds of the first important hero. For example, there is a tendency to think that the modern history of England began with William the Conquerer. Many things happened in England before 1066, but most laymen remember little of what took place earlier except for the names of a few minor heroes such as Ethelred the Unready, Edward the Confessor, Swayne Forkbeard and the Venerable Bede. In the case of France, the first major hero is Charlemagne, and people tend to forget the leaders of minor significance who came before him, such as Vercingetorix, Galswintha and Pippin. Students make puns about Pippin, but everybody takes Charlemagne seriously.

Heroes generally belong to one of two classes: leaders or members of the group apparatus. The most important hero psychologically is the one who is traditionally regarded as the founder of the group and thus may be called its primal leader. Primal leaders are canonmakers. They make possible in practice the constitution, the laws and the culture. Later leaders may bring about important changes in the canon or save it from destruction, and to that extent they also are primal leaders. The mark of the primal leader is not that he actually sets up the canon, but that he gives it existential reinforcement. The historical canon-maker is the one who writes the constitution, but the traditional primal leader is the one who, by heroic deeds, gives it meaning in action by fighting or dying to make it possible. Thus, George Washington is *the* primal leader of our country because he made the constitution possible, and Abraham Lincoln is a later primal leader because he was willing to shed blood to preserve it.

After his death a primal leader tends to become subject to a process which may be called euhemerization. In fact the impact of a primal leader may be measured by the degree of his euhemerization, i.e., by the mythical qualities that are attributed to him after he is dead. The early psychological history of older groups is based on such myths. Charlemagne is a typical example. The folk history of early France revolves around his figure. For centuries peasants believed that he rose from the dead to take part in the Crusades. He was immortalized in song and story, canonized with the Christian attributes of holiness and the pagan attributes of magic and resurrection, and, in Germany and England, the astronomers even named the Great Bear after him.

This process whereby ancient kings and heroes took on mythical attributes in the popular mind until they became godlike, with the original connections lost or disregarded, was first publicized in the Western world by the Greek philosopher Euhemerus, although the idea was already known in the Orient. Therefore, in his honor those individuals whose memory has undergone the process of euhemerization may be called euhemeri. Thus, Charlemagne is an outstanding example of a euhemerus. The euhemeri of a group which has survived for a long period include "The Euhemerus," representing the dead primal leader, and a number of "later euhemeri," representing later heroes in the group's tradition. The most dramatically successful primal leaders are the ones with the greatest impact, and hence the ones most likely to be euhemerized.

There are two main types of near-heroes, or *héros manqués*: 1. It can be noted that a leader or agitator who kills or is killed but fails to save or change the structure of the group (such as Trotsky) is not euhemerized. 2. The leader who is required to have courage or genius but not actually to kill or be killed (such as Freud) may be euhemerized to some extent but never as decisively as the killer. "The Euhemerus" may be the first primal leader such as Washington, Lenin or Mahomet, or a later one who has greater impact than his predecessors, such as Charlemagne.

Sometimes the process of euhemerization may begin before a primal leader dies, if it is thought that he has departed permanently. In a small way this was the case with a dancing teacher named Abe. Abe taught folk dancing, and his whole class was enthusiastic about him. When war came he was called into the service, and they got a new teacher. They were continually making comparisons between Abe and the new man, always favorable to Abe. As time passed Abe became greater and greater. There was nobody like old Abe. He became more and more glorious and splendid, and the members of the class actually believed what they said about him. Then one day, Abe walked in, back from the army and ready to take over. When he went out on the floor there was a great letdown when they saw that he was an ordinary folk dancing teacher, just as ordinary as the man who had replaced him. All the newcomers who had heard about the mythical figure of Abe could hardly believe their eyes when he actually appeared in the form of an ordinary human being. This is a relatively rare case of a euhemerus who came back.*

Many euhemeri such as Hippocrates, Washington, Lincoln, Lenin and Freud are well known, but a newcomer to a more restricted group might have some difficulty at first in deciding who were the euhemeri. In past centuries a euhemerus could be picked out from the songs and the folk tales which were traditional for the group. Now a euhemerus is seen rather than heard. The euhemerus of a group is the dead person whose picture is most likely to be found on the walls of both the meeting places and the homes of the members. In the case of Buddha or the Catholic saints the representation is often in the form of a statue rather than a picture. In some religions in which such replicas are forbidden, they are replaced by quotations from the writings of the euhemerus, as in the cases of Mahomet and Moses.

A euhemerus serves as a rallying point for the cohesive forces of the group and also increases its effectiveness by lending authority to the canon. The primal leader establishes customs concerning the manner in which the group work is carried on, and these customs become traditions after his death and are referred to him as the authority. The members of the model tribe described above fish with nets of hemp, always address their mothers-in-law in the third person, and are allowed to laugh at men who commit adultery and to sing a song when the wronged husband takes his revenge. All this is traditional because it is said that that is the way Glub did it when he came down from the

* This anecdote was related to me by Dr. Lauren Carter.

moon and showed it all to the first man and woman and their children after he made them out of tapioca. Hence, Glub is The Euhemerus of this fictitious society. He was the primal leader, and he made the primal canon. The primal canon was changed slightly by Chief Blug, who lived several hundred years later. He saw to it that sisters-in-law were included in the third-person taboo, and, because he had the courage to change this part of the canon without consulting the medicine men, he became a minor euhemerus, especially among sisters-in-law, who ever since his death have worn his carven figure in their headdresses.

The dynamic influence of euhemeri is most clearly seen in times of stress. So long as things go smoothly for the group and the process can be handled by everyday police and morale work, the euhemeri seem to be of little importance. During such periods they may be ignored or even made fun of. But if someone makes a forceful attack on the group structure, either from within or from without, so that ordinary methods are no longer sufficient to control the turbulence, the euhemeri are brought out, often in reverse chronologic order. For example, in this country when the Constitution is threatened by a strong minority, both sides begin to quote Lincoln in support of their positions, and, if the difficulties continue, then the names of the Founding Fathers begin to appear more and more frequently.

THE GROUP FUNCTIONS

There are certain things that happen regularly in the histories of different kinds of groups, and these may be called group functions. The internal process of any group can be broken down into a series of such functions. Some of them seem to occur, if not full-blown, at least in embryonic form in every kind of group, as though no group could survive without them; these may be called obligatory functions. Others occur frequently, but not in every group; these may be called incidental functions. The first sections of this chapter have dealt with the functions of organization and euhemerization, and these both appear to be obligatory. Organization is obligatory because a group, by definition, could not come into being without it, while the historical evidence is that euhemerization takes place in any group that survives several generations and may very well be necessary for its survival. It is difficult to think of any enduring group that does not or did not have a euhemerus. The founders of all religions are euhemerized, and so are the founders of cities, states, empires and dynasties, such as Cadmus, Byzas, Romulus and Remus, Jimmu Tenno of the Japanese and Jacob of the Jews. The traditional professions have theirs, such as Aesculapius of the doctors and Solon of the law-givers. Since there seems to be a kind of euhemerus-hunger in most groups, it would be psychologically incredible if a group survived for more than two generations without euhemerizing someone. In modern industry and finance the process of euhemerization is already in progress with living and recently deceased leaders, as shown in the legendary quirks and exploits of Samuel Goldwyn, Henry Ford and John D. Rockefeller.

Another obligatory function is getting acquainted. If people are already acquainted outside the group, they must become reacquainted in their new roles as group members.

There may be other obligatory functions, but at present it is not possible to state them with any degree of certainty. Additions to the list beyond organization, getting acquainted and euhemerization would require a careful study of the histories of a large number of groups from this particular point of view, and such a collection is not yet available.

Incidental functions include proceedings which are

commonly put under the heading of "contagion": for example laughing together, crying together and singing together. The ancient Greeks had hundreds of words that described such proceedings in which members of groups participated together.

It should be possible to think up experiments for testing the properties and the effects of obligatory functions. For example, a speaker is introduced before his talk and not afterward—a formal way of getting acquainted by means of a warrant. What would happen if this program were reversed without the audience's knowing that it was a deliberate experiment? By discovering additional obligatory functions and shifting them around, many aspects of group dynamics might be clarified.

The idea of functions is related to certain well-known observations in social psychiatry. Bion has described what he calls "basic assumptions." He has names for different states of the group—the work group, the dependency group, the pairing group and the fight or flight group. Bion is one of the few people who have tried to observe what goes on in a group from a naturalistic point of view, not trying to prove or disprove anything but merely asking themselves: "What's going on here?" In some ways Bion's work is more interesting than the usual commonplace statistical studies. He observed very acutely what happened in his particular groups. The group states that he describes seem to be incidental functions, but it is possible that they are obligatory. The question is whether all groups have to be in one or other of these states or even pass through them in the course of development or whether that is unnecessary in some cases. The answer awaits further study. Trigant Burrow, the first man who practiced group therapy as we know it today, was also a great observer. The special state which he calls cotention, in which the subjects' breathing patterns, eye movements and even electroencephalograms seem to be altered, is probably related to an incidental function of his groups.

The evidence so far is that obligatory functions proceed in a certain unchanging order: organization is first, and euhemerization can only take place late in the life of a group after many other functions have been completed. It has already been noted that the central person of a ritual-like activity, such as a lecturer, is introduced beforehand, rather than afterward; his warrant is always presented before the activity begins. The directing force that determines this order may be related to the biologic force that regulates the order in which the functions of a growing organism develop. Perhaps it is something like the Physis of the Stoics, or perhaps it is only that certain things are possible at certain times.

SUMMARY

The important hypotheses outlined here are as follows:

1. The internal group process results from the tension between two sets of mental images: what the individual wants the group to be like, and what he perceives it to be.

2. Those who organize a group try to make the reality correspond as closely as possible to their images of what it should be like, but since the organizers have different images, compromises are always necessary; such compromises are never final, due to hypothesis 1.

3. The function of a primal leader is to regulate the group work through the process of canon-making.

4. Every group has a hunger for heroes and tends to glorify primal leaders after their deaths by a process of euhemerization.

5. These euhemeri are strong influences in making the group meaningful.

6. The internal group process can be broken up his-

torically into a series of functions. Certain functions, such as organization and euhemerization, are obligatory if the group survives, and they proceed in a certain order.

SPECIAL TERMS INTRODUCED
IN THIS CHAPTER

Group imago	Autotelic provision
Provisional group imago	Existential reinforcement
Negotiation	Tradition
Group canon	Hero
Existential provision	Primal leader
Teleologic provision	Euhemerus
Structural provision	Obligatory function
Regulatory provision	Incidental function

TECHNICAL NOTES

THE BIRTH OF A NATION

Machiavelli's precepts may be found in his *Discourses*. The material concerning the organization of the United States of America is outlined in *Essentials of American Government*, by F. A. Ogg and P. O. Ray (New York, Appleton-Century Company, 1932). Hitler's views can be found in *Mein Kampf*. The Armenians were uprooted under Ataturk by Kiazim Kara Bekir in 1920. (*Grey Wolf*, by H. C. Armstrong, Harmondsworth, Penguin Books, 1937). An intimate picture of their tribulations is given by Franz Werfel in *The Forty Days of Musa Dagh* (New York, Viking Press, 1934).

It is evident that the word "patriotism" is subject to vulgarization and exploitation by special interests in various countries.

HISTORY AND TRADITION

The historical details mentioned in connection with euhemeri may be found in the *Encyclopaedia Britannica*.

Tapioca comes from the root of Janipha Manihot (cassava, manioc). Anthropologists who may take exception to Glub as a mere individual euhemerus, rather than as a representative of a whole historical era, may be overlooking evidence that cultural history often proceeds in jumps rather than slow walks, e.g., (1) the Tongan invasions of Fiji; (2) Cakombau's Lotu, which radically changed the character of Fijian culture in a very few years (cf. Plekhanov vs. the Narodniks); and (3) the rapidity with which in practice a whole culture can develop in a new group. This last must be experienced to be believed. This phenomenon was well demonstrated during the growth of the San Francisco Social Psychiatry Seminars, with the evolution of its own folkways and its own jargon in the course of a very few years.

THE GROUP FUNCTIONS

Liddell and Scott give a long list of words under *syn-* and *sym-* which describe what people can do in groups but do not necessarily do in every group. This list makes it clear that incidental functions are intimately connected with the group culture.

W. R. Bion's series of 7 papers concerning what he calls "basic assumptions" in groups can be found in the periodical *Human Relations* from 1948 to 1951, as follows: Vol. 1, Nos. 3 and 4, 1948; Vol. 2, Nos. 1 and 4, 1949; Vol. 3, Nos. 1 and 4, 1950; and Vol. 4, No. 3, 1951. He summarizes his ideas in "Group Dynamics: A Re-view," (*International Journal of Psycho-Analysis, 33:*235-247, 1952) but this is difficult to follow even for readers who are well acquainted with the original papers. All this has now appeared in book form (*Experiences in Groups,* New York, Basic Books, 1961). Some experienced group therapists, such as D. A. Shaskan in San Francisco, use Bion's work as a nucleus for their approach.

The papers of Trigant Burrow referred to in this section are "The Basis of Group Analysis" (1928) and "The Neurodynamics of Human Behavior" (1943).

The concept of Physis is discussed in *The Stoic Age*, by Gilbert Murray (London, Watts, 1915) and may be comprehended in an elementary way through my book, *A Layman's Guide to Psychiatry and Psychoanalysis* (New York, Simon & Schuster, 1957).

7

The Group Authority

THE LEADER

The group authority consists of two sectors, the leadership and the group canon. These fit together so that a member can appeal from the leader's decision to the canon, from the judge's verdict to the body of laws; or he can appeal from the canon to the leader, from the legal punishment to the Governor's pardon.

There are three kinds of leadership, corresponding to the three aspects of the group structure. The responsible leader is the front man, the man who fills the role of leader in the organizational structure. The effective leader, who makes the actual decisions, may or may not have a role in the organizational structure. He may be the man in the back room, but he is the most important person in the individual structure. The psychological leader is the one who is most powerful in the private structures of the members and occupies the leadership slot in their group imagoes. All three types of leadership may be invested in the same individual, but there are all sorts of combinations. Thus, in the British Government, the Prime Minister is the responsible and effective leader, and the monarch is the psychological leader. In certain of our cities, the mayor is the responsible and psychological leader, and the ward boss is the effective leader. In certain criminal groups the front men are the responsible leaders, while another man who has no fixed role in the organizational structure is the effective and psychological leader.

The distinction between the three kinds of leadership is not always easy to make. For example, the psychological leader, who belongs to the private structure (which is often unconscious), can sometimes only be identified by psychiatric methods. But since the private structure usually comes out into the open in times of stress or over the long term, the psychological leadership may become clearer in historical situations. For example, in the case of the British Empire, it is quite certain that Queen Victoria, even when she was not constitutionally responsible or effective, was psychologically supreme. No matter how distinguished her prime ministers were, this period is still known as the Victorian era, and the Queen was very likely the most influential person of her time.

The effective leader can be distinguished by studying the group in action. He is the one whose questions are most likely to be answered or whose suggestions are most likely to be followed in situations of stress. There is some resemblance between effective leaders and the so-called "subleaders" found in various types of experimental groups. "Subleaders" have been carefully studied in experiments with soldiers and college students. They are members who attract attention because they are dominant, popular or show a special interest in the group activity. One object of these experiments is to study the personality characteristics of such influential people as an aid to selecting officer candidates, executives or student leaders. However, in judging such experiments, it is often overlooked that the effective leader of an experimental group is usually the experimenter himself.

The responsible leader is the individual who is going to be called to account by higher authority if things go wrong—the experimenter in an experimental group and the executive in a business group. Since in many organizations the responsible leader is only a front, it is here that dominance, popularity and helpfulness find their usefulness. A man who possesses these qualities may be attractive to the members and thus serve the purposes of the effective leadership.

The psychological leader of a group occupies a special position, whether or not he is also the responsible and effective leader. The members demand certain qualities of the psychological leader, the one who is likely to survive in the group tradition as a euhemerus. And these are the qualities of a god. The leader is supposed to be omnipotent, omniscient, immortal, invulnerable, irresistible, incorruptible, unseducible, indefatigable and fearless. These are the same qualities that were attributed in ancient times to emperors such as "the unequalled, almighty, invincible, unwavering Assur-nasir-pal." If a leader in real life fails in any one of these respects, there will always be those who will criticise him for it. For example this happens if an American president shows weakness, ignorance, sickness, touchiness, corruptibility or fear. The effects soon begin to show in the stock market, the political cartoons and the letters to the editor. Even a group therapist is supposed to have most of these qualities. In many groups, the members will become uneasy if he so much as has a cold. He will be teased, some patients will say that they feel insecure because he got sick, and some of them will ask how he can cure them if he gets sick himself.

It will be noted that the qualities required of a psychological leader already resemble the attributes of a euhemerus. The ancient emperors who expected to be treated like gods while they were still alive were actually insisting that they be euhemerized before they were dead, as shown by the inscription about Assur-nasir-pal.

In addition to classifying leaders according to the three aspects of leadership it is also desirable to classify them according to their positions in the group. The one who first establishes the group is the primal leader. Leaders who follow in his footsteps may be called executives. Subsequent leaders who change the constitution are to that extent again primal leaders. The actual living leader at any given moment may be called the personal leader. Leaders who have certain independent powers but are answerable to higher authority for other decisions may be called subleaders. Leaders who are answerable for everything are personal leaders in their subgroups, but, in relation to the whole group, they may be called delegates. A practical test of leadership is the power to make decisions that are not subject to revision or veto by anyone else present; most convincingly, decisions concerning the group structure, such as who is allowed to remain in the group, when the meeting ends and when another meeting will be held. If no one else can override an individual's authority in such matters, then that individual is the leader of the group. If the so-called leader plays the king but someone else can play the ace (to paraphrase Eugene Field's epigram), then he is more a subleader or delegate than a true leader.

Leadership is most strongly confirmed by existential reinforcement. Historically, great leaders have always been able to kill or be killed and to take responsibility for everything, including death. In our own country the three most euhemerized presidents, Washington, Lincoln and Roosevelt, were all war presidents and all able to take the responsibility for killing. Assurnasir-pal, Cheops, Pericles, Mahomet, Napoleon, Ataturk, Hitler and Stalin were all able to order bloodshed; Socrates and Jesus were men who knew how to die. Under more civilized conditions banishment replaces killing, and a good leader must have the ability to enforce this when it is required. Thus Freud banished agitators who tried to twist his theories, and every good professor must be able to fail a student when circumstances require it. So the basic tests of leadership are the responsibility and the right (organizationally) to apply sanctions and give rewards, and the ability (individually) to do so irrevocably. In a small way, even the chairman of a PTA meeting must be ruthless so that he can keep people from getting out of hand.

THE GROUP CANON

After the death of the primal leader, the course of the group work is regulated by the canon that he has established. As already mentioned, the canon consists of three parts: the constitution, the laws based on it and the culture. The basic canon follows that of the mother group; but each group develops its own peculiar departures from the mother canon, and it is these departures which distinguish the canon of one group from that of another in the same society.

The main features of a typical constitution were listed previously. First, there is the naming of the group, the existential provision that gives it its responsibility toward other groups and toward society in general. Secondly, there is a statement concerning the activity, the teleologic provision which gives the group its goal. Thirdly, the structure is described in the structural provision. Fourthly, the process is regulated by the regulatory provision. And fifthly, the changing of the constitution itself is authorized by the autotelic provision.

The first canon is made by the primal leader, who through his authority is able to establish a tradition of behavior which in some respects is different from what the members are accustomed to outside the group. This is the primal canon and has a very forceful appeal for the members in later generations. Anyone who changes,

adds to or subtracts from the primal canon is himself to
that extent a primal leader. The appeal to the traditional canon in times of doubt is nearly always made in
a personal way by bringing up the name of the appropriate euhemerus. Thus, we have, "Confucius said,"
"Lincoln said," "Freud said," "Lenin said." That is
the way in which the euhemerus exerts his authority on
the posterity of his group. Ataturk and Lenin were typical primal leaders. They set up new constitutions and
new cultures with organizational and personal relationships radically altered from the old ways of their
mother groups. Constitutionally, both of them changed
the form of government, and culturally, both of them
changed the relationships between men and women, for
example.

Because the euhemerus and the primal canon have a
sacred quality in even the most "irreligious" groups, a
good executive rarely tries to become a primal leader.
Instead, he changes the canon according to his needs or
the demands of the times in such a way that he appears
to be interpreting it rather than changing it. In this way
he lessens the risk of a diminished cohesion. However,
if he wishes to form his own group in a revolutionary
operation, he must boldly attack the old canon and often weaken the authority of the old euhemeri as well.
But he must carefully consider how far he can go
safely. A simple way out is to attack the personal
leader without attacking the euhemeri, to overthrow
Emperor Nicholas without derogating Peter the Great,
to depose Abdul Hamid without destroying the prestige
of Sultan Achmet, to attack Kennedy without attacking
Lincoln.

As noted, the object of the canon is to regulate the
group work, and particularly the internal group process, which consists of operations meant to change the
organizational, the individual or the private structure of
the group. The roles in the organizational structure are

maintained by the constitutional contract, which reads: "I promise to support the constitution of this group." The rest of the internal group process is regulated by the social contract, which reads: "You respect my persona, and I'll respect yours." The social contract is enforced by the group etiquette, but each group develops certain relaxations in the etiquette, and these relaxations form part of the group character.

Since the social contract is the most important influence in the group culture, its meaning should be clearly understood. The way in which an individual chooses to present himself to a group is called his persona. The social contract states that his presentation must be accepted courteously at face value, according to the group etiquette. Every group must find its own ways of legitimately violating the social contract; otherwise life would become intolerably dull. These departures from strict etiquette belong to the group character.

This can be illustrated by comparing the culture of news photography in the Soviet Union with that in America (in 1956). The material aspects, the equipment and the technic are similar in both countries. But in the Soviet Union the persona is protected by a strict etiquette. For example, athletes and political figures can only be photographed while they are engaged in their official occupations, and, to make certain that the photographers abide by the social contract, they must get permission beforehand in both cases. Thus, Soviet news photography tends to be dull. In America, it is much more lively because it is full of character. There is hardly any etiquette, and every possible exception to the social contract is taken full advantage of. In fact, our photographers delight in playing with the personas of their subjects: taking pictures of athletes at nightclubs and of bankers with midgets on their knees.

In the culture of police activity, the situation is reversed. It is the Soviets who disregard the social contract, and the crudest violations of personas by their secret police apparatus are (or were) tolerated by the membership and even encouraged by the leadership. In America there is a strict legally controlled etiquette that forces the police to observe the social contract, and violations are not tolerated except by the lowest elements. Thus, in the U.S.S.R., in the culture of press photography the etiquette predominates with strict adherence to the social contract, while in the culture of police activity, character predominates to permit gross insults. In the American group culture, it is the other way round.

It should be noted that the culture does not change with the individual but with the group he is in. For example, a husband may be quite unrestrained toward his wife at home, but he must treat her differently at a PTA meeting. It is the individual who adjusts to the culture and not vice versa, except in the case of a primal leader.

THE GROUP CULTURE

For a practical understanding of organizations and groups it is necessary to have a workable theory of group culture, since the culture influences almost everything that happens in a social aggregation. The following approach, based on the personality structure outlined in Part III, has been found to be the most useful in dealing with ailing groups.

Culture is divided into three segments—technical culture, group etiquette and group character. The technical culture is used principally in the work and the combat groups and includes all sorts of useful (and decorative) artifacts, from quartz chips to space ships; all sorts of practical technics for changing the environment, from daubing pigments to making plutonium; as well as all sorts of practical intellectual operations, from counting reindeer to programming computers. It includes those aspects of culture that require the use of a logical mind directed toward reality, that part of the personality which later will be called the Adult.

The group etiquette is based on the general social etiquette and includes all items of etiquette which are different from the general etiquette but are acceptable in the given group. Etiquette deals with standards of behavior and ways of presenting an acceptable persona or of reinforcing or guiding the personas of others. What makes people comfortable socially is to feel that other people see them as they want to be seen. Most people want to be seen as generous, intelligent, courageous, sincere and loyal—in general, acceptable according to the standards of the group. Each group has its own special standards and its own favored ways of presenting or reinforcing a persona. There is a different standard and a different approach for presenting oneself as courageous at a scientific meeting, at a revival meeting or in a group of skin-divers. And there is a different etiquette for acknowledging courage in each of these situations. Etiquette is usually traditional and in most cases only changes slowly or under special conditions. This part of the group culture originates from that aspect of the personality which later will be called the Parent.

The group character includes departures from the social contract which are established as legitimate in a particular group through relaxations of the group etiquette. Sometimes these freedoms are surprising to outsiders. For example, Bell, Cuppy and Q, being inexperienced spiritualists, were a little startled to find that it was all right to tease some of the spirits and to laugh at certain times. The social contract was relaxed with Ruby, but no liberties were permitted with Dr. Murgatroyd.

Character is more "primitive" than etiquette. Etiquette requires a restraint, an understanding and a knowledge of social behavior that an infant, for example, does not have. Character is a more direct expression of instinctual life. It includes many things that infants can do, such as laughing, singing and weeping. The group character is chiefly an expression of that aspect of the personality which later will be called the Child.

The usefulness of this three-pronged view of culture can be illustrated by analyzing some items of group behavior which are often thought of as typically "cultural."

1. Circumcision may be regarded as an initiation rite, i.e., a constitutional requirement for membership. When the constitution is a written one, as in the Old Testament, for example, the primal canon can be found in its original form. Rituals surrounding the operation then would be part of the group etiquette—the etiquette of circumcision. In many localities the ceremonies include a feast where more relaxed expressions of feeling are permissible as part of the group character.

2. The organizational structure of the United States of America provides a slot for the Presidency. The man who occupies this slot is known officially as the President or Mr. President, and unofficially by his surname and nickname. As the President, his role cannot be attacked, under the constitutional contract, except by constitutional means. If there are changes to be made in the manner of his election or the maximal number of terms that he can serve, this must be done by due process, and the changes then apply not to any specific individual but to whoever fills the Presidency slot in the role of President.

However, the incumbent at any moment presents himself as an acceptable person with a certain kind of courage, generosity, sincerity and loyalty in regard to certain specific problems, such as racial integration and interstate commerce.* Mr. President can be attacked on the floor by marshalling facts against his viewpoint, but these facts must relate to the matter in hand, and the personality of the President must not be brought into the argument; his deeds can be scrutinized courteously, but his persona must not be questioned, as this would be considered a breach of etiquette. Thus, it was regarded as rude when, several years ago, the head of another state referred to Mr. Eisenhower as insincere. One of the official manuals for this etiquette is *Robert's Rules of Order*. In unofficial reports, the President's title is replaced by his surname, which belongs to the individual structure.

However, in accordance with the American group character, Ike the personality could be teased in a decent way about his golfing and criticized for some of his friendships. But there were definite limits as to how far this could go publicly, and to transgress them was an insult. These aspects of the canon relating to the Presidency are shown in Table 8.

While there is often a manual or authority concerning a group's etiquette, the character comes so naturally and is so plastic that it is difficult to pin down or formulate in words. The political cartoonist carries his

TABLE 8. CANON OF THE AMERICAN PRESIDENCY

Structure	Canonical Provision	Aspect	Contract	Requirement	Violations
Organizational	Constitution	Role: The President	Constitutional	Due Process	Revolution
Individual	Etiquette	Persona: Mr. President, Eisenhower	Social	Courtesy	Breach of Etiquette, Rudeness
Private	Character	Personality: Ike	Social	Decency	Insult

* In general, roles in the organizational structure are defined by verbs ("He makes decisions") and personas by adjectives ("He is a decisive person").

Rules of Satirical Order mostly in his head. The distinction between rudeness and insult should be noted. Rudeness is a mere neglect of etiquette or an exhibition of character ("familiarity") when etiquette is called for. An insult goes beyond even the latitude allowed by the group character.

3. Secret societies, primitive or otherwise, with their elaborate concern over dignity, are good examples to consider. They are boring to many people because they have so much etiquette and so little character; i.e., everyone has to take everyone else very seriously. But in many of them, if a member breaks a rule, it is legitimate to attack him, and this is where the character comes out and the fun begins. For example, some American service clubs derive much of their fun from fining members 10 cents each time they use a swear word.

The psychological aspects of culture as outlined here may be summarized as follows. The technical culture, what one has to do, is based on an objective, realistic, "adult" approach to the environment. The group etiquette, what one is supposed to do, is a matter of tradition, dealing with behavior standards and their maintenance, and is passed down from one generation to another, being learned from the parents, as it were. The group character deals with what one might like to do, and, with proper restraint, allows the expression of more archaic aspects of the personality. The culture of clothes in our society illustrates the integration of these three aspects. Women wear clothes to protect themselves from the weather, which is a rational or Adult view; for reasons of modesty, which is a traditional or Parental view; and to decorate themselves and make themselves appear more interesting and sometimes provocative. Thus, clothes are a part of the technical culture in being useful, part of the etiquette in being modest, and part of the character in allowing self-expression even when this conflicts with the persona of modesty. From the organizational point of view clothes are also worn for constitutional reasons; i.e., in most places they are required by law.

This approach to culture has two advantages. On the one hand it is based on the personality of the individual, and on the other it fits into the dynamics of the group as a whole. Thus, it has a natural place in the consideration of what happens between specific individuals in any particular group.

SUMMARY

The following hypotheses are offered:

1. The proceedings of any group are regulated by two authorities: the leadership and the group canon.

2. There are three kinds of leadership: the responsible leader, the effective leader and the psychological leader.

3. The members demand certain absolute qualities of their leaders so that fundamentally every successful leader is a charismatic leader.

4. The culture of a group can be divided into three aspects: the technical culture, the group etiquette and the group character. The last two are based on an implicit contract that the members will respect each others' personas. Each group evolves its own standards of behavior, its own ways of reinforcing the contract and its own ways of violating it in certain respects.

5. Each of the three aspects of a group culture is derived from a special aspect of the members' personalities: the technical culture from the realistic (adult) aspect; the group etiquette from the traditional (parental) aspect; and the group character from the emotional (archaic) aspect.

SPECIAL TERMS INTRODUCED
IN THIS CHAPTER

Responsible leader	Constitutional contract
Effective leader	Persona
Psychological leader	Adult
Primal leader	Parent
Executive	Child
Personal leader	Manual
Subleader	Rudeness
Delegate	Insult
Primal canon	

TECHNICAL NOTES

THE LEADER

The results of the investigation of the International Boxing Guild and the International Boxing Club, which illustrates the relationship between the effective leader and the responsible front, were reported regularly in *Sports Illustrated*, e.g., December 19, 1955, p. 15, and January 16, 1956, p. 9. An example of the academic approach to leadership may be found in "Leadership Among Patients in Group Therapy," by R. Sears, *International Journal of Group Psychotherapy*, 3:191-197, April, 1953. A similar study is described in "How People Interact in Conferences," by R. F. Bales, *Scientific American*, 192:31-35, March, 1955.

For the description of the "glorious" personality of the monstrous murderer Assur-nasir-pal, see *Annals of Assur-nasir-pal*, Column I (*Worlds Great Classics*, New York, Colonial Press, 1901).

The existentialist point of view is set forth in simple language by J. P. Sartre in *Existentialism*, translated by B. Frechtman (New York, Philosophical Library, 1947).

THE GROUP CANON

The background of the word "autotelic" may be found in Liddell and Scott, and is discussed by K. F. Leidecker in *Dictionary of Philosophy* (D. D. Runes, [ed.], New York, Philosophical Library, n.d.).

Ataturk: see *Grey Wolf, loc. cit.* Lenin: see *Lenin,* by James

Maxton (New York, Appleton & Company, 1932). The term "social contract," as used here, has less strict implication than the "social contracts" of Hobbes, Locke and Rousseau, which would correspond more to what is here called the "constitutional contract," with its connotations of legal force, although all these cases are similar because they are essentially based on a *volonté générale*. See article on "Social Contract" in Runes, *Dictionary of Philosophy* (*loc. cit.*), and *The Encyclopaedia Britannica*.

The attitude of a Russian Olympic athlete toward being photographed is recounted in *Sports Illustrated,* February 6, 1956, p. 17.

THE GROUP CULTURE

The etiquette concerning modesty *in medias res* is shown in *A House Is Not a Home,* by Polly Adler (New York, Popular Library, 1954), p. 87, for example.

Regarding the written canonical provision for circumcision, see: Genesis xviii, 10-14.

E. Crawley, in *The Mystic Rose* (London, Macmillan & Company, 1902), propounds the following questions "after the fashion of Plutarch" at the outset (pp. 2 & 3): "Why do husbands and wives, brothers and sisters, engaged couples, men and their mothers-in-law, and men and women generally, avoid each other in certain ways?" On the basis of Crawley's material, most of these avoidances can be brought under the rubric of etiquette; they represent idiosyncratic methods of enforcing the social contract in the groups concerned. In our society, a more joking character would intrude on the etiquette of some of the relationships.

A perusal of H. Webster's *Primitive Secret Societies* (New York, Macmillan Company, 1932) or a visit to a service club luncheon will easily demonstrate how seriously the members of such societies take themselves. In regard to clothing, see J. C. Flugel's monograph on *The Psychology of Clothes* (London, Hogarth Press, 1930).

8

The Classification of Groups

A SYSTEM FOR CLASSIFICATION

So far we have been concentrating on things that all groups have in common. Now it is time to consider the differences between them. There are prison groups and social groups, obligatory groups and voluntary groups. Some are born members, some achieve membership, and others have membership thrust upon them. There are groups that are easy to get into but hard to get out of, like marriage or the army. And groups that are hard to get into and easy to get out of, like the high school football team. In fact, it would not be difficult to make a kind of anthology or the thesaurus with almost innumerable systems of classification, each one admirably suited to its purpose. J. F. Brown gives a good classification of classifications: biologic-social, based on class theory; functional-sociologic based on goals; economic-functional, based on Bukharin; in-group versus out-group, based on Sumner; primary versus secondary groups, based on Cooley; open versus closed groups, based on Alverdes. Krech and Crutchfield offer such descriptive distinctions as rigid and flexible, organized and unorganized. Kimball Young divides groups into race, society, and community; primary and secondary; permanent and impermanent; we-group and others-group.

However, in order to deal systematically with ailing

groups, it is necessary to have a classification that includes all of the important aspects dealt with in the previous chapters: the group structure, the group forces, the group work and the group authority. In this way, something akin to a scientific approach to the practical problems of all sorts of groups becomes possible. Experience has shown that such a system enables the investigator to make accurate diagnoses, and, as every clinician knows, that is the most important step toward improving the situation.

It is convenient to begin with the group structure, starting at the external boundary. The first characteristic to be considered is its permeability: the open boundary, which almost anyone may cross in either direction at any time, in such open groups as the S.P.C.A. or the Red Cross; the closed boundary, which it is impossible to cross inward once the group is formed, in such closed groups as the complement of a ship at sea, the alumni of the class of '23 or the veterans of the Spanish-American war; and the sealed boundary which prevents outward crossing from sealed groups such as a prison or a closed psychiatric ward. Sealed groups correspond to what some writers call by the unfortunate name of "captive" groups. The sealing of a boundary is relative and is rarely as complete as in the well-known "sealed trains" of Hitler's Germany.

Closely related to the permeability of the external boundary are the circumstances under which it may be crossed. This leads to a distinction by classes of membership: voluntary, by application; optional, by invitation; conditional, by achievement; and obligatory, by draft. To these may be added memberships which are accidental, as by accident of birth.

Moving on to the internal structure, it is useful to speak of simple, compound, complex and complicated groups. A simple group is one with a single internal boundary, as illustrated in Figure 17, so that it consists only of a leadership and a membership with no subdivisions. This is the typical structure of a psychotherapy group. A compound or graded group is one with a simple hierarchy corresponding to the concentric structure of Figure 18A. It consists of a leader, subleaders in order of rank, superior members and inferior members. Examples might be a union local or a stock company with preferred and common shareholders. A complex group consists of an assembly of subgroups, each with its own internal organization, corresponding to the segmented structure of Figure 18B, typically a confederation like the United States or Canada. A complicated group is one in which the authority is split, as in a hospital or corporation; the financial responsibility, the administrative responsibility and the working responsibility are divided among different subgroups that cannot encroach directly on each other's fields. A stockholder cannot tell the foreman how to puddle steel, and a surgeon cannot tell the hospital administrator how to train the bookkeeper. In practice there are various combinations of these types, and such structural distinctions also depend to some extent on the observer's point of view, but usually a simple group is always just a simple group.

The relationship between the organizational and the individual structures gives rise to the classes of overorganized, completely organized and incompletely organized groups, depending on the ratio between roles and slots, and overmanned, fully manned and undermanned groups, depending on the number of members as compared to the available slots. The degree of differentiation in the group imagoes provides another opportunity for classification, but that is a special problem that will have to be discussed in more detail later. This completes the important items of the structural classification, which raises some interesting questions. For example, what are the results of the fact that all simple groups of more than two people are incompletely organized?

Dynamically, groups may be classified according to the strengths of the forces engaged at a given moment and also according to whether the forces are active or merely potential: the cohesive forces, the individual proclivities and the external disruptive forces. Concerning cohesion, a group that looks weak and is not functioning effectively under ordinary circumstances may in time of danger be able to mobilize strong active cohesive forces. Thus, a group can be graded not only on its active strength but also on its potential strength. This is one aspect of the problem of morale.

Individual proclivities may also be either active or potential. When the members are not actively engaged or are holding back, the group may be either relaxed or tense, depending on how they judge the possibilities. If the internal group process is actively under way, it may be either mild or intense. For example, the Swiss seem to have found satisfactory solutions for certain internal problems, so that when things are quiet on the national scene they go about their business in a relaxed way, and if disputations do break out, they are usually mild. A South American country, on the other hand, may be tense in anticipation of an assassination or a revolution, and if it occurs, it may be followed by intense fighting. Thus, the relaxation or tension of a group depends on what is under the surface, and its mildness or intensity depends on what comes out into the open in the way of individual proclivities.

The same classification may be used in regard to external forces. The strength of the potential external pressure as judged by the members determines whether the group is relaxed or tense toward the external environment; if the external disruptive forces become active, the external group process may be mild or intense. One country may handle a number of actual spies with only a mild disturbance, while another may be whipped into a state of acute tension over an imaginary enemy.

The dynamic classifications raise many questions for investigation. Some examples, with the answers found in specific cases, are as follows. Under what conditions may a tense group be (a) more effective, or (b) less effective than a relaxed group? (a. When the tension is related to the external environment, and b. When the tension is related to the leadership.) How does increasing intensity of the internal process affect the intensity of the external process? (By draining forces from the external apparatus into the internal apparatus.) How does it affect the cohesion? (By draining forces from the morale apparatus into the police apparatus.)

The classification of groups according to the phases of the group work in which they are engaged has already been discussed in detail. A group may be primarily either a work group, a combat group or a process group.

An attempt to distinguish groups according to the nature of the group authority immediately raises questions which have always been controversial, such as the distinction between democratic and authoritarian groups. From one point of view, nearly all groups are authoritarian in that the members have to obey the group canon. This can be shown by taking two extreme cases: one canon says that every member has an equal vote, and the other says that no member has any vote. Now if someone in the first group tries to deprive another member of his right to vote, there may be just as much trouble as if someone in the second group tries to interfere with the decisions of the autocrat. The Civil War, which was an attempt to enforce democracy, was no milder than the Revolutionary War, which was an attempt to enforce autocracy. In both cases those who tried to upset the canon were treated in an equally authoritarian manner, namely, they were shot at.

Every group that wishes to survive has to enforce obedience to its canon, sometimes by drastic measures, and to that extent is authoritarian. However, the canons themselves may be graded as more or less democratic according to popular standards by examining the three main components of the group authority: the leadership, the constitution and the group culture. In this way groups can be placed on a scale with democratic governments at one end and totalitarian governments at the other. This is a vast topic which is the province of political science, but a few simple classifications are useful to any student of organizations and groups. For example, the leadership may be fluid, viscid or frozen. With a fluid leadership, the leader is responsible to the members and can easily be replaced; with a viscid leadership, he is responsible only to a special class of privileged people and is harder to displace; a frozen leadership is self-perpetuating and may be irresponsible and autocratic. The constitution may be flexible and easily adapted to the needs of the members, or it may be rigid and unchangeable. The culture may be permissive, restrictive or prohibitive, according to how freely the membership may criticize.

A clearly democratic canon would have a fluid leadership, represented by such procedures as cross-filing; a flexible constitution which could be changed easily on the initiative of the people; and a permissive culture, represented by a free press. In our country, California for example, seems to have all of these features, while some other states have leaned in the opposite direction, with rigged elections, little real constitutional initiative in the hands of the people and a one-sided press.

It is worth keeping in mind, in considering ailing groups, that there is one subgroup which even the most autocratic leader must think twice about, and that is his own group apparatus. Otherwise he may find himself confronted with something resembling the famous

revolutionary juntas of Latin America or the aroused
Janissaries of the palace guard. When Mahmud the
Second finally overthrew the Janissaries, who had kept
some of his predecessors virtual prisoners, he had to be
careful how he treated his new apparatus, which consisted of gardeners from the Top Kapi Sarai and a reorga-
nized army.

Besides the political aspects of a group's canon, there
are other important characteristics to investigate, particularly its firmness and its severity. Firmness is a matter
of "communication" and refers to the clarity with
which the canon is stated. In a firm culture everyone
knows (or can find out) when he is doing something
legitimate and when he is not. In a soft culture he is often in doubt and this causes difficulties, very much as
an inconsistent parent causes difficulties for his family.
A culture that is too soft may impair the morale of a
group and make it flabby.

Severity refers to the exercise of sanctions and includes four different aspects. A canon may be restrictive, as in certain convents, or permissive, as in certain
kindergartens. It may be retributive, with the emphasis
on punishment, as in prisons, or remunerative, with the
emphasis on rewards, as in sales organizations. It may
be harsh, like the English law of bygone times which
called for severe punishments for small transgressions,
or mild, like the modern probation system which may
result in a minimum of punishment for serious crimes.
It may be strict, with every possible infraction pun-
ished, as in concentration camps, or tolerant, as in
towns which want to encourage tourist trade. In many
cases these aspects all go to the same extreme, so that
some canons are very severe: restrictive, retributive,
harsh and strict, as in certain prisons; or very lax: permissive, remunerative, mild and tolerant, like the Pro-
hibition era in America. Often a lax canon merely
means that the leadership is not effective so that inter-

nal disorder is not controlled, as in some kindergartens and classrooms.

Since firmness and severity are independent of each other, a "good" leader must be careful to distinguish these two aspects and think about each of them separately. The best group is not necessarily the one with the firmest and severest culture. What the members seem to need is a well-balanced degree of freedom: not so little as to frustrate them unduly and not so much as to disconcert them. As far as the individual is concerned, a social situation is a grateful opportunity and a welcome invitation, but it is also an anxious threat and a dangerous temptation. This comes out clearly with individual proclivities motivated by exhibitionism or suppressed rage. A "good" leader defines the group culture firmly enough to channelise without obstructing and exercises the right degree of severity to control without intimidating. At least, this is the modern approach in England and North America. For each group there is probably an ideal degree of firmness and severity, and too little or too much of either is likely to cause difficulties.

PSYCHOLOGICAL TYPES

It appears that the actual experiences of people in groups are influenced as much by certain psychological factors as by the other characteristics we have considered. Hence, the psychological situation which determines whether a group is personal, constrained or obligatory is important.

The individual joins a personal group because of the people in it. He is not so much concerned with his role in the organizational structure as with his place in the individual structure. A personal group consists of people of his own psychological class—people with whom he shares certain interests, social attitudes, experiences and distinctions from the rest of the population. This is the attraction of sparetime activity groups, fraternities and social clubs. Personal groups are usually (but not necessarily) what have been previously classified as voluntary, optional or conditional groups; in time, almost any group takes on a personal aspect for its members.

A constrained group is one that the individual joins not so much because of its individual structure but because of its organizational structure; that is, he becomes a member because there is a slot for him, and he needs the advantages that go with the slot. He may even be willing to suffer a very uncongenial individual structure for the sake of keeping his membership. The typical example is taking a job in order to earn a living. If a member joins because of a compelling need for the advantages, whether they be moral, social or material, then for him that group is a constrained one, although it may not be obligatory. The psychological distinction of a constrained group is that for the constrained member reliability and responsibility are not optional. He is thrown in with people he did not choose himself, a world he never made, and it is necessary for him to adjust to them as they are. He can neither choose his associates nor change them; neither his work assignment nor his attendance at meetings is optional. Adjusting to a slot in a business office is a different problem from getting along with the boys at the club. At the club he can come and go as he pleases and deal only with associates of his own choosing. This is not true at the office. There, not only are his movements and associations under constraint, but he is forced to resign some of his individual proclivities in favor of the survival and the growth of the group, whether he likes it or not, or he may lose his position and its advantages.

The personal group is a social problem; the constrained group is an "existential" one: the member has to settle his mode of existence within himself as a "necessary choice." The obligatory group, such as a prison, is neither; it is primarily a problem in individual survival. There a member may be forced to contribute to the group activity, but he cannot be forced to be sociable or to contribute to the cohesion. However, he may elect, with profit, to act as if he were in a personal or a constrained group rather than in an obligatory one, in which case he may enjoy the privileges of a "good guy" with his fellow members or of a "model prisoner" with the administration.

Another psychological factor that influences the actual experiences of people in groups is the group's attitude. American and European work groups typically show a rational attitude; Group S, like many groups in primitive societies, showed one of childlike superstitition. Missionary organizations, both political and religious, show a third kind of attitude: a moralistic or parental one. These are examples of the three types of group attitudes: rational, archaic, and parental. Attitude is a matter of ego states, which will be discussed in the next chapter.

Attitudes must be distinguished from Bion's "basic assumptions" (dependency, pairing, fight or flight). Bion himself stresses the instability of his "basic assumption" groups, and it has already been suggested that they be regarded as incidental functions.

The demeanor of a group is another psychological characteristic and is not the same thing as its attitude. Some work groups, such as bank employees and surgical teams, have a serious demeanor, while others, such as lunch counter employees, are more casual. (For some reason, people seeking a bank loan are supposed to look serious.) Interesting poles of demeanor can be found in regard to certain religions, which sound formidable as written down, but are actually practiced with a much more casual air. The Buddhist worshippers of the lower classes in Thailand do not wrestle grimly with *Koans* but go by the temples to have their illnesses cured very much as an American housewife runs down to the drugstore for some aspirin. The impressive feature of a Voodoo meeting in the forests of Haiti is the gossiping and the gum-chewing of many of the participants. The interesting thing about many an idol-worshipper in the mountains of Guatemala is the casual and uninspired way in which he addresses the god.

Attitude and demeanor, along with some of the other characteristics discussed previously, such as tension and intensity, contribute to what some authors call the "group climate." In practice, it is better to break down the term "climate" into specific components and deal with each one separately as far as possible.

SOCIOLOGIC TYPES

Groups may be classified according to the nature of their activities. Such a classification might be extensive if it went into any amount of detail. Some of the broad classes would be athletic, commercial, educational, military, political, religious, scientific, social, and so forth.

The variables mentioned in this chapter are summar-

TABLE 9. A SUGGESTED CLASSIFICATION OF GROUPS

ASPECT	VARIABLE	CHARACTERISTICS	CLASSES OF GROUPS
Structure	External boundary	Permeability	Open Closed Sealed
		Membership	Voluntary Optional Conditional Obligatory Accidental
	Internal structure	Complexity	Simple Compound Complex Complicated
	Individual structure	Completeness	Undermanned Fully manned Overmanned

·ized in Table 9. This concludes the discussion of groups as a whole, and with this background it is now appropriate to consider the individual member as he functions in a group. This will be done in Part III.

TABLE 9 (*Continued*)

ASPECT	VARIABLE	CHARACTERISTICS	CLASSES OF GROUPS
	Organizational structure	Completeness	Incompletely organized
			Completely organized
			Overorganized
Dynamics	Cohesion	State	Potential
			Active
		Strength	Weak
			Strong
	Agitation and pressure	Potentiality	Relaxed
			Tense
		Activity	Mild
			Intense
Work	Nature of forces	Direction	Activity
			Process
			Combat
Authority	Canon	Democracy	Democratic
			Totalitarian
	Leadership	Fluidity	Fluid
			Viscid
			Frozen
	Constitution	Rigidity	Flexible
			Rigid
	Culture	Permissiveness	Permissive
			Restrictive
			Prohibitive
		Firmness	Soft
			Firm
		Severity— 4 variables	Lax
			Severe
Psychological	Situation	Necessity	Personal
			Constrained
			Obligatory
	Attitude	Ego state	Archaic
			Rational
			Parental
	Demeanor	Seriousness	Casual
			Serious
Sociologic	Activity	Descriptive	Educational
			Commercial
			Social, etc.

SUMMARY

The following hypotheses are stated:

1. Groups can be consistently and usefully classified on the basis of their structure, their dynamics, their work, the group authority and their "psychological" aspects.

2. All groups are "authoritarian" because the members must comply with the group canon.

SPECIAL TERMS INTRODUCED IN THIS CHAPTER

Permeability	Permissive culture
Open boundary	Restrictive culture
Closed boundary	Prohibitive culture
Sealed boundary	Firmness
Strong group	Softness
Weak group	Severity
Relaxed group	Laxity
Tense group	Retributive
Mild group	Remunerative
Intense group	Harsh
Democratic	Mild
Totalitarian	Strict
Fluid leadership	Tolerant
Viscid leadership	Personal group
Frozen leadership	Constrained group
Flexible constitution	Attitude
Rigid constitution	Demeanor

TECHNICAL NOTES

A System for Classification

J. F. Brown's excellent discussion of classification can be found in Chapter 6 of *Psychology and the Social Order* (New York, McGraw-Hill Book Company, 1936). D. Krech and R. S. Crutchfield (*Theory and Problems of Social Psychology,*

New York, McGraw-Hill Book Company, 1948) do not discuss it systematically but mention it here and there (e.g., p. 397). Kimball Young begins his book *An Introductory Sociology* (New York, American Book Company, 1934) with this problem.

One of the most interesting historical examples of a closed group is the Bourgeoisie of Zermatt (Switzerland), the temporal and spiritual guardians of the Matterhorn. "No one can be a member of this society whose family was not resident in Zermatt before the year 1619. The only exception to this rule is the Seiler family to whom special permission was granted at the end of the nineteenth century." (Lehner, K.: *A Pocket History of Zermatt*, p. 8. Translated by C. Williams. Zermatt, Wega, n.d.).

For the history of the Janissaries and their relationships to the Sultans and their gardeners or *bostanji*, see *The Harem*, by N. H. Penzer (pp. 88-94, Philadelphia, J. B. Lippincott Company, n.d.).

The classification of cultures given here is rather different from that of J. and J. M. Arsenian in "Tough and Easy Cultures," (*Psychiatry 11*:377-385, 1948).

For a background in the political aspects of group dynamics, the reader is referred to the standard works of Bryce, Hegel, Mill, Rousseau and, above all, Gierke's *Natural Law and the Theory of Society* (translated by Ernest Barker, Boston, Beacon Press, 1957).

PSYCHOLOGICAL TYPES

Rather than using the word "superstitious," I would prefer to employ the more general term "apotropaic" to describe certain groups with an archaic attitude of a religious nature. The apotropaic attitude is one which hopes to avert evil through the use of magic or the expectation of a miracle and is found in religious, occult, superstitious and ritualistic groups, as well as in some psychotherapy groups, especially during certain kinds of silences. For the same reasons given in connection with the word "anancasm," I have refrained from using "apotropaic" in the text. It is another one of these words used by Freud (e.g., *A General Introduction to Psychoanalysis,* p. 146, New York, Garden City Publishing Company, 1938, *apotropaea*) which are not easy to find in English dictionaries in spite of their honorable history. The Latin cognate is *averruncus,* especially applied to *iram deorum.* Liddell and Scott give *apotropaios,* averting evil; *apotropiazo*, to avert evil by sacrifices; *apotro-piasma,* a sacrifice to avert evil, etc.

The unlettered classes in Bangkok are just as apt, or perhaps more apt, to go to the Buddha as to the physician for their ailments and have their usual charmingly casual approach to the procedure. Good Voodoo ceremonies are not easy to find in Haiti but still exist. Idol worship can be seen in the mountains around Chichicastenango in Guatemala by those who are adept at finding such things.

Part 3

The Individual in the Group

9

Personality Structure

INTRODUCTION

The unit of action in any social aggregation is called a transaction. One individual who may be called the agent behaves in a certain way with the intention of getting a response. This behavior, in words or otherwise, is called the transactional stimulus. Another individual, who may be called the respondent, responds to the stimulus, giving the transactional response.

The intention of getting a response is what makes the aggregation a social one. If a number of people are assembled in the same place but there is no intention on the part of any of them to get responses from any of the others, then that aggregation is not a social one. Such a situation may occur on a ward full of withdrawn patients in a mental hospital or, under more ordinary conditions, before the curtain goes up at a public performance. An aggregation in which this intention is not present in any of the members may be called a dissocial aggregation. Thus it may be said that the New York subway is one of the greatest inventions ever devised by mankind for the collection of dissocial aggregations. Since such aggregations are the exceptions rather than the rule, it may be said that the desire to get responses is easily aroused in man, which is another way of saying that man is a social animal.

The inner causes and the motives that result in specific transactional stimuli and responses are the individual's private concern and lie within the field of social psychiatry. The study of the outward effects of such stimuli and responses is the science of social dynamics. Both of these may be considered to be branches of sociology or social psychology, in the broadest meaning of those terms.

The establishment of a unit of social action makes it possible to begin an analysis of any type of social situation at any point by taking up a specific transaction and going backward or forward from that point. The analysis of such units is called transactional analysis. In order to analyze transactions it is first necessary to study the structure of the human personality as it is observed to function in social aggregations.

PERSONALITY STRUCTURE

If a number of people come together in one place and participate in transactions with each other, it can usually be observed that the attitudes of the individuals change from time to time. On such occasions, an experienced observer can note shifts in almost every aspect of the human organism: posture, muscle tone, facial expression, gestures, voice, vocabulary, emotional intensity, emotional quality and content of speech. Many frameworks have been offered for the analysis of such observations. The psychiatrist or clinical worker who spends much of his time observing behavioral, emotional and physiologic changes in his patients, and in addition has the privilege of investigating the individual's state of mind at each moment, is in a particularly good position to see relationships between all these factors. Comparing various patterns of behavior and the states of mind that go with them gives rise to the idea of ego states. From the objective point of view there is a set of integrated behavior patterns; from the subjective point of view there is a corresponding system of feelings; the two together, the behavior and the state of mind, form an active ego state.

There are only a limited number of ego states available to each individual. The ego states of grownups usually fall into one of three classes:

1. Those that resemble the ego state of a parent, i.e., of someone who is acting parentally;

2. Those in which the facts offered by the environment are dealt with objectively;

3. Archaic ego states that resemble closely those found in infants and young children of various ages.

Ego states are regarded as products of mental organs: the exteropsyche, the neopsyche and the archaeopsyche. The exteropsyche deals with those that are borrowed from other people, usually the parents, and are imitative; the neopsyche deals with those that are concerned with the objective analysis of the internal mental and the external physical environments; and the archaeopsyche contains ego states that are left over from early childhood and are still active under certain conditions.

The diagram of any personality may then be represented very simply as in Figure 21 by 3 circles. The top circle represents his collection of borrowed ego states. Since these are typically patterned after parental figures, this aspect of the personality is conveniently called the Parent. The middle circle represents those ego states in which he is objectively appraising the mental and the physical environment. Since this type of activity is most commonly found in responsible grownups and is popularly called "mature behavior," this set of ego states is said to constitute the Adult aspect of the personality. Ego states that represent breakthroughs or fixations of early attitudes are collectively called the Child aspect of the personality.

It should be emphasized again that the total number

of ego states available to any individual is quite limited. Thus, he may have available two parental ego states, one adult ego state, and two childlike ego states, and no more. The diagram in Figure 21 is called a structural diagram of a personality and is to be distinguished from the structural diagram of a group. In this section of the book, the term "structural diagram" will be used in the personality sense, and the words Parent, Adult and Child, when capitalized, will refer to ego states rather than to people.

Personality structure as outlined here can be studied wherever people are participating in transactions with each other—at the dinner table, at school, at social gatherings and at work. However, it is investigated most conveniently in psychotherapy groups, where the information needed for verifying the diagnosis of each aspect of the personality is more readily available than in other situations.

A classic example of the distinction between ego states emerged during the treatment of a male psychiatric patient, who told the following anecdote:

An 8-year-old boy vacationing on a ranch in his

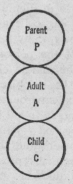

FIG. 21. A structural diagram.

cowboy suit helped the hired man to unsaddle his horse. When they were finished, the hired man said, "Thanks, cowpoke!" To which his assistant answered: "I'm not really a cowpoke; I'm just a little boy."

The man who told this story remarked: "That's just the way I feel. I'm not really a lawyer; I'm just a little boy." Away from the psychiatrist's office, he was an effective and successful courtroom lawyer of high repute. He reared his family decently, did a lot of community work and was popular socially. But in the psychiatrist's office he often did have the attitude of a little boy. Thus it was clear in his case that at certain times he behaved like a grown-up lawyer and at other times like a child. He became so familiar with these two different attitudes that sometimes during his treatment hour he would ask the therapist: "Are you talking to the lawyer or to the little boy?" It was soon possible to speak familiarly of these two attitudes as the Adult and the Child. It then appeared further that in his community work he was neither rational (Adult), as he was in the courtroom, nor lonely and apprehensive (Child) as he often was in the psychiatrist's office; rather he was inclined to feel emotionally involved with the downtrodden: sympathetic, philanthropic and helpful. And he recognized this as a duplication of his father's attitude; hence, it was doubly easy for him to accept the idea of calling this state of mind "parental."

His three states of mind, or ego states, were clearly distinguished in his ways of handling money. At times he would give away large sums, often to the detriment of himself and his family. At other times he would handle his finances with a banker's shrewd foresight. On still other occasions he would get into petty disputes or difficulties over a few pennies. As noted, he recognized the philanthropic attitude as resembling that of his father. In the second condition he was shrewdly appraising the information offered by the environment. In the third condition he recognized relics of the way he had behaved about money when he was a little boy. The clear distinction between the three ego states was brought out by the conflicts that each of these forms of behavior aroused. When he was philanthropic, the lawyer in him would rebel against the unwise use of his funds, and the child-like part of him would resent the fact that he had to give away money that he might use for his own pleasure. In structural language, both his Adult and his Child objected to his Parental way of handling money. When he was being shrewd, his Parent would reproach him with being inconsiderate of other people's needs, while his Child would regard his financial manipulations with a kind of awe. When his Child was being petty, his Parent would express disapproval and his Adult, the lawyer, would caution him that he might get into a great deal of trouble over a triviality, such as cheating a shopkeeper out of a few pennies. Sometimes these various protests would take the form of ill-defined feelings, but at other times they would take well-verbalised forms so that he would engage in a triologue with himself.

From this brief description it can already be seen that it was possible to analyze in structural terms any of his financial operations, whether it was donating a large sum to the Community Chest, buying securities or stealing chewing gum from a grocery store. In each case it was possible to say which of the three aspects of his personality was executing the transaction. This type of analysis, in which the executive ego state involved in any transaction is diagnosed, is called structural analysis.

For a clear understanding of what an individual is up to in a group, accurate structural analysis is necessary. However, this should not rest merely on the opinion of the observer, and unless the diagnosis is thoroughly verified, if should always be regarded as tentative. The diagnosis is complete when it can be supported from four different viewpoints.

1. The diagnosis made by the observer is behavioral. For example, a behavioral diagnosis can be made if someone unpredictably and somewhat inappropriately bursts into tears, so that the observer is irresisibly reminded of the behavior of a child at a certain age; or if the agent exhibits coyness, sulkiness or playfulness which is reminiscent of a special phase of childhood.

2. Those participating in transactions with the agent make the diagnosis on social grounds. If he behaves in such a way as to make them feel fatherly or motherly, he is presumably offering child-like stimuli, and his behavior at that moment can be diagnosed as a manifestation of his Child. Conversely, the respondents' behavior can be diagnosed as Parental. If the agent elicits objective responses related to the outside environment, then the respondents are in the Adult ego state, and the chances are that the agent is also in this ego state. Conversely, if two people are building a boat and one says (Adult): "Pass me the hammer," the respondent's reply will reveal his ego state. If he says: "Always be careful to keep your fingers out of the way when you're hammering," this response may be presumed to come from his Parent. If he says: "Which hammer?" he response may be assumed to come from his Adult. If he says petulantly: "Why do I have to do everything around here?" his complaint may be diagnosed as coming from his Child.

3. The subjective diagnosis comes from self-observation. The individual himself realises that he is acting the way his father did, or that he is objectively interested in what is going on before him, or that he is reacting the the way he did as a child.

4. The historical diagnosis is made from factual information about the individual's past. He may remember the exact moments when his father behaved in a

similar way; or where he learned how to accomplish this particular task; or exactly where he was when he had a similar reaction in early childhood.

The more of these standards that can be met, the sounder the diagnosis is. The full psychiatric diagnosis of an ego state requires that the observer, the individual's associates, his self-observation and his personal history all point in the same direction.

Since in most situations the social, the subjective and the historical diagnosis cannot be obtained, the behavioral diagnosis is the most important to the general student of groups. For example, a PTA meeting cannot be interrupted to ask whether everyone agrees that a certain member made them feel like children when he spoke; or whether the member felt Parental when he said what he did; or whether his father often spoke in the same tone, and if so, under what circumstances he did it. Therefore, behavioral observations are particularly valuable to collect. A few selected items will illustrate the point.

1. Demeanor. The sternly paternal uprightness, sometimes with extended finger, and the gracious mothering flexion of the neck soon become familiar as Parental attitudes. Thoughtful concentration, often with pursed lips or slightly flared nostrils, are typically Adult. The inclination of the head which signifies coyness, or the accompanying smile which turns it into cuteness, are manifestations of the Child. So is the aversion and fixed brow of sulkiness, which can be transformed into reluctant and chagrined laughter by Parental teasing. Observations of family life will reveal other characteristic attitudes belonging to each type of ego state: parents being Parental, students being Adult, and children being Child-like. An interesting exercise is to go through the text and especially the illustrations of Darwin's book on emotional expression, with structural analysis in mind.

2. Gestures. The Parental origin of forbidding and refusing gestures is often obvious if the observer is acquainted with the agent's family. Certain kinds of pointing with the index finger come from the Adult: a professional man talking to a colleague or client, a foreman instructing a workman, or a teacher assisting a pupil. A warding off gesture of the arm, when it is out of place, is a manifestation of the Child. Some gestures are easily diagnosed by intuition. For example, sometimes it is easy to see that pointing with the index finger is not Adult but is part of an exhortation by the Parent or of a plaintive accusation by the Child.

3. Voice. It is quite common for people to have two voices, each with a different intonation, although in many situations one or the other may be suppressed for very long periods. For example, one who presents herself in a therapy group as "little old me" may not reveal for many months the hidden voice of Parental wrath (perhaps that of an alcoholic mother); or it may require intense group stress before the voice of the "judicious workman" collapses, to be replaced by that of his frightened Child. Meanwhile, intimate friends and relations may be fully aware of both intonations. Nor is it exceedingly rare to meet people who have three different intonations: under favorable circumstances one may literally encounter the voice of the Parent, the voice of the Adult and the voice of the Child all coming from the same individual. When the voice changes, it is usually not difficult to detect other evidences of the change in ego state. One of the most dramatic illustrations is when "little old me" is suddenly replaced by the facsimile of her infuriated mother or grandmother.

4. Vocabulary. Certain words and phrases are characteristic of particular ego states. An important example is the distinction between "childish," which is invariably a Parental word, and "childlike," which is

Adult. "Childish" means "non acceptable" while "childlike," properly used, is an objective biologic term.

Typical Parental words are: cute, sonny, naughty, low, vulgar, disgusting, ridiculous, and many of their synonyms. Adult words are: unconstructive, apt, parsimonious, desirable. Oaths, exclamations and name-calling are often manifestations of the Child. Nouns and verbs are in themselves Adult, since they refer without prejudice, distortion or exaggeration to objective reality, but they may be employed for their own purposes by Parent or Child. Diagnosis of the word "good" is an intriguing exercise in intuition. With a recognized or unrecognized capital G it is Parental. When its use is strictly rational and defensible, it is Adult. When it means instinctual gratification, and is really an exclamation, it comes from the Child, being then an educated synonym for something like "Yum yum!" or "Mmmmm!" Very commonly, it expresses Parental prejudices which are faked out as Adult: it is said as if it had a small g, but if it is questioned, the capital G begins to show through. The speaker may become angry, defensive or anxious at the questioning, or at best the evidence he brings up to support his opinion is flimsy and poorly thought out.

These examples merely illustrate some of the possibilities. There is a very large number of behavior patterns available to the human being. Anthropologists have compiled long lists of deportments, and specialists (pasimologists) estimate that some 700,000 distinct elementary gestures can be produced by different muscular combinations. There are enough variations in timbre, pitch, intensity and range of vocalization to occupy the attention of whole schools of students and teachers. The problems of vocabulary are so complex that they are divided between different disciplines. And these are only four categories out of the almost innumerable types of indicators available to the structural analyst.

The only practical course for the serious student is observation: to observe parents acting in their capacity as parents; adults acting in their capacity as thoughtful and responsible citizens; and children acting like children at the breast, in the cradle, in the nursery, the bathroom and the kitchen, and in the schoolroom and the play-yard. By cultivating his powers of observation and intuition, he can add new dimensions of interest to his work.

Mr. Mead's presentation of three ego states to Group S has already been noted. When he gave his preliminary discussion, he was in an Adult ego state, talking objectively about the problems of the spiritualist medium and about what the members were going to become involved in. Ruby exhibited a typical child-like ego state. Dr. Murgatroyd at first presented an authoritative Parental ego state; later, during the experiments, he switched into that of a hurt child.

SPECIAL CHARACTERISTICS

The special characteristics of each type of ego state will now be reviewed in more detail. This will help in understanding further the relationships between the individual member and the other people in a group.

A. A Parental ego state is a set of feelings, attitudes and behavior patterns that resemble those of a parental figure. The diagnosis is usually made first by observation of demeanor, gestures, voice, vocabulary and other characteristics. This is the behavioral diagnosis. It is supported if the particular set of patterns is especially apt to be aroused by child-like behavior on the part of someone else in the group. This is the social diagnosis. In psychotherapy groups, the diagnosis may be further investigated through the family history and the individual's reports of his own feelings—the historical and the subjective diagnoses. The Parent usually shows in one of two forms: prejudiced or nurturing. The prejudiced

Parent has a dogmatic and disapproving attitude. If the prejudices happen to be the same as those of other people in the group, they may be accepted as rational, or at least justifiable, without adequate examination. The nurturing Parent is often shown in "supporting" and sympathizing with another individual.

The Parental ego state must be distinguished from the Parental influence. The Parental ego state means "Your Parent is talking now; you are talking like your mother." The Parental influence means "Your Child is talking that way to please your Parent; you are talking as mother would have liked you to."

The value of the Parent is that it saves energy and lessens anxiety by making certain decisions "automatic" and not to be questioned.

B. The Adult ego state is an independent set of feelings, attitudes and behavior patterns that are adapted to the current reality and are not affected by Parental prejudices or archaic attitudes left over from childhood. In each individual case, due allowances must be made for past learning opportunities. The Adult of a very young person or of a peasant may make very different judgments from that of a professionally trained worker. The question is not the accuracy of the judgments, nor their acceptability to the other members (which depends on their Parental prejudices) but on the quality of the thinking and the use made of the resources available to that particular person. The Adult is the ego state which makes survival possible.

C. The Child ego state is a set of feelings, attitudes and behavior patterns that are relics of the individual's own childhood. Again, the behavioral diagnosis is usually made first by careful observation. If that particular set of patterns is most likely to be provoked by someone who behaves parentally, that gives the social diagnosis. The historical diagnosis comes from memories of similar feelings and behavior in early childhood. The subjective diagnosis, the actual reliving of the original childhood experience, should only be attempted in the course of psychotherapy under the guidance of a fully qualified therapist.

The Child comes out in one of two forms: adapted or natural. The adapted Child acts under the Parental influence and has modified its natural way of expression by compliance or avoidance. The natural Child is freer, more impulsive and self-indulgent. The Child is in many ways the most valuable aspect of the personality, and if it can find healthy ways of self-expression and enjoyment, it may make the greatest contribution to vitality and happiness.

SUMMARY

The most significant hypotheses offered in this chapter are as follows:

1. The behavior of any individual in a group at any given moment can be classified into one of three categories, colloquially called Parent, Adult and Child.

2. Behavioral, social, historical and phenomenologic data converge to validate such classifications.

3. Parent, Adult and Child, on the basis of clinical evidence, are treated primarily as states of mind, or ego states, and it is proposed that such organizations arise from one of three psychic organs: exteropsyche, neopsyche and archaeopsyche, respectively.

4. Accurate structural analysis is necessary (or at least desirable) for precise understanding of the behavior and the function of each individual in a group.

SPECIAL TERMS INTRODUCED IN THIS CHAPTER

Transaction	Parent
Agent	Adult
Transactional stimulus	Child

Respondent	Structural analysis
Transactional response	Behavioral diagnosis
Social aggregation	Social diagnosis
Dissocial aggregation	Subjective diagnosis
Social psychiatry	Historical diagnosis
Social dynamics	Prejudiced Parent
Transactional analysis	Nurturing Parent
Ego state	Parental ego state
Exteropsyche	Parental influence
Neopsyche	Adapted Child
Archaeopsyche	Natural Child

TECHNICAL NOTES

The word "dissocial" is preferred to "unsocial" for describing non-transacting aggregations because "unsocial" has an unfair implication of sulkiness.

The case of the philanthropic lawyer has been presented in more detail in several of the writer's publications (e.g., "Ego States in Psychotherapy," *American Journal of Psychotherapy 11*:293-309, 1957). It should be emphasized that Parent, Adult and Child are not neologisms or synonyms for Superego, Ego and Id. The former are ego states, the latter are concepts. This question is discussed at more length in my book on *Transactional Analysis in Psychotherapy* (New York, Grove Press, 1961). The exposition given in the present chapter is in effect an attempt to summarize pertinently the contents of the first part of that book, which should be read by anyone who desires more information about the physiologic and psychological bases of structural analysis, or who is critical of the formulations as presented here.

E. T. Hall offers an excellent account of the anthropologic study of deportment ("The anthropology of manners", *Scientific American 192*:84-90, April 1955), while the linguist Mario Pei discusses pasimology (*The Story of Language*, Philadelphia, J. B. Lippincott Company, 1949).

10

Analysis of Transactions

SIMPLE COMPLEMENTARY TRANSACTIONS

The object of transactional analysis is to diagnose which ego states give rise to the transactional stimulus and the transactional response in any transaction that is being investigated. Anyone who proposes to deal with ailing groups should become familiar with this procedure. A simple transaction is represented by drawing two structural diagrams side by side, one for the agent and one for the respondent, as in Figures 22 and 23. An arrow is then drawn from the active ego state of the agent to whichever aspect of the respondent he is addressing. This represents the transactional stimulus.

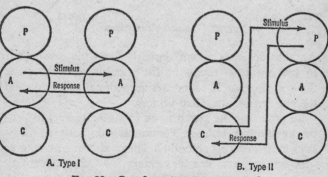

FIG. 22. Complementary transactions.

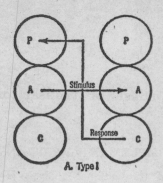

A. Type I

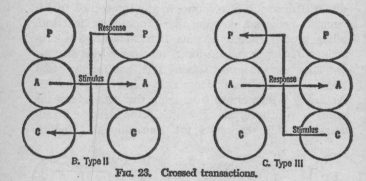

B. Type II   C. Type III

Fɪɢ. 23.   Crossed transactions.

Another arrow is drawn similarly from the respondent
to the agent to represent the transactional response.
Such a diagram is called a transactional diagram, and
the two arrows are called vectors.

In order for the group work in all its aspects to proceed without turbulence, communication between members must progress smoothly. This will occur as long as
transactions are complementary. A complementary
transaction is one in which the two vectors are parallel.
Most commonly, such transactions are Adult-to-Adult,
or between Parent and Child.

The complementary Adult-to-Adult transaction typically occurs in the course of the group activity. In everyday life it is exemplified by the question "What time is it?" and the response "Three-thirty." This Adult-to-Adult stimulus evoking Adult-to-Adult response may be classified as Complementary Transaction Type I and is represented in Figure 22A.

The second type of common complementary transaction—that taking place between Parent and Child—is easily observed in family life where actual children ask actual parents for help, reassurance or protection. Corresponding transactions occur between grownups when one of them is in difficulties and needs a helpful, reassuring or protective type of response. For example, a feverish husband, who learned how to be sick when he was a little boy, reverts to a Child ego state and goes to bed. His wife, who learned how to take care of sick people from her mother, shifts into a Parental ego state and takes care of him. If she falls sick, their roles will be switched, and so will their ego states. Such mutual loving care in time of need is an example of Complementary Transaction Type II and is represented in Figure 22B. The Adult ego state is particularly vulnerable to certain drugs and bacterial toxins. Usually anyone with a high fever will be unable to maintain his Adult and will revert to a Child ego state, thus activating the nurturing Parent in those concerned with his welfare. They will then go beyond the strictly Adult medical requirements of treatment to comfort and reassure him.

CROSSED TRANSACTIONS

Returning now to the Adult agent who wanted to know the time, suppose the respondent, instead of telling him, answers differently. Suppose he says like a sulky child "Why do I have to keep track of the time?" or alternatively, in the tone of a reprimanding parent, "If you had your own watch, you'd be more punctual!"

In either case, the agent becomes disconcerted. The respondent has raised new questions which are no longer concerned directly with the time of day. Communication is broken off on that subject and has to be re-established in a different direction. The agent at this point is likely to be distracted by resentment or self-defense. The first example, in which an Adult-to-Adult stimulus ("What time is it?") finds a sulky Child-to-Parent response, is illustrated in Figure 23A, and is called Crossed Transaction Type I. The second example, in which Adult-to-Adult stimulus gets a reprimanding Parent-to-Child response, is illustrated in Figure 23B and is called Crossed Transaction Type II. The important thing to notice about these two transactional diagrams is that the vectors are not parallel, as in a complementary transaction, but cross each other. This gives rise to one of the most important rules in the therapy of ailing groups, the rule of communication: communication is broken off when a crossed transaction occurs. This can also be put the other way round: if communication is broken off, there has been a crossed transaction.

A study of a simple transactional diagram makes it evident that there are 9 possible types of complementary transactions, including Adult-to-Child and Child-to-Adult, Parent-to-Parent and so forth, but most of these occur only rarely in comparison with Types I and II. There are a larger number of possible crossed transactions, but, again, most of them are rare in comparison with Types I, II and III illustrated in Figure 23. Since the diagrams are not (topologically) perfect, some of the crossed transactions when drawn will not show an actual cross. Therefore, strictly speaking, a crossed transaction is better defined as one in which the vectors are not parallel. But in the commonest cases, the cross will show clearly.

The detection of crossed transactions is of great

practical importance. For example, Crossed Transaction Type I (Fig. 23A) gives rise and has always given rise to most of the difficulties in the world—historical, marital, occupational and otherwise. If this type of transaction is found to be frequent in any relationship, it can be predicted that the relationship will go badly and will probably end in a misunderstanding or rupture. Many of the problems of psychiatry and group therapy can be studied from this point of view. Crossed Transaction Type I is the major concern of psychoanalysis and constitutes the typical "transference reaction." For example, if the (Adult) analyst says something like: "Your behavior reminds me of the way you behaved during the incident which occurred when you were 3 years old," in a sense he is entitled to expect a response like: "That's worth thinking about!" This would indicate that the patient's Adult is interested in the declared purpose of the treatment, which is to obtain increased understanding of himself. A transference reaction would go something like: "You're always criticising me!," clearly a Child-to-Parent response. The "counter-transference reaction," to which more and more attention is being devoted, is typified by Crossed Transactions Types I (Fig. 23A) and II (Fig. 23B), in which the patient makes an objective (Adult) statement and the analyst becomes either irritated in a child-like way or pompously Parental.

INDIRECT TRANSACTIONS

It can be observed in many groups that something is said by A to B which is intended to influence C indirectly. This timid approach is often thought of as tact or diplomacy. Such transactions commonly occur in so-called "well-run" groups, in which questionable methods of influencing people are considered to be good form. For example, instead of facing the boss directly, a suggestion may be made in his hearing to

someone else in the hope that it will influence the boss.
Since such devices are evidence of a poor relationship
between the agent and the boss and originate from fear
or insecurity, the question of whether this is really good
practice may be raised. It will be noted that indirect
transactions are really three-handed transactions in
which the respondent is used as a kind of go-between
in transacting psychological business with a third party.

DILUTED TRANSACTIONS

In the course of any group activity, no matter how
businesslike, nearly everybody becomes personally involved to some extent sooner or later. In this country, a
common approach is this is for workers to kid each
other. Here certain transactions which are half-hostile,
half-affectionate, take place through the material of the
activity. A may ask B to pass the hammer and say it in
a kidding way ("Hey, squarehead, where's the hammer?"), and B may throw the hammer instead of passing it, which is a kind of retaliative kidding or testing
of A. Such transactions which are embedded in the material of the group activity may be called diluted transactions.

A direct transaction is one which is neither indirect
nor diluted. The evidence is that even if "playing it
smart" by the use of indirect or diluted transactions
may lead to a certain kind of material success, the more
admirable members of the human race tend to use direct transactions in important situations.

INTENSITY

Transactional analysis deals with what actually happens rather than with what is going on in the minds of
the individuals concerned. Someone who uses indirect
or diluted transactions may be motivated by very intense feelings, but the feelings are deflected or watered

down in the actual transactional exchanges. When the transaction itself can be observed or judged to have a strong emotional intensity at the time of its occurrence, it is more likely to be direct than indirect or diluted. It is often useful to classify transactions according to their intensity. The most intense are passionate murder or impregnation, the one the most intense expression of hostility, the other the most intense expression of love. If murder takes the form of accidental manslaughter, or impregnation takes place in the course of more or less perfunctory love-making, then the transaction as carried out may not have been very intense. Similarly, the transactions which are more open to everyday observation should be carefully considered before their intensity is estimated.

The important items to be considered in analyzing single, simple transactions are therefore complementarity (or crossing), directness (or indirectness), purity (or dilution) and intensity (or weakness). Thus in intimate love relationships, people talk to each other relevantly, directly, without distractions, and intensely.

ULTERIOR TRANSACTIONS

Simple transactions are those that can be regarded as involving only a single ego state in each of the people concerned. However, a large number of transactions are obviously based on ulterior motives. An ulterior transaction is one that involves major activity from more than one ego state in one or all of the individuals concerned.

In certain situations ulterior transactions are deliberately cultivated, and their properties are carefully studied, although not under that name. For example, an insurance salesman who takes an authoritative, paternal interest in the welfare and the future of a potential client is engaging in an ulterior transaction, since, however genuine his Parental interest in the client, his chief goal is the Adult one of getting money from him. Good salesmanship, advertising and promotion always involve ulterior transactions in which a real or apparent concern with the welfare of the prospective buyer conceals quite another interest. The fact that salesmen speak of "making a killing," and are not referring entirely to their own financial gain but to a kind of childlike victory over the client, shows that in most cases the Child of a salesman is involved in his work, as well as his carefully cultivated Parental attitude and his Adult skill in closing sales. This ulterior aspect is more or less frankly acknowledged in referring to "the insurance game," "the real estate game" and, among criminals, to "the con game." Some ulterior transactions, such as cultivating acquaintances at parties with the ulterior motive of selling them something later, or playing golf with the ulterior object of exploiting the relationship later, are socially acceptable in many circles. Such operations must conform to the etiquette of informal commerce. Expert sales work requires social and psychological sophistication in order to appeal to more than one ego state of the client.

Diagrams of some ulterior transactions will be found in the next chapter.

SUMMARY

The following hypotheses are proposed:

1. Simple transactions can be usefully and pertinently classified according to certain significant variables: complementarity, directness, purity and intensity.

2. As long as transactions are complementary, communication can be maintained indefinitely. It is broken off if a crossed transaction occurs and must be re-established at a new level.

SPECIAL TERMS INTRODUCED
IN THIS CHAPTER

Transactional diagram

Vector

Complementary transaction

Crossed transaction

Indirect transaction

Diluted transaction

Direct transaction

Intensity

Purity

Simple transaction

Ulterior transaction

TECHNICAL NOTES

For further information regarding the analysis of transactions, my book on this subject (*Transactional Analysis in Psychotherapy, loc. cit.*) or, for a shorter account, the paper on this subject cited previously (*American Journal of Psychotherapy 12*:735-743, 1958) may be consulted.

11

Analysis of Games

INDIVIDUAL PARTICIPATION

The analysis of single transactions may be very useful in certain situations, but for a more thorough understanding of the nature of the individual's participation in the proceedings of a group, it is necessary to consider chains of transactions. Such chains can be usefully classified into six important types, including the extreme cases of nonparticipation (withdrawal) and "total" participation (intimacy). This gives the individual six options or choices as to how he will conduct himself in a group.

1. Withdrawal. Some people may be physically present but are in effect mentally absent from the gathering. They do not participate in the proceedings, and on inquiry it is found that they are engaged in fantasies. These generally fall into one of two classes:

a. Extraneous fantasies in which the individual mentally leaves the group and imagines himself elsewhere doing something quite unrelated to the proceedings.

b. Autistic transactions in which he is interested in what is going on but for various reasons is unable to participate. He spends his time imagining things that he might say or do with various members of the group. Autistic transactions are sometimes concerned with the possibility of participating in an acceptable way and at other times are less well adapted to the situation and may be concerned with direct assaults or sexual advances which would be quite unacceptable to the other members. Thus, autistic transactions may in turn be classified as adapted or unadapted.

2. Rituals, ceremonies and ceremonials. The preliminary and closing stages of the proceedings of any social aggregation, including groups, are often ritualistic in nature. These ritualistic phases may be abortive, consisting only of standard greetings and farewells, or they may be more prolonged, with formalities such as reading the minutes and votes of thanks. At formal ceremonies, such as weddings, not only the initial and terminal phases, but also the body of the meeting is ritualistic. From the point of view of social dynamics, the characteristic of ritualistic behavior is predictability. If at the beginning of a meeting one member says to another "Hello," it can be predicted with a high degree of confidence that the response will be "Hello" or one of its equivalents. If the first member then says "Hot enough for you?" it can likewise be predicted that the response will be "Yes," or some variant—similarly with the farewells at the end of a meeting. In a traditional ritual such as a church service, the stimuli and the responses are well known to all present and are completely predictable under ordinary conditions.

The unit of ritualistic transactions is called a stroke. The following is an example of a typical 8-stroke American greeting ritual:

A. "Hi!"

B. "Hi!"

A. "Warm enough for you?"

B. "Sure is. How's it going?"

A. "Fine. And you?"

B. "Fine."

A. "Well, so long."

B. "I'll be seeing you. So long."

Here there is an approximately equal exchange comprising a greeting stroke, an impersonal stroke, a personal stroke and a terminal stroke. Such rituals are part of the group etiquette.

At a group meeting the first six strokes may be exchanged at the beginning and the last two at the end. The problem then remains how the time is filled in between these two segments.

3. Activity. Most groups come together for the ostensible purpose of engaging in some activity which, as noted, is usually mentioned at least in a general way in the constitution. Pure activity in transactional language consists of simple, complementary, Adult transactions starting with something like "Pass the hammer!" or "What is the sum of 3 plus 3?" If there is no planned activity, as at many social parties, and in some psychotherapy groups, then the time is usually filled in with either pastimes or games.

4. Pastimes. Pastimes consist of a semi-ritualistic series of complementary transactions, usually of an agreeable nature and sometimes instructive. At formal meetings the time between the greeting rituals and the beginning of formal proceedings is often filled in with pastimes. During this period the gathering has the structure of a party rather than that of a group. At social parties, pastimes may occupy the whole period between the greeting and the terminal rituals. In psychotherapy groups, they may continue or be initiated even after the entrance of the therapist which signals the beginning of the formal proceedings.

5. Games. As members become acquainted with each other, generally through pastimes carried on in the course of the group activity, they tend to develop more personal relationships with each other, and ulterior transactions begin to creep in. These often occur in chains, with a well-defined goal, and are actually attempts of various people to manipulate each other in a

subtle way in order to produce certain desired responses. Such sets of ongoing transactions with an ulterior motive are called games.

6. Intimacy comes out transactionally in the direct expression of meaningful emotions between two individuals, without ulterior motives or reservations. Under special conditions, as in family life, more than two people may be engaged. Since such "pairing" may distract from the activity of a group, it is not encouraged in large work groups. For example, some organizations have a rule that if two members marry, one of them must resign. Because the subjective aspects are so important in true intimacy, and because it rarely comes out in groups because of external prohibitions and internal inhibitions, its characteristics are difficult to investigate. Indeed, this is one of the cases in which attempts at investigation are likely to destroy what is being investigated, since true intimacy is by nature a private matter. Few people would care to have their honeymoons tape recorded by a third person. There are certain sacrifices that should not be expected, even for the sake of science.

Pseudo-intimacy (with ulterior motives or reservations) is quite another matter and is frequently observed and erroneously described in the scientific literature as real intimacy. Some special groups are set up so that physical freedom, including sexual intercourse, is encouraged, but these are ritualistic, commercialized or rebellious and do not necessarily promote the subjective binding of two personalities. Pseudo-intimacy usually falls into the category of rituals, pastimes or games.

These six options have been listed roughly in order of the complexity of engagement and the seriousness of the commitment. The two extremes, withdrawal and intimacy, properly belong to the field of psychiatry. The two that stand out as most needful of further clarification for the student of social dynamics are pastimes and games, since these are the ones that most commonly affect the course of the internal group process.

PASTIMES

A pastime may be described as a chain of simple complementary transactions, usually dealing with the environment and basically irrelevant to the group activity. Pastimes are appropriate at parties, and they can be easily observed in such unstructured enclaves. Happy or well-organized people whose capacity for enjoyment is unimpaired may indulge in a social pastime for its own sake and for the satisfactions which it brings. Others, particularly neurotics, engaged in pastimes for just what their name implies—a way of passing (i.e., structuring) the time "until": until one gets to know people better, until this hour has been sweated out, and on a larger scale, until bedtime, until vacation-time, until school starts, until the cure is forthcoming, or until a miracle, rescue or death arrives. (In therapy groups the last three are known colloquially as "waiting for Santa Claus.") Besides the immediate advantages which it offers, a pastime serves as a means of getting acquainted in the hope of achieving the longed-for intimacy with another human being. In any case, each participant tries to get whatever he can out of it. The best place to study pastimes systematically is in psychotherapy groups.

The two commonest pastimes in such groups are variations of "PTA" and "Psychiatry," and these may be used as illustrations for analysis. At an actual Parent-Teachers Association meeting, "PTA," officially at least, is not a pastime, since it is the constitutionally stated activity of the group. But in a psychotherapy group it is basically irrelevant because very few people are cured of neuroses or psychoses by playing it. In that situation it occurs in two forms. The projective type of "PTA" is a Parental pastime. Its subject is delinquency in the general meaning of the word, and it may deal with delinquent juveniles, delinquent husbands, delinquent wives, delinquent tradesmen, delinquent authorities or delinquent celebrities. Introjective "PTA" is Adult and deals with one's own socially acceptable delinquencies. "Why can't I be a good mother, father, employer, worker, fellow hostess?" The motto of the projective form is "Isn't It Awful?"; that of the introjective form is "Me Too!"

"Psychiatry" is an Adult or at least pseudo-Adult pastime. In its projective form it is known colloquially as "Here's What You're Doing"; its introjective form is called "Why Do I Do This?"

People in therapy groups are particularly apt to fall back on pastimes in three types of situations: when a new member comes in, when the members are avoiding something, or when the leader is absent. The superficial nature of these interchanges is shown in the following two examples, the analyses of which are represented in Figures 24 and 25.

I. "PTA"—projective type.

Mary: "There wouldn't be all this delinquency if it weren't for broken homes."

Jane: "It's not only that. Even in good homes nowadays the children aren't taught manners the way they used to be."

II. "Psychiatry"—introjective type.

Mary: "Painting must symbolize smearing to me."

Jane: "In my case, it would be trying to please my father."

In most cases pastimes are variations of "small talk," such as "General Motors" (comparing cars) and "Who Won" (both "man-talk"); "Grocery," "Kitchen" and "Wardrobe," (all "lady-talk"); "How To" (go about doing something), "How Much" (does it cost?), "Ever Been" (to some nostalgic place), "Do You Know" (so-and-so), "Whatever Became" (of good old Joe),

"Morning After" (what a hangover), and "Martini" (I know a better drink).

It is evident that at any given moment when two people are engaged in one of these pastimes, there are thousands of conversations going on throughout the world, allowing for differences in time zones, in which essentially the same exchanges are taking place, with a few differences in proper nouns and other local terms. The situation brings to mind those printed postal cards which were supplied to the soldiers in the trenches in World War I, in which the terms that did not apply could be crossed out; or those box-top contests that require the completion of a sentence in less than 25 words. Thus, pastimes are for the most part stereotyped sets of transactions, each element consisting of what a

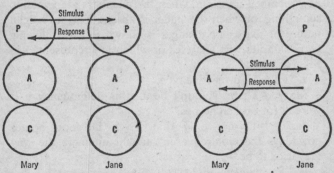

FIG. 24. "PTA"—projective type.   FIG. 25. "Psychiatry"—introjective type.

PASTIMES

psychology student might call a multiple choice plus a sentence completion; e.g., in "General Motors": "I like a (Ford, Plymouth, Chevrolet) better than a (Ford, Plymouth, Chevrolet) because . . ."

The social value of pastimes is that they offer a harmless way for people to feel each other out. They provide a preliminary period of noncomittal observation during which the players can line each other up before the games begin. Many people are grateful for such a trial period, because once he is committed to a game, the individual must take the consequences.

GAMES

The game called "If It Weren't For You," which is the commonest game played between husbands and wives, can be used to illustrate the characteristics of games in general.

Mrs. White complained that her husband would not allow her to indulge in any athletic or social activities. As she improved with psychiatric treatment, she became more independent and decided to do some of the things she had always wanted to do. She signed up for swimming and dancing lessons. When the courses began, she was surprised and dismayed to discover that she had abnormal fears of both swimming pools and dance-floors and had to give up both projects.

These experiences revealed some important aspects of the structure of her marriage. There were good Parental and Adult reasons why she loved her husband, but her Child had a special interest in his domineering Parent. By prohibiting outside activities, he saved her from exposing herself to situations that would frighten her. This was the psychological advantage of her marriage. At the same time, as a kind of bonus, he gave her the "justifiable" right to complain about his restrictions. These complaints were part of the social advantages of the marriage. Within the family group, she could say to him: "If it weren't for you, I could . . . etc." Outside the home, she was also in an advantageous position, since she could join her friends, with a sense of gratification and accomplishment, in their similar complaints about their husbands: "If it weren't for him, I could . . . etc."

"If It Weren't For You" was a game because it exploited her husband unfairly. In prohibiting outside activities, Mr. White was only doing what his wife's Child really wanted him to do (the psychological advantage), but instead of expressing appreciation, she took further advantage of him by enjoying herself in complaining about it (the social advantage).

But it was an even exchange, and that is what kept the marriage going; for Mr. White, on his side, was also using the situation to get questionable satisfaction out of it. As an important by-product, the White children's emotional education included an intensive field course in playing this game, so that eventually the whole family could and did indulge in this occupation skillfully and frequently. Thus, the social dynamics of this family revolved around the game of "If It Weren't For You."

In the pastime the transactions are simple and complementary. In a game they are also complementary, but they are not simple; they involve two levels simultaneously, called the social and the psychological. The transactional analysis of "If It Weren't For You" is shown in Figure 26. At the social level, the scheme is as follows:

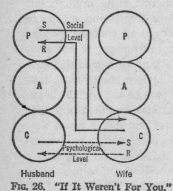

Husband   Wife
FIG. 26. "If It Weren't For You."

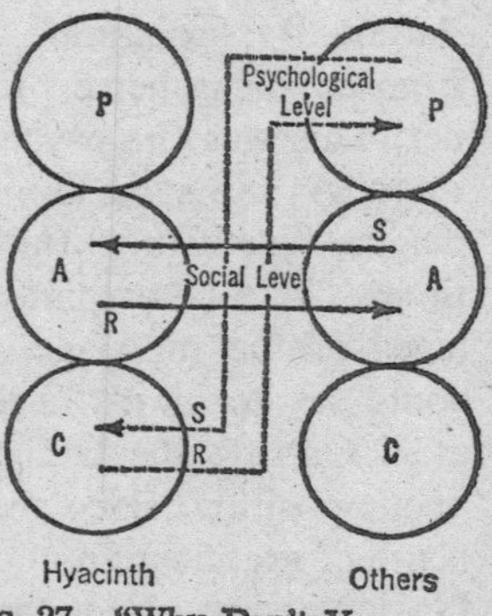

FIG. 27. "Why Don't You . . . Yes, But."

Husband: "You stay home and take care of the house."

Wife: "If it weren't for you I could be having fun."

Here the transactional stimulus is Parent to Child, and the response is Child to Parent.

At the psychological level (the ulterior marriage contract) the situation is quite different.

Husband: "You must always be here when I get home. I am terrified of desertion."

Wife: "I will be, if you help me avoid situations that arouse my abnormal fears."

Here both stimulus and response are Child to Child. At neither level is there a crossing, so that the game can proceed indefinitely as long as both parties are interested. Such a transaction, since it involves two complementary levels simultaneously, is a typical ulterior transaction.

A game can be defined as a set of ongoing ulterior transactions with a concealed motivation, leading to a well-defined climax. Because each player has a definite goal (of which he may not be aware), the innocent-looking transactions are really a series of moves with a snare or "gimmick" designed to bring about the climax or "pay-off."

The most common game in parties and groups of all kinds including psychotherapy groups, is "Why Don't You . . . Yes, But."

Hyacinth: "My husband never builds anything right."

Camellia: "Why doesn't he take a course in carpentry?"

Hyacinth: "Yes, but he doesn't have time."

Rosita: "Why don't you buy him some good tools?"

Hyacinth: "Yes, but he doesn't know how to use them."

Holly: "Why don't you have your building done by a carpenter?"

Hyacinth: "Yes, but that would cost too much."

Iris: "Why don't you just accept what he does the way he does it?"

Hyacinth: "Yes, but the whole thing might fall down."

"Why Don't You . . . Yes, But" can be played by any number. One player, who is "It," presents a problem. The others start to present solutions, each beginning with "Why don't you?" To each of these the one who is "It" objects with a "Yes, but . . ." A good player can stand off the rest of the group indefinitely, until they all give up, whereupon "It" wins. Hyacinth, for example, successfully objected to more than a dozen solutions before Rosita and the therapist broke up the game.

Since all the solutions, with rare exceptions, are rejected, it soon becomes evident that this game must serve some ulterior purpose. The "gimmick" in "Why Don't You . . . Yes, But" is that it is not played for its apparent purpose (an Adult quest for information or solutions) but to reassure and gratify the Child. In writing it may sound Adult, but in the living tissue it can be observed that the one who is "It" presents herself as a Child inadequate to meet the situation; whereupon the others become transformed into sage Parents anxious to dispense their wisdom for the benefit of the helpless one. This is exactly what "It" wants, since her object is to confound these Parents one after another. The analysis of that game is shown in Figure 27. The game can proceed because, at the social level, both stimulus and response are Adult to Adult, and at the psychological level they are also complementary, a Parent-to-Child stimulus ("Why don't you . . .") bringing out a Child-to-Parent response ("Yes, but . . ."). The psychological level may be unconscious on both sides.

Some interesting features come to light by following through on Hyacinth's game.

Hyacinth: "Yes, but the whole thing might fall down."

Dr. Q: "What do you all think of this?"

Rosita: "There we go, playing 'Why Don't You . . . Yes, But' again. You'd think we'd know better by this time."

Dr. Q: "Did anyone suggest anything you hadn't thought of yourself?"

Hyacinth: "No, they didn't. As a matter of fact, I've actually tried almost everything they suggested. I did buy my husband some tools, and he did take a course in carpentry."

Dr. Q: "It's interesting that Hyacinth said he didn't have time to take the course."

Hyacinth: "Well, while we were talking I didn't realize what we were doing, but now I see I was playing 'Why Don't You . . . Yes, But' again, so I guess I'm still trying to prove that no Parent can tell me anything, and this time I even had to lie to do it."

One object of games is to prevent discomfort by structuring an interval of time. This was clearly brought out by another woman, Mrs. Black. As is commonly the case, Mrs. Black could switch roles in any of her favorite games. In "Why Don't You . . . Yes, But," she was equally adept at playing either "It" or one of the sages, and this was discussed with her at an individual session.

Dr. Q: "Why do you play it if you know it's a con?"

Mrs. Black: "When I'm with people, I have to keep thinking of things to say. If I don't I feel uncomfortable."

Dr. Q: "It would be an interesting experiment if you stopped playing 'Why Don't You . . .' in the group. We might all learn something."

Mrs. Black: "But I can't stand a lull. I know it and my husband knows it too, and he's always told me that."

Dr. Q: "You mean if your Adult doesn't keep busy, your Child is exposed and you feel uncomfortable?"

Mrs. Black: "That's it. So if I can keep making suggestions to somebody or get them to make suggestions to me, then I'm all right. I'm protected."

Here Mrs. Black indicates clearly enough that she fears unstructured time. Her Child can be soothed as long as her Adult can be kept busy in a social situation, and a game is a good way to keep her Adult occupied. But in order to maintain her interest, it must also offer satisfactions to her Child. Her choice of this particular game depended on the fact that, for psychiatric reasons, it suited the needs of her special kind of Child.

Other common games are "Schlemiel," "Alcoholic," "Uproar," "You Got Me Into This," "There I Go Again," and "Let's You and Him Fight." Such games have many similarities to popular contests such as chess or football. "White makes the first move," "East kicks off," each have their parallels in the first moves of social games. After a definite number of moves the game ends in a distinct climax which is the equivalent of a checkmate or touchdown. This should make it clear that a game is not just a way of grumbling or a hypocritical attitude but a goal-directed set of ulterior transactions with an unexpected twist which is often overlooked.

The sequence of moves is illustrated in the game of Schlemiel. In this game the one who is "It" breaks things, spills things and makes messes of various kinds, and each time says "I'm sorry!" The moves in a typical situation are as follows:

1. White spills a highball on the hostess's evening gown.

2. Black responds at first with anger, but he senses (often only vaguely) that if he shows it, White wins. Black therefore pulls himself together, and this gives him the illusion that he wins.

3. White says, "I'm sorry!"

4. Black mutters forgiveness, strengthening his illusion that he wins.

It can be seen that both parties gain considerable satisfaction. White's Child is exhilarated because he has enjoyed himself in the messy moves of the game and has been forgiven at the end, while Black has made a gratifying display of suffering self-control. Thus, both of them profit from an unfortunate situation, and Black is not necessarily anxious to end the apparently unpromising friendship. It should be noted that as with most games, White, the aggressor, wins either way. If Black shows his anger, White can feel "justified" in his own resentment. If Black restrains himself, White can go on enjoying his opportunities.

The "gimmick" in such games almost always has an element of surprise. For example, a careless observer might sympathize with Mrs. White because of her autocratic husband, but the "gimmick" is that while she is complaining about him he is really serving a very important purpose in protecting her from her abnormal fears. In "Why Don't You . . . Yes, But" the "gimmick" has remained concealed from serious investigation through the thousands of years that this game has been played. It may have been observed facetiously that the one who is "It" rejects all the suggestions offered, but the possibility that this in itself might be a source of reassurance and pleasure has not been taken seriously enough to stimulate scientific interest. The clumsiness of the Schlemiel, and the possible secret pleasure he may derive from it, have been discussed, but this pleasure is merely a dividend; the "gimmick" and the goal of the whole procedure, which lie in the apology and the resulting forgiveness, have been overlooked.

The kinds of games, such as those mentioned above, which are of interest to the student of social dynamics, are of a serious nature, even thought their descriptions may bring to mind the English humorists. They form the stuff out of which many lives are made and many personal and national destinies are decided. Any set of transactions that occurs repeatedly in a group, and that can be analyzed on two levels like the illustrations in Figures 26 and 27, is probably a game. The diagnosis is confirmed if an ulterior motive can be found which leads progressively to the same climax again and again.

SUMMARY

The most significant hypotheses offered in this chapter are as follows:

1. With appropriate classification of group proceedings, it can be said that there are only a limited number of behavioral options open to an individual member.

2. The social function of pastimes is to serve as an innocuous matrix for tentative excursions of the Child.

3. Certain repetitive sets of transactions have an ulterior motive and lead to a climax which is concealed by the superficial indications.

SPECIAL TERMS INTRODUCED IN THIS CHAPTER

Withdrawal	Intimacy
Extraneous fantasies	Pseudo-intimacy
Autistic transactions	Psychological advantage
Ritual	Social advantage
Stroke	Psychological level
Pastimes	Social level
Games	

TECHNICAL NOTES

The elements of rituals, especially of greeting and farewell rituals, are called "strokes" for reasons which will become clearer in the next chapter.

The word "gimmick" is particularly appropriate to games. Its original technical meaning referred to a device placed behind a wheel of fortune so that the operator could stop it in order to prevent a player from winning. Thus it is the hidden snare which is controlled by the operator and assures him of an advantage in the pay-off. It's the "con" that leads to the "sting."

For further information and descriptions of some of the other games mentioned, the reader is again referred to my book *Transactional Analysis in Psychotherapy* (*loc. cit.*). Stephen Potter is the chief representative of the humorous exposition of ulterior transactions (e.g., *Lifemanship*, New York, Henry Holt & Company, 1951; *Gamesmanship*, ibid., n.d.). An extensive discussion and thesaurus of pastimes and games is contained in my book *Games People Play* (New York, Grove Press).

12

Adjustment of the Individual
to the Group

Each individual enters a group with the following
necessary equipment: (1) biologic needs, (2) psychological needs, (3) drives, (4) patterns of striving, (5)
past experience, and (6) adjustive capacities. It is just
this equipment which makes it possible for leaders to ex-
ploit their members for good or evil, and which ham-
pers the independent flowering of individual personalities. But that is another matter which does not belong in
a technical book on group dynamics, any more than a
discussion of human morality belongs in a textbook of
medicine. After he sees what forces people are up
against when they join groups, the reader will be better
able to form his own philosophy.

BIOLOGIC NEEDS

The well-known sensory deprivation experiments indicate that a continual flow of changing sensory stimuli
is necessary for the mental health of the individual.
The study of infants in foundling hospitals, as well as
everyday considerations, demonstrates that the preferred
form of stimulation is being touched by another human being. In infants, the withholding of caresses and
normal human contact, which René Spitz calls "emotional deprivation," results directly or indirectly in

physical as well as mental deterioration. Among transactional analysts, these findings are summarized in the inexact but handy slogan: "If the infant is not stroked, his spinal cord shrivels up."

As the individual grows up, he learns to accept symbolic forms of stroking instead of the actual touch, until the mere act of recognition serves the purpose. That is why the elements of greeting rituals are called "strokes." What is said is less important than the fact that people are recognizing each other's presence and in that way offering the social contact which is necessary for the preservation of health. Thus, both infants and grownups show a need for, or at least an appreciation of, social contact even in its most primitive forms. This can be easily tested by anyone who has the courage to refuse to respond when his friends say "Hello." The desire for "stroking" may also be related to the fact that outside stimulation is necessary to keep certain parts of the brain active in order to maintain a normal waking state. This need to be "recharged," as it were, by stimulation, and especially by social contact, may be regarded as one of the biologic origins of group formation. The fear of loneliness (or of lack of social stimulation) is one reason why people are willing to resign part of their individual proclivities in favor of the group cohesion.

PSYCHOLOGICAL NEEDS

Beyond that, human beings find it difficult to face an interval of time which is not allotted to a specific program: an empty period without some sort of structure, especially a long one. This "structure hunger" accounts for the inability of most people simply to sit still and do nothing for any length of time. Structure hunger is well known to parents. The wail of children during summer vacation and of teenagers on Sunday afternoon—"Mommy, there's nothing to do!"—recurrently taxes their leadership and ingenuity.

Only a relatively small proportion of people are able to structure their time independently. As a class, the most highly paid people in our society are the ones who can offer an entertaining time structure for those whose inner resources are not equal to the task. Television now makes this advantage available in every home. In a group, it is principally the leader who performs the necessary task of structuring time. Capable leaders know that few things are more demoralizing than idleness, and soldiers have said that risking their lives in active combat is preferable to sitting out a "bore war." Psychotherapists see the same thing in a milder degree when their group patients beg them for instructions as to how to proceed and resent it if a program is not forthcoming. One product of structure hunger is "leadership hunger," which quickly emerges if the leader refuses to offer a program or is he is absent from a meeting and there is no adequate substitute. No doubt there are other factors involved here, but the fact remains that a long unexpected silence at any group meeting or on the radio arouses increasing anxiety in most people.

Because a group offers a program for structuring an interval of time, the members are willing to pay a price for their membership. They are willing to resign still more of their individual proclivities in favor of ensuring the survival of the group and its structure. They also appreciate the fact that the leader is the principal time-structurer, and that is one factor in awakening their devotion.

The reason given by Mrs. Black for playing her games throws some light on why people seek time-structuring. Unless the Adult is kept busy, or the Child's activities are channeled, there is a danger that the Child may run wild, so to speak, in a way the individual is not prepared to handle. The need to avoid this kind of chaos is one of the strongest influences which sends people into groups and disposes them to make the sacrifices and the adjustments necessary to remain in good standing.

The need for social contact and the hunger for time-structure might be called the preventive motives for group formation. One purpose of forming, joining and adjusting to groups is to prevent biologic, psychological and also moral deterioration. Few people are able to "recharge their own batteries," lift themselves up by their own psychological bootstraps, and keep their own morals trimmed without outside assistance.

DRIVES

On the positive side, the presence of other human beings offers many opportunities for gratification, and everyone intuitively or deliberately acquires a high proficiency in getting as many satisfactions as possible from the people in the groups to which he belongs. These are obtained by means of the options for participation listed in the previous chapter. The surrounding people contribute least to the satisfactions reaped from fantasy and most to those enjoyed in intimacy. Intimacy is threatening for various reasons, partly because it requires independent structuring and personal responsibility; also, as already noted, it is not well suited to public situations. Hence, most people in groups settle for whatever satisfactions they can get from games, and the more timid ones may not go beyond pastimes.

Nevertheless, hidden or open, simple or complicated, a striving for intimacy underlies the most intense and important operations in the group process. This striving, which gives rise to active individual proclivities, may be called the individual anancasm, the inner necessity that drives each man throughout his life to his own special destiny. Four factors lend variety to its expression: (1) the resignations and compromises that are necessary to ensure the survival of the group. This is the individual's contribution to the group cohesion. (2) The disguises resulting from fear of the longed-for intimacy. (3) Individual differences in the meaning of intimacy: to most it means a loving sexual union, to some a one-sided penetration into the being of another through torture; it may involve self-glorification or self-abasement. There are differences in the kind of stroking received or given. Most want a partner of the opposite sex, some want one of the same sex, in love or in torment. All of these elements are influenced by the individual's past experiences in dealing with or being dealt with by other human beings. From the very day of birth, each person is subjected to a different kind of handling: rough and harsh or soft and gentle or any combination or variation of these may signify to him the nature of intimacy. (4) Differences in the method of operation, the patterns of behavior learned and used in transacting emotional business with other people.

PATTERNS OF STRIVING

Each person has an unconscious life plan, formulated in his earliest years, which he takes every opportunity to further as much as he dares in a given situation. This plan calls for other people to respond in a desired way and is generally divided, on a long-term basis, into distinct sections and subsections, very much like the script of a play. In fact, it may be said that the theatre is an outgrowth of such unconscious life plans or scripts. The original set of experiences which forms the pattern for the plan is called the protocol. The Oedipus complex of Sigmund Freud is an example. In transactional analysis the Oedipus complex is not regarded as a mere set of attitudes, but as an ongoing drama, divided, as are Sophocles's *Oedipus Rex, Elec-*

tra, Antigone, and other dramas, into natural scenes and acts calling for other people to play definite roles.

Partly because of the advantages of being an infant, even under bad conditions, every human being is left with some nostalgia for his infancy and often for his childhood as well; therefore, in later years he strives to bring about as close as possible a reproduction of the original protocol situation, either to live it through again if it was enjoyable, or to try to re-experience it in a more benevolent form if it was unpleasant. In fact, many people are so nostalgic and confused that they try to relive the original experience as it was even if it was very unpleasant—hence the peculiar behavior of some individuals who are willing to subject themselves to all sorts of pain and humiliation, repeating the same situation again and again. In any case, this nostalgia is the basis for the individual anancasm. This is something like what Freud calls the "repetition compulsion," except that a single re-enactment may take a whole lifetime, so that there may be no actual repetition but only one grand re-experiencing of the whole protocol.

Since the script calls for the manipulation of other people, it is first necessary to choose an appropriate cast. This is what takes place in the course of pastimes. Stereotyped as they are, they nevertheless give some opportunity for individual variations which are revealing of the underlying personalities of the participants. Such indications help each player to select the people he would like to know better, with the object of involving suitable ones in his favorite games. From among those who are willing and able to play his games, he then selects candidates who show promise of playing the roles called for in his script; this is an important factor in the choice of a spouse (the chief supporting role). Of course, if things are to progress, this process of selection must be mutual and complementary.

Because of its complexity, it is fortunate that it is not necessary to consider the script as a whole in order to understand what is going on in most group situations. It is usually enough to be aware of the favorite games of the people concerned.

THE PROVISIONAL GROUP IMAGO

There are various forces which determine group membership, and the individual is not necessarily attracted mainly by the activity of a group. If it is the kind of group in which he will meet other members face to face, his more personal desires become important. As soon as his membership is impending, he begins to form a provisional group imago, an image of what the group is going to be like for him and what he may hope to get out of it. In most cases, this provisional group imago will not long remain unchanged under the impact of reality; but, as already noted, the internal group process is based on the desire of each member to make the actual, real group correspond as closely as possible to his provisional group imago. For example, a man may join a country club because that will offer him an opportunity to engage in his favorite pastimes. If the club is not equipped for one of them, he may try to introduce it. Membership in any group that includes unmarried people is nearly always influenced by the hope of finding a mate, and this may give rise to a very lively and colorful provisional group imago.

Psychotherapists often have to deal with provisional group imagoes when they suggest that a patient join a therapy group. The patient questions the therapist either to adjust an imago he has already formed from reading or gossip or to start forming one so that he will know what to expect. If the picture offered by the therapist does not meet his desires, the patient will not be favorably inclined and may join only to please the doctor rather than with the hope that "the group" will be of value to him.

While the script and the games that go along with it and set it in action come from older levels of the individual's history, his provisional group imago is based on more recent experiences: partly first-hand, from groups he has been a member of, and partly second-hand, from descriptions of groups similar to the one he desires or expects to join. One branch of the advertising and procurement professions is particularly concerned with favorably influencing provisional group imagoes.

It should be clear now that each member first enters the group equipped with: (1) a biologic need for stimulation; (2) a psychological need for time-structuring; (3) a social need for intimacy; (4) a nostalgic need for patterning transactions; and (5) a provisional set of expectations based on past experience. His task is then to adjust these needs and expectations to the reality that confronts him.

ADJUSTMENT

Each new member of a group can be judged according to his ability to adjust. This involves two different capacities: adaptability and flexibility.

Adaptability is a matter of Adult technics. It depends on the carefulness and the accuracy with which he appraises the situation. Some individuals make prudent estimates of the kinds of people they are dealing with before they make their moves. They are tactful, diplomatic, shrewd or patient in their operations, without swerving from their purposes. The adaptable person continually adjusts his group imago in accordance with his experiences and observations in the group, with the practical goal of eventually getting the greatest satisfaction for the needs of his script. If his script calls for him to be president, he picks his way carefully and with forethought through the hazards of political groups.

On the other hand, the arbitrary person proceeds blindly on the basis of his provisional group imago. This is typical of a certain type of impulsive woman, who will launch a sexually seductive game immediately on entering a group, hardly glancing around the room to see what company she has to reckon with. Occasionally her crude, unadapted maneuvers may be successful, and she will get the responses her script calls for: advances from the men and jealousy from the women. However, if the other members are not so easily manipulated, she may be ignored or rebuffed by both sexes. Then she is faced with the alternatives of either adjusting or withdrawing; otherwise, she may be extruded by the other members.

The second variable, flexibility, depends on the individual's ability and willingness to modify or sacrifice elements of his script. He may decide that he cannot obtain a certain type of satisfaction from a group and may settle for other satisfactions which are more readily available. Or he may settle for a lesser degree of satisfaction than he originally hoped for. The rigid person is unable or unwilling to do either of these things.

Adaptability, then, concerns chiefly the Adult, whose task it is to arrange satisfactions for the Child. The adaptable person may keep his script intact by modifying his group imago in a realistic way. Flexibility becomes the concern of the Child, who must modify his script to accord with the possibilities presented by the group imago. From this it can be seen that adaptability and flexibility often overlap, but they may also be independent of each other, as consideration of four extreme cases will demonstrate.

The adaptable, flexible individual will carry out his operations smoothly and with patience and will settle for what is expedient. ("Politics is the science of the possible.") He is the rather uninspiring "socially adjusted" person that some school systems take as their ideal, the "common-ground finder" who sacrifices principle to convenience in a "socially acceptable" way. In certain professions, such capacities may be desirable or profitable and may be deliberately cultivated.

The adaptable, inflexible member will carry on patiently and diplomatically but will not yield on any of the goals he is striving for. In this class are many successful business men who do things their own way. The arbitrary, flexible person will shift from one goal to another, showing little skill or patience, and will settle for what he can get without changing his tactics. The arbitrary, inflexible person is the dictator: ready to accomplish his aims without regard to the needs of others and inflexible in his demands. The others play it his way, and he gets and gives what he wants to.

The above descriptions are transactional and refer to the individual's behavior in a group situation, but they resemble character types described from other points of view.

It should be noted that it is the group process and not the group activity that leads to adjustment. For example, a certain type of bookkeeper may never adjust himself to the office group; he may concentrate on his work and do it well while remaining an isolate year in and year out except for participating in greeting rituals.

THE GROUP IMAGO

The complete process of adjustment of the group imago involves four different stages. The provisional group imago of a candidate for membership, the first stage, is a blend of Child fantasy and Adult expectations based on previous experience. This is modified into an adapted group imago, the second stage, by rather superficial Adult appraisals of the other people, usually made by observing them during rituals and ac-

tivities. At this point, the member is ready to participate in pastimes, but if he is careful and not arbitrary,
he will not yet start any games of his own, although he
may become passively involved in the games of others.
Before he begins his own games, his adapted imago
must be changed into an operative one, which is the
third stage. This transformation works on the following
principle: the imago of a member does not become operative until he thinks he knows his own place in the
leader's group imago, and this operative group imago
remains shaky unless it has repeated existential reinforcement. To become operative, an imago must have a
high degree of the differentiation mentioned in Chapter
5.

Grim examples may be found in the memoirs of officers of secret police forces. Many of these officers felt
uncertain of their positions in the hierarchy until they
thought they knew how they rated with their superiors,
whom they were continually trying to impress in the
course of their work. Once they felt that their positions
were established, they were then able to differentiate
themselves and their colleagues more clearly in their
own group imagoes, whereupon they felt free to un-
leash the full force of their individual proclivities. They
grew more and more confident in their atrocious actions
and in their relationships with other party members as
the approval of their leaders was reinforced.

A more commonplace example of operative adjustment is the case of the inhibited boy in kindergarten.
He may find it difficult to associate with the other children until he feels sure that he knows how he stands
with the teacher. Of course, this principle is intuitively
known to all capable teachers, and they act accordingly. If they are successful, they will then note
that "this boy has improved his adjustment and has
now made some friends," i.e., he has differentiated
some of the other children in a meaningful way. Simi-

larly, in a psychotherapy group, an adaptable member will not begin to play his games until he thinks he knows how he stands with the leader. If he is arbitrary and not adaptable (e.g., the impulsive type of woman mentioned in the previous section), he may act prematurely and pay the penalty.

The operative principle may sound complicated, but it is really very simple. After a new child is born into a family, the other children treat him cautiously until they think they know how they stand in relation to the baby in the group imagoes of their parents, which they find out by testing. If a father is replaced by a stepfather, the wise child walks softly with the other children until he finds out how he and they stand with the new parent.

The operative principle is what makes it advisable to draw an authority diagram in considering an ailing group. The imago of each person on such a diagram operates according to how he thinks he stands with his superiors, and what he thinks they expect from him; this determines how he will behave in his role in the organizational structure. The primal leader, or the leader who is on his own, has to raise his imago by its own bootstraps, as it were. But even here the operative principle may come into play. An independent leader, such as a group therapist in private practice, may feel responsible to his own Parent, and his group imago becomes operative on that basis. Thus it may be said that the true leader of some psychotherapy groups is the therapist's father. The leadership slot in such an imago is occupied by a phantom, and the therapist operates as the executive of his father's canon. (Incidentally, a phantom is also left whenever a well-differentiated member leaves a group, and it persists until the mourning process is completed, if it ever is. Since only autistic transactions are possible with phantoms, they give rise to many interesting and complex events.)

The fourth phase of the group imago is secondary adjustment. At this stage the member begins to give up his own games in favor of playing it the group's way, conforming to its culture. If this occurs in a small group or subgroup, it may prepare the way for game-free intimacy. However, activity may be carried on effectively regardless of the state of an individual's group imago.

The four stages of adjustment of the group imago and their suitability for structuring time are: (1) the provisional imago for rituals; (2) the adapted imago for pastimes; (3) the operative imago for games; and (4) the secondarily adjusted imago for intimacy.

Knowledge of this progression makes it possible to define with some exactness four popular terms which are usually used carelessly and even interchangeably: participation, involvement, engagement and belonging.

An individual who gives any transactional stimuli or transactional responses, in words or otherwise, is to that extent participating. Thus, participation is the opposite of withdrawal. It may occur at any stage of adjustment. A member may participate in activities, rituals, pastimes or games, depending on how far his provisional group imago has been adjusted.

A person who plays a passive role in the game of another member, without taking the initiative, is involved. Involvement may occur with an adapted group imago which is not yet operative.

A member who takes the initiative in starting one of his own games, or who actively tries to influence the course of someone else's game to his own advantage, is engaged. This occurs only after his group imago becomes operative. As already noted, this may happen prematurely and inappropriately in arbitrary individuals.

Belonging is more complicated. A member belongs when he has met three conditions: eligibility, adjustment and acceptance. Eligibility means that he can meet the requirements for membership. Adjustment means that he is willing to resign his own games in favor of playing it the group's way. Such a resignation results from secondary adjustment of an operative group imago. Those who are "born to belong" are taught very early certain rituals, pastimes and games which are acceptable to their class; their secondary adjustment takes place during their early training. Acceptance means that the other members recognize that he has given up some of his individual proclivities in favor of the group cohesion, and that he will abide by the group canon. If he fails to do so, acceptance may be withdrawn. The sign of belonging is assurance, and the sign of acceptance is that the members give the responses required by the canon. If they break the social contract and show rudeness, the member loses his assurance. All this is well illustrated in the process of naturalization. The foreigner must first be eligible to cross the external boundary by immigration. Then he is required to study the canon of his adopted country. The better he adjusts his group imago, the more he is accepted and the more he belongs.

THE SCRIPT

The script is the most important item and, at the same time, the most difficult to investigate of all the items of equipment which the individual brings with him when he enters a group. For example, in choosing a new president from among the vice-presidents of a corporation, a psychologist can test the capacities of the various candidates for the job, but the script will determine what use each individual will make of his capacities, and the script cannot be reliably brought to light by any form of testing. Its unmasking requires a long period of psychiatric investigation by a skilled script analyst. Fortunately, however, the intuition of the member's associates or superiors, especially those who have known him a long time and have seen him react to a variety of pressures, is sometimes fairly reliable in this respect. There are outstanding vice-presidents whose scripts call for them to excel the deceased president in effectiveness, and there are equally capable vice-presidents who may give no indication to an untrained observer that their scripts call for them to destroy what the deceased president has built up and also destroy themselves in the process.

The adjustment of a script is similiar to the adjustment of a group imago, but the preparatory stages occur before the individual enters the group.

The original drama, the protocol, is usually completed in the early years of childhood, often by the age of 5, occasionally earlier. This drama may be played out again in more elaborate form, in accordance with the growing child's changing abilities, needs and social situation, in the next few years. Such a later version is called a palimpsest. A protocol or palimpsest is of such a crude nature that it is quite unsuitable as a program for grown-up relationships. It becomes largely forgotten (unconscious) and is replaced by a more civilized version, the script proper: a plan of which the individual is not actively aware (preconscious), but which can be brought into consciousness by appropriate procedures. The script proper is closely related to the provisional group imago and can be found along with it among the fantasies of a candidate about to enter a group. Once he becomes a member, the script goes through the same processes of adjustment as the provisional group imago, depending on the individual's flexibility. In a clear-cut case there is an adapted script, called the adaptation, then an operative script and finally a secondary adjustment. The similarity to the development of theatrical and movie scripts is evident, and sometimes it is remarkable.

Since some scripts may take years or even a whole lifetime to play out, they are not easily studied in experimental situations or in groups of short duration. They are most efficiently unmasked by a careful review of the life history or in long term psychotherapy groups, which are much better than individual therapy for this purpose. But in some measure, the script influences a large percentage of the individual's transactions in any group meeting in which he participates actively.

One of the easiest scripts to observe in action is that of the man whose individual anancasm tragically drives him to failure. He can be followed through his expulsion from college to his discharge from one job after another, and the acute observer can soon spot the decisive moments in each of these performances which set the stage for the final outcome and can see the same drama being played over and over again with a different cast.

The adjustment of a script can be illustrated by a more constructive example. A therapist whose protocol had to do with "curing lots of people" (siblings) had a palimpsest by the age of 5 where he would invite his neighborhood contemporaries en masse to his house to play doctor. The protocol was based on a beloved family physician and much illness in the family. The palimpsest was necessary because Davy's siblings, being of various ages up to adolescence, were not readily available for his performances, so that he had to fill his cast with extras off the street. The script proper was active for a while during his grade-school years when he would invite various clubs to "meet at my house," hoping in this way to become a leader. The adaptation occurred years later when he was able to become a group therapist, which was a socially acceptable way of trying to "cure a lot of people who meet at my house." During the period of the adaptation, his efforts were tentative and not very successful. During the phase of his operative script when he took more initiative in structuring his therapy groups, he was more efficient but became heavily involved ("identified") with his patients. Finally, his script underwent a secondary adjustment, in which his therapeutic efforts were better controlled, involved fewer games, and were still more successful. He still had "lots of sick people meeting at my house" but was flexible enough to give up the magical satisfactions of "curing" them, acting in accordance with Ambroise Paré's dictum "I treated them, but God cured them." This "meeting at my house" was the first act of a long script which led to a satisfactory professional career when it was properly adjusted.

SUMMARY

We have now studied the individual's course from infancy until the time he belongs to a group, the kinds of transactions he may participate in and the manner in which he sets up and becomes engaged in chains of transactions. This is sufficient information to understand the operations of any individual in any group in terms of social dynamics and complements the study of the structure and the dynamics of groups as a whole.

The most important hypotheses on which this discussion of the adjustment of the individual to the group is based are as follows:

1. Social contact and time-structuring are necessary for psychological survival and probably for biologic survival as well.

2. Therefore, the problem of the healthy individual is primarily to find a suitable group for structuring his time. Secondarily, he strives to attain the maximum possible satisfactions from the facilities available.

3. The secondary considerations lead to the emergence of a provisional group imago before entering the group.

4. The individual then adjusts his operations in the group according to his adaptability and flexibility.

5. His participation is programmed by a mental picture of the group, its social customs, certain idiosyncratic patterns of manipulation and specific predetermined long-term goals, or more concisely, his group imago, the group culture, his games and his script.

6. He will not take the initiative in the group process until he thinks he knows his place in the leader's group imago, although he may be premature in his inferences.

7. The group imago and the script go through well-defined phases of adjustment.

SPECIAL TERMS INTRODUCED IN THIS CHAPTER

Stroking	Operative group imago
Structure hunger	Operative principle
Leadership hunger	Phantom
Individual anancasm	Secondary adjustment
Script	Participation
Protocol	Involvement
Adjustment	Engagement
Adaptability	Belonging
Flexibility	Acceptance
Adapted group imago	Palimpsest
Arbitrary	Script proper

TECHNICAL NOTES

The need for time structuring is discussed by W. Heron in "The Pathology of Boredom" (*Scientific American 196*:52-56, 1957). The survival value of physical contact is demonstrated by René Spitz: "Hospitalism, Genesis of Psychiatric Conditions in Early Childhood" (*Psychoanalytic Study of the Child 1*:53-74, 1945). See also his articles on "Hospitalism: A Follow-up Report" and "Anaclitic Depression" (*ibid. 2*:113-117 and 313-342). Cf. the confirmatory experimental work of H. F. and M. K. Harlow on "Social Deprivation in Monkeys" (*Scientific American 207*:136-146, November 1962).

The significance of unstructured time—i.e., boredom—as an existential problem is discussed by Soren Kierkegaard and others (R. Bretall, [ed.]: *A Kierkegaard Anthology,* pp. 22 ff., Princeton, Princeton University Press, 1947).

For a demonstration of leadership hunger, see E. Berne, R. J. Starrels and A. Trinchero: "Leadership Hunger in a Therapy Group" (*Archives of General Psychiatry 2:*75-81, 1960). Also Bion's first paper (*loc. cit.*).

The term "anancasm" has already been discussed in the Notes to Chapter 4, p. 107.

"Protocol" comes from *Proto-Kollon,* the first leaf of a volume, a fly leaf stuck to the outside case by glue and containing some account of the MS (Liddell & Scott, *loc. cit.*).

The need for careful definition of words relating to various forms of participation is evident to anyone reading the literature, especially the literature of group psychotherapy, which tends to be particularly careless in this respect.

As to palimpsests, in clinical practice what at first looks like an original protocol (e.g., phallic) often turns out to be an elaborated version of an earlier protocol (e.g., anal or oral). Or, from the developmental viewpoint, an oral protocol may have anal and phallic palimpsests. From the example given no implication is intended that group therapists tend to come from large families.

Part 4

Applied Social Psychiatry

13

Group Psychotherapy

Only the group dynamic aspects of psychotherapy groups will be discussed here, since the technical aspects belong to the psychiatric literature.

THE LOCATION DIAGRAM

The location diagram, which incorporates the roster and the schedule as shown in Figure 1 (p. 2), raises several important practical questions. Trigant Burrow noted as early as 1928 that membership in psychotherapy groups should be limited to 10 if there is to be adequate opportunity for individual self-expression. Nowadays many therapists prefer 8, and some like to work with 6. Theoretically, a smaller number would be sufficient, but the difficulty is that in practice the absences of 2 or more members may coincide, leaving the therapist with only one or 2 people to work with at some sessions, and such a situation is not desirable from the point of view of using the group as a therapeutic instrument. Therefore, 5 members would be a practical minimum. With a group larger than 10, it becomes almost impossible to be aware of every patient at every moment, so that group psychotherapy with larger groups is of a different order than with smaller groups.

Some therapists prefer 2-hour sessions. A 1-hour session is too short because a kind of warm-up period is necessary and termination also may be a distinct phase, leaving insufficient time in between to accomplish the necessary work of gathering information and observing and interpreting enough of the group process to obtain the best therapeutic results. However, it will be found that shortening the 2-hour session to 1½ hours does little damage. An erroneous impression may be given by certain patients whose policy is to abstain from their significant transactions until the end of the session. The error is to assume that it takes them 2 hours to make their minds up. Actually, such terminal activity is part of a game and will occur no matter how long or short the group session is. If a 2-hour session is shortened to 90 minutes, it will be found that the patients who formerly made their plays at the end of the 2 hours will now do so at the end of the hour-and-a-half. Therefore, shortening the session does not appear to impair the efficiency of therapy; in fact it may increase it by tightening things up. It also leaves the therapist free to handle more groups per day, which is desirable in the present state of psychotherapy because of the relative scarcity of therapists all over the world. This is particularly applicable to Africa and the Orient where the ratio of psychiatrists to the general population is extremely low.

As to the arrangement of the room, the principle factor is the presence or absence of a table; or more precisely, the presence or absence of an empty space in the middle of the room. Whatever is in the middle of the room tends to become endowed with special properties, and if it is a space, it is treated differently from a large object such as a table. A table has the additional property of tending to conceal the lower halves of the bodies of the members, which has some effect on the proceedings of the group, particularly if it includes both sexes. There is not sufficient information at present to make firm statements about the presence or absence of a table, but there is no doubt that it has some significance.

THE AUTHORITY DIAGRAM

Group psychotherapists in public facilities are understandably reluctant to accept the idea that their groups are dynamically different from those in private practice. These differences arise from the authority diagram and the operative principle which influence to some degree everything that a psychotherapist in an institutional setting does. An authority diagram for a psychotherapy setup in a clinic is given in Figure 29 (p. 249). Anyone doing group therapy in this situation is responsible primarily to the Chief of Clinic and secondarily to the Chief Public Health Officer and the others shown in the diagram. He carries with him at all times a preconscious concept of what these people expect from him. Under ordinary conditions many of these suppositions may never become conscious, but in time of stress they will emerge full blown. Everyone in the clinic knows in the back of his mind that at any moment some patient might write a letter to the governor or some other official which, in rare instances, and however remote the possibility, might be of decisive importance to the official's own career.

In institutions under Federal jurisdiction, such as the Veterans Administration, the authority diagram must be traced right back through the head of the Department in Washington to the President of the United States because it is just possible that the case of an individual patient in a psychotherapy group might become a national issue, and this is known to Federal employees. More commonly, the therapist is aware of the expectations of his immediate supervisor and the chief of his clinic and knows that if those expectations are not met, difficulties may arise. Hence, before setting up a psychotherapy group, it is important to draw an authority diagram to clarify what the therapist thinks is expected of him. Often he is surprised at what that brings out, since pride may have kept him from acknowledging the influence of these factors.

The authority within the group itself depends on the capabilities of the leader. If the appointed therapist is weak, his patients may appeal to higher authority and undermine his leadership. If he is competent, this will rarely occur.

The physician in private practice is for all practical purposes responsible only to himself and therefore does not have to take into account the expectations of a hierarchy of superiors. All this may be summarized by saying that the senior leader of a therapy group in an institution is the Chief of Clinic, and the invisible leader of a therapy group in private practice, as already noted, is the father (or mother) of the therapist. Interestingly enough, in those therapy groups which are conducted by psychoanalytically trained therapists, there is an active euhemerus in the person of Freud. And this is often well-known to the patients, so that in such groups the influence of a euhemerus may make itself felt in times of stress.

THE STRUCTURAL DIAGRAM

Psychotherapy groups have the structure of simple groups, with two classes only: the leadership, represented by one individual, the therapist; and the membership, represented by one class of individuals, the patients. The commonest departure from this simple structure is to have a compound or complex minor structure within the leadership, represented by an observer or recorder or by an assistant or co-therapist.

A phantom complexity may be introduced if the sessions are mechanically recorded. The group then becomes a complex one because of the fantasies the patients will have about the recording instrument. It is said that the patients get used to having their sessions recorded, but that is always done at some cost and with some warping of the proceedings; i.e., their anxiety is controlled by the marshalling of defenses, and those defenses alter the nature of the proceedings. This is easily validated when a patient transfers from a regularly recorded group. If he enters a group where the proceedings are not recorded or goes into individual therapy, it soon appears that fantasies of what would be done with the recording were active throughout his membership in the previous group. These fantasies can easily be revived and are often surprising to the patient himself, who has successfully forgotten that they ever existed even though actually they were there as an active artifact all the time.

Some groups are set up in the public structure as having a co-therapist when it is well-known to the patients that the so-called co-therapist is really an assistant therapist who is subject to the authority of the senior therapist in a show-down. This hypocrisy of the leadership is recognized in the group imago of the patients and introduces cant as an element of the group culture. Overlooking this psychological reality does more harm than good, and the myth of the "co-therapist" (if it is a myth in a given instance) will impair therapeutic efficiency. In any case, the presence of more than one individual in the leadership region alters the proceedings in a way which cannot be foreseen at present and is not sufficiently understood. Therefore, the introduction of another person as an arm of the leadership must always be undertaken with caution and with the knowledge that there are certain disadvantages which in many cases outweigh the advantages of having an observer or co-therapist.

In this simplest kind of group, the leader acts as his own external and internal apparatus. That is, it is usually his job to select the members, arrange the time and the place of the meetings, set up the furniture and other equipment required, answer the telephone, deal with outside authorities, collect the fees and keep internal order. At times these duties may be delegated to the "co-therapist" or to the observer.

THE DYNAMICS DIAGRAM

For most psychotherapy groups, the external pressure is negligible. Most commonly in time of war, and in rare cases in a hurricane, earthquake or epidemic area, it may affect the proceedings. In an institution the external pressure generally is represented by the people who have the authority to transfer the therapist or terminate permanently the meetings of the group. If situations arise in which this pressure becomes active, the therapist may deal with it without mentioning it to the patients or he may discuss it with them.

By and large, however, it is unusual for a therapy group to go into the combat state; in most cases it remains a simple process group. The patients' transactions can be divided into those in the major process, which are commonly labelled transference phenomena, and those in the minor process—i.e., transactions between the patients that do not directly involve the therapist. Theoretically, every transaction that takes place in such a group is influenced by the transference—i.e., by the major process—but it is still possible in practice to separate the proceedings into those of the major internal process and those of the minor internal process; or, put in group dynamic terms, those in which individual proclivities are engaged with the group cohesion, and those in which two or more individual proclivities are engaged with each other.

An elementary classification of chains of transactions which is particularly useful to beginners in group therapy is the triad discussion-description-expression. Discussion is concerned with the external environment (pastimes and activity). Description is concerned with personal feelings—talking about them rather than expressing them; these are Adult descriptions of Child and Parent attitudes and are often part of a game of Psychiatry. Description is often marked by the use of "this" in place of "that" as a demonstrative ("This is what I did yesterday" rather than "That is (or was) what I did yesterday."). Expression refers to the direct, undiluted expression of feelings toward another member of the group.

THE GROUP IMAGOES

The real aim of most dynamic psychotherapy groups is to clarify the group imagoes of the individual members, although this may be stated in different words. Some therapists believe that the protocol for all therapy groups is based on early family life. Hence, the group imago is a facsimile of an infantile or childhood group imago. However, it is probably an error to accept this too easily, and valuable insights may be lost by making unwarranted assumptions in this respect; in particular, the careful study of adjustments is apt to be neglected.

TRANSACTIONAL DIAGRAMS

The advantage of using transactional analysis in group therapy is that it raises the theoretical efficiency of this treatment to 100 per cent. In principle, each stimulus and each response, no matter how trivial it appears, is a potentially fruitful subject for analysis. There is no need to wait for "material," and there is no such thing as an "unproductive" session unless the therapist makes it so. The old joke about the psychiatrist who said "Hello!" to his colleague and was asked in reply "What do you mean by that?" becomes a serious central question in transactional analysis.* The fact

* Too often a patient who asks the therapist "How are you?" really means "When are you going to drop dead?"

that the therapist has a well-defined, progressive program leading from structural analysis through transactional analysis proper and game analysis to script analysis, gives him a confidence and forthrightness which is in itself therapeutic and eliminates the gingerly, tentative approach which is the hallmark of technics borrowed from individual therapy. Transactional analysis is a strong instrument in group therapy because it is based on a theory native to and derived from the group therapy chamber. Thus, it not only is highly efficient, but the results so far indicate that it is also of superior therapeutic effectiveness.

Transactional diagrams of what occurs in psychotherapy groups are the models for all other transactional diagrams, since only in such a group can the characteristics of transactions be adequately investigated. Hence, it is from psychotherapy groups that most knowledge of the relationship between individual dynamics and group dynamics is derived. For this reason it is common for all sorts of people who work with groups to become interested in group therapy and to enter psychotherapy groups as patients, particularly if they wish to learn the principles of structural analysis, transactional analysis and game analysis. It appears that group leaders of many kinds can benefit from such experiences both in regard to their own inner problems and as an aid to understanding the proceedings of their own groups; but only if they genuinely feel a need for personal psychotherapy.

TECHNICAL NOTES

The work of Trigant Burrow, the first systematic psychiatric group therapist, is discussed at some length in the appendix on the literature of group dynamics, together with the ideas of other creative group therapists. C. Beukenkamp ("Further Developments of the Transference Life Concept in Therapeutic Groups," *Journal of the Hillside Hospital* 5:441-498, 1956) is the ablest exponent of the theory that a psychotherapy group recapitulates the family situation. G. R. Bach (*Intensive Group Psychotherapy,* New York, Ronald Press Company, 1954) has noted the occurrence of chains of transactions which he calls "set-up operations," and which are actually parts of games.

For further discussion of the problems of group psychotherapy and group treatment, see Eric Berne, *Principles of Group Treatment,* (New York, Oxford University Press, 1966).

14

The Therapy of Ailing Groups

APPLIED GROUP DYNAMICS

Applied social psychiatry deals on the one hand with unhealthy transactions between individuals, where it finds its chief usefulness in group psychotherapy; and on the other hand with unhealthy aspects of organizations and groups, where it becomes a branch of applied group dynamics.

The therapy of ailing groups, like the therapy of individuals, depends on a clear understanding of the problems at issue. In both cases, the ailments may be considered under the classic headings of pathologic structure (anatomy), pathologic function (physiology), symptoms, diagnosis, outlook and treatment. In order to understand the malfunctioning of a group, one should have at least enough information to draw the 6 basic diagrams: Location, Authority, Structural, Dynamics, Imago and Transactional. In addition, it is necessary to know something about the history of the group and the motivations of the leadership and the membership. The actual proceedings at a given moment then can be considered or reconsidered in an attempt to find a remedy.

At the present time, the therapy of ailing groups is mostly in the hands of industrial psychologists. But all chiefs of state and their internal apparatuses, legislators, public officials, political scientists, economists, sociologists, educators, criminologists and sometimes (as in the islands of the South Pacific (anthropologists are concerned with the questions involved. In fact, this applies to anyone in a position of leadership and to any member of a group apparatus.

One of the most important contributions of industrial psychology is the following principle: No conflicts between two classes of membership can be settled satisfactorily by consultation with each class separately. For example, if there is a conflict between factory managers and factory workers, little will be accomplished by a consultant who meets first with the managers and then with the workers, or vice versa. The increase in cohesion and the decrease in agitation which favor productivity can best be brought about by joint meetings of both subgroups. From this principle, the usefulness of "family group therapy" can be deduced logically.

However, the personal leader is the personal representative of the group cohesion, and his group imago influences the behavior of all the members in accordance with the operative principle. Therefore, a shift in his group imago will have the greatest effect in changing the private structure of the group, with a resulting change in effectiveness. Hence, consultations with the leadership are the most powerful weapon in the therapy of ailing groups.

Four examples will be used to illustrate the practical application of this method: an outpatient clinic, a psychotherapy group, a state hospital and a boy's club. The best way to learn the therapy of ailing groups is to practice the use of this approach at a regular professional seminar, each weekly session of which should last at least 2 hours: 1 hour for presentation and 1 hour for diagnosis. Once an accurate diagnosis has been made, the treatment is usually easy to work out, and the results can be checked by a follow-up presentation a few weeks or months later. Almost any kind of a group or organization will do, provided that the leader or a regular member is willing and able to give the required information; e.g., a rowdy classroom, a postgraduate school, a county health department, a social welfare clinic, a disorganized theatrical company, a housing development, a hospital, a teen-age activity group—any group which is not producing the best it should be capable of. The most instructive is a psychotherapy group, since a psychotherapist knows more about his members than the leaders of most other groups. In order to head off idle speculation and rambling discussions, the person who presents the situation should be requested to ask a specific question right at the beginning, so that the members of the seminar can direct their attention to the particular symptom which is causing uneasiness.

AN AILING CLINIC

Dr. Lebon had recently been appointed Chief of Staff of a psychiatric outpatient clinic in a medium-sized inland city. His predecessor, Dr. Fabel, had resigned in order to go into private practice. Dr. Lebon had not had previous administrative experience but felt that he had abilities along these lines and wanted to use them to the best advantage. A colleague referred him to Dr. Q.

Dr. Fabel had given little attention to the organizational aspects of the clinic. He had preferred to devote himself to seeing patients, leaving the rest of the staff to do pretty much as they pleased. Dr. Lebon said that he found the morale poor. No one spoke up at staff conferences, which tended to be perfunctory and lackadaisical. He had attempted to review some of the medical and therapeutic procedures so that he would have a clearer idea of how the staff was performing its duties, and this had aroused resentment.

A. THE FIRST SESSION

At their first session, Dr. Q encouraged Dr. Lebon to present whatever problems were uppermost in his mind. He then questioned him for details that would help to set up the 6 basic diagrams. Since this was a private consultation and not a teaching seminar, Dr. Q did not draw all the diagrams on the blackboard, but constructed them in his mind. He did not attempt to give Dr. Lebon a course in group dynamics. He focused his opinions and suggestions on the points which Dr. Lebon raised and said enough so that Dr. Lebon could follow his train of thought; when he had to use a technical term for the sake of precision, he explained it sufficiently so that Dr. Lebon would know what it referred to in his particular situation. This approach was quite acceptable to Dr. Lebon. Being a practical clinician himself, he did not want a course in theory at that time but workable answers to concrete problems, and he trusted Dr. Q's judgment just as he would trust a consultant in any other branch of psychiatry or medicine.

It was not necessary to go into much detail to set up an adequate Location Diagram, shown roughly in Figure 28. Dr. Lebon described briefly the layout of the clinic, with larger offices for himself, the chief psychologist and the chief social worker and smaller ones for the other members of the staff; a waiting room, reception desk, emergency treatment room, secretaries' offices and conference room. The most important point established here was that the physical facilities of the clinic were satisfactory to him.

More attention was paid to the Authority Diagram. The clinic was financed by the city, with some state funds as well. The finances were administered by the Public Health Officer, to whom the Chief of Clinic was directly responsible. The Public Health Officer was responsible to the Mayor and the Board of Supervisors.

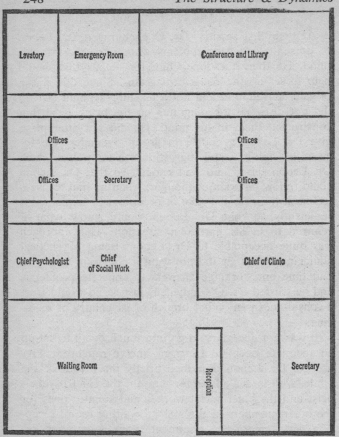

Fig. 28. Location diagram.

The local newspaper was actively interested in the clinic and so was the general public, since it was expected to diminish the need for welfare funds and to provide superior psychiatric care for the segment of the population who could not afford private treatment. At this session it appeared that the senior portion of the chain of authority was not directly involved in the problem, so this aspect was soon dropped. However,

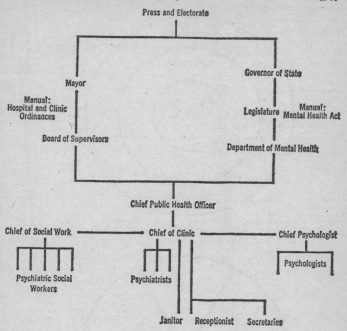

Note: Psychiatrists, Psychologists and Social Workers work
independently on the same echelon.

FIG. 29. Authority diagram.

the junior portion seemed more disturbed and, therefore, was investigated in more detail. The senior echelons are partly represented in Figure 29; the junior echelons include the janitor and the secretaries, but in this case it turned out that they were not implicated, as far as could be determined.

By this time the structural diagram was becoming clear. Unlike some clinics, which are structured as compound groups in which the psychologists and the social workers are supervised by and responsible to the medical personnel (Fig. 30A), this clinic was structured as a complex group. The psychiatrists, the psychologists and

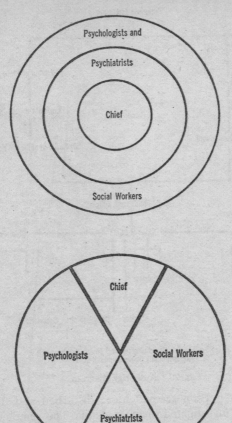

Fig. 30. A (*top*). A typical clinic. B (*bottom*). An ailing clinic.

the social workers each functioned as an independent subgroup, so that the Chief of Clinic served only as an administrative buffer who protected them from external pressures (Fig. 30B). Dr. Lebon indicated this by saying that procedures for the clinic were poorly out-

Fig. 31. Dynamics diagram.

lined. Everyone did pretty much as he pleased. The social workers in particular resented any interference.
The chief social worker was an energetic, well-organized woman of large build, much more aggressive than
Dr. Fabel, for example.

It was the social workers who had been most upset
when Dr. Lebon had reviewed the therapeutic procedures. They felt this was an invasion of their field
and an abrogation of their rights (the social contract as
they saw it). In an attempt to mollify them, Dr. Lebon
explained that he had undertaken this review as part of
his duties under the State Mental Health Act.

The important aspects of the Dynamics Diagram
were now clear in Dr. Q's mind (Fig. 31). The external
pressure was negligible. The social workers were weakening the group cohesion by agitation across the major
internal boundary and also by intrigues across the Psy-
chiatrist-Social Worker minor internal boundary, freely
expressing their individual proclivities with little com-

promise in favor of the effectiveness and the survival of
the group as a whole.

At this point, Dr. Q made three observations to Dr.
Lebon. 1. He explained the principle that the members
of a group do not engage in the group process until
they think they know their positions in the group imago
of the leader and then engage accordingly. The former
chief, by his "hands-off" policy, had given the social
workers no indications to go by. Therefore, during his
régime there had been no engagement in the major
process, and Dr. Fabel and the social workers had
treated each other like strangers, with consequent
weakening of the group cohesion. But, in their own
subgroup, the chief social worker had been a good psychological leader. They knew where they stood with
her, and this enabled them to go ahead with their
subgroup process. As Dr. Lebon made clear, they were
engaged in a competitive game. At one level they were
emotionally involved by their patients, and at another
level they vied with each other for the chief social
worker's approval by using a rather stereotyped therapeutic approach which she favored. (This was a version
of the game called "I'm Only Trying to Help You.")
What they resented was his interference with this game,
and they feared him because they could not guess how
far he might go in this direction. The culture of the
group as a whole was soft and lax.

2. He suggested that leaders exist partly to provide
an object for the hostility of the members, and that Dr.
Lebon should not be surprised or ruffled at their reaction to his inquiries, since to them his questions indicated that there might be trouble in the future if he was
dissatisfied with their work. Dr. Fabel had acted more
like an external apparatus than like a real Chief. Now
they were confronted with someone who wanted to be a
responsible and effective leader, instead of merely an
administrator who only did the undesirable paper work

and acted as a buffer. Hence, they too must become responsible and effective. If they did not fight him, their Adults would have to take over their clinical work, leaving the Parent in each of them frustrated and resentful. Therefore, although he could understand their feelings, this should not deter him from doing what had to be done.

3. In saying that he had undertaken the review of procedures, because of the Mental Health Act, he had started a 3-handed game in which he was in effect calling in the State Legislature as his backer. Since they could not attack the Legislature, this left them helpless. He could always brush off their resentment by referring it to someone they could not deal with instead of meeting it directly himself. This "successful" maneuver, as he thought of it, might be successful in keeping him from having the anxieties of responsibility, but its effect would probably be to arouse even more resentment. Since he was dodging his responsibility, in their helplessness they might fall back on passive resistance, which would further damage the group cohesion. Furthermore, they might interpret his explanation quite rightly as a sign of weakness, which would decrease their respect for him and make it more difficult for them to accept his leadership. The fact that this device of falling back on the protection of higher authorities was common did not necessarily mean that it was good practice; perhaps its popularity only indicated how difficult it was to be a courageous leader.

B. The Second Session

At the next session, 2 weeks later, Dr. Lebon described a staff conference. Some transactional analysis became possible, and the Group Imagoes of the social workers could be visualized (Fig. 32A). It appeared that they viewed the staff, including themselves, as a group of precocious children, all on an equal level, un-

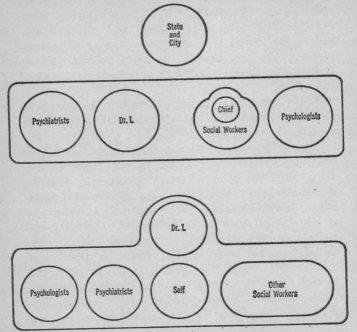

Fig. 32. A (*top*). Group imago of member of disjunctive subgroup (weak cohesion). B (*bottom*). Group imago of a conjunctive member (strong cohesion).

der the benevolent protection of the state and the city governments.

According to Dr. Lebon's description, the 3 psychologists stood apart as a small subgroup and concentrated on doing their jobs; their talk was confined to matters concerning their own profession, and they did not join in more general discussions as the social workers did. The psychiatrists tended to work as independent individuals, each primarily interested in his own patients, with little participation in the group process. The staff conferences were repetitious and ritualistic, with strict adherence to the etiquette of the social contract. There was no frank discussion, no real thought; no one wanted or ventured any criticism. After a case was presented, the attitude of the members was: "Don't say anything destructive. Please look on the constructive side." This was said aloud by more than one social worker. The proceedings consisted only of reinforcing the speaker's persona as a "good" therapist. In the face of such a rigid ritual, no real activity was possible, and little or no benefit came to the patients from the conferences.

The problem here was how to develop a more useful group culture. The first step must be to change the poorly differentiated group imagoes of the social workers, which actually represented the situation as a party rather than as a group or organization, into something more effective, and to get the psychologists and the psychiatrists to participate more. Dr. Lebon had to make clear that it was his right and duty as a leader to question their personas and to differentiate himself from the other members. In order to do this, he must be willing to take the consequences of occupying the leadership slot instead of just another membership slot. The desired change in the imagoes of the members is represented in the shift from Figure 32A to Figure 32B. One question was how rapidly the shift should be attempted. The dilemma was: the quicker, the better for the patients; the slower, the more time for the staff to adjust and the less likelihood of resignations. It was agreed that the kind of social worker who becomes too personally involved with her patients does not give up her psychological position easily and sometimes under pressure would flee rather than make an orderly retreat.

Besides the need for careful timing, there was also a transactional difficulty. The chances were that any questioning of the persona of the "good therapist" would result in a crossed transaction. No matter how objective the leader was, his remarks would likely be

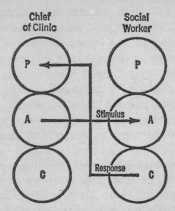

FIG. 33. (A) Crossed transaction (Type I). (S) "Let's
discuss it." (R) "Why do you
criticize me?"

regarded (in the beginning at least) as a Parental criticism of the Child, resulting in the situation represented
in Figure 33, with a resentful response. The best approach would be to "hook" their Adults by stressing
"good clinic practice" before questioning any particular
procedure. By thus arousing Adult pride, the leader
would have a valuable ally, an inner check against resentful rebellion on the part of any member's Child.
How Dr. Lebon would accomplish this preparation was
left to his judgment.

He asked whether he should do it by talking quietly
to the subleader, the chief social worker, and letting her
handle it from there, or whether he should take over.
The first alternative, hiding behind her skirts, did not
promise to be constructive. She was getting considerable satisfaction out of being an independent leader,
and he would be asking her to give that up and come
over to his side. She would only do this if she thought
she would get something in return. That meant he
would have to "seduce" her into bringing her subgroup

into his fold. A seduction, however subtle and hidden, always contains unspoken promises and holds unpredictable possibilities. It is some kind of a "deal." It was suggested that he tell the subleader first, to prepare her, and then take over himself. If he shows her clearly that he is not making a deal, but that he is the leader and expects her co-operation, then he is organizing a group and not a seduction. She then has the alternatives of open rebellion or of acknowledging and respecting his leadership, both of which are easier to handle than the possible consequences of his first proposition.

In discussing the problem of firmness as outlined above, Dr. Lebon's special characteristics as a leader came out more strongly than before, and he readily acknowledged them. He had a tendency in his declarations of policy to be Parentally sermonizing and over-justifying, rather than practical and Adult. And if he was challenged, he would, like a little boy, bring up external authorities instead of standing on his own ground. He was recognizing these things more clearly, but he still found himself doing them occasionally; nevertheless, he felt that there was some improvement in these respects and looked for more.

C. The Third Session

At the third session, which took place a month after the first, Dr. Lebon said that the clinic staff was now in better shape and that the discussions had been a great help. After the previous session, he had spoken privately to the chief social worker. He had simply asked her what the role of a social worker was and stopped there without defending or embroidering his question, which was unusual for him and even felt a little unnatural. Much to his surprise, instead of becoming defensive, she had at first appeared to be confused by his new approach, but had then proceeded to answer in a matter of fact way, reciting the well-established tasks

which were the legitimate concern of her profession. He
had listened quietly and had then mentioned that many
of the items she listed were beyond the capacity of a
psychiatrist to deal with and clearly indicated the need
for social workers at the clinic. He had suggested that
the social work staff at the next clinic conference talk
about the things they could contribute. The presentations
had been poor, and Dr. Lebon thought this meant that
they were worried and displeased at his suggestion. Dr.
Q agreed that the issue had now been joined, and that
they were fighting what they rightly felt was an intrusion into the private preserve they had set up.

But in spite of themselves, the presentations had had
a good effect. The psychiatrists had hitherto been igno-
rant of the proper usefulness of a social worker because
the social workers had set themselves up as envious
competitors of the medical staff. Now the psychiatrists
saw for the first time and readily acknowledged that the
social workers, if they went legitimate, could make a
definite and unique contribution to the effectiveness of
the clinic. With all its deficiencies, this one conference
had made a strong impression on the staff, so that the
different members were beginning to "appreciate" each
other (i.e., listen to each other) for the first time since
the clinic had been activated.

Dr. Lebon went on to another problem. He wanted
to open an inpatient ward in the local hospital, and the
social workers objected because it would give the public
the idea that the clinic dealt with "crazy" people. Dr
Lebon wanted to go secretly to the Superintendent of
the hospital and persuade him to say that it was his, the
Superintendent's, idea to start an inpatient psychiatric
ward. Dr. Lebon thought that in this manner he could
avoid taking responsibility for the ward and thus escape
the criticism of the social workers.

Dr. Q said that in his opinion that would be a very
bad move, since once more it amounted to setting up a

3-handed game between himself and his staff, with the Superintendent as his ally, except that this time it was worse because it involved keeping a secret. Since Dr. Lebon's aim at the moment was to break up the games that the staff was now playing with him, it seemed inadvisable meanwhile for him to set up a game from his side.

At this point, Dr. Q thought to himself that if Dr. Lebon went ahead with his plan, sooner or later he would unconsciously arrange for the secret to leak out and thus get himself into difficulties, very likely at precisely the moment when "at last everything is going well." However, he did not say this aloud, because Dr. Lebon had come for therapy for his ailing group and not for treatment of his personal problems. It is always an easy out for a psychiatric consultant in group dynamics to suggest that the leader is in need of personal psychotherapy, but that merely amounts to a confession that the consultant has reached the end of his rope, as far as his knowledge of group dynamics is concerned. If that is the best he has to contribute, he should resign before he begins.

Dr. Lebon's thoughts were evidently running along similiar lines because the very next thing he said was that he realized things had now come to the point where he had to choose between psychotherapy for himself and studying more about the theory of social dynamics. He added that he thought he was "not very sick." Dr. Q replied:

"I don't feel that you're 'sick' at all. It's not a question of 'sick' or 'not sick' behavior on your part, as you've often said it was. It's a question of procedures that work, and procedures that don't work."

Thus it was agreed between them that further consultations could be postponed. Dr. Lebon concluded:

"A lot of things have been straightened out in my mind, and the situation is considerably improved. I think now I know enough about everybody's weaknesses, including my own, to go ahead."

Subsequent events confirmed his confidence.

AN AILING PSYCHOTHERAPY GROUP

Psychotherapy groups are similiar in most respects to simple work gangs such as rural classrooms and small plantations. The main differences are in the group cultures. In all three, the location diagrams allow people to talk to each other face to face, and the manning tables and the structural diagrams are simple, with only two roles ("overseer" and members). There are only small differences in the authority diagrams; as long as the job gets done, there is not likely to be any interference from above, and if anything goes wrong, the leader knows exactly whom he is responsible to: the clinic head, the school board or the manager. If the groups are healthy, the dynamics diagrams are equally simple: internally, the leader has almost absolute authority to impose certain restrictions, and the members have no authority over each other. For the most part, the work proceeds without any interruption from external pressure, although a flood or a hurricane might disrupt any of these groups. The imagoes are of an elementary type if the group cohesion is strong, and transactions tend to be Adult-to-Adult in the activity and Parent-to-Child in the major process.

The ailments that affect classrooms are often due to softness and some form of laxity in the culture. On the plantations, according to responsible press reports, difficulties usually seem to arise from the opposite condition of overfirmness and overseverity. For example, tropical planters whose fathers settled their lands in the face of crocodiles and cannibals, often exert rigid and sometimes irritable discipline over their indentured native laborers. Thus, unhealthy cultures may be divided into flabby and brittle types. Flabby cultures are soft

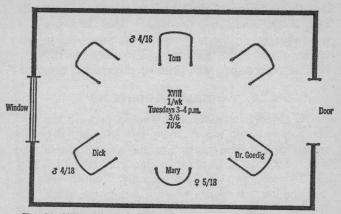

FIG. 34. "Discussion Diagram" of a therapy group. A diagram like this is drawn on the blackboard whenever a therapy group is discussed. It gives on inspection the answers to many different questions. If a recording is being played the therapist can indicate which patient is talking.

Key

XVIII: 18th meeting
1/wk: meets once weekly
3/6: 3 out of 6 active members present
70%: average attendance during life of group (indicates cohesion)
4/16: Tom came 2 weeks after the group was activated and has been to 4 out of 16 possible meetings since.
Other information can be included, such as age or diagnosis of each patient, but here it is irrelevant.

and lax, and the activity is not sufficiently structured and goal-directed to engage the Adult seriously. Brittle cultures are too firm and severe, and the activity is too highly structured, with the result that the Child becomes sullen from suppression, or completely cowed. A flabby culture encourages decay, and a brittle one passive resistance or open rebellion. Nobody can learn anything in the classroom, or the natives refuse to pay their head-tax, and spears and bullets fly.

The therapy of an ailing psychotherapy group is usually easy to prescribe. Because of the simple structure and dynamics, the difficulty rarely lies in those areas. Unhealthy therapy groups are almost always flabby, so

that the cohesion is weak and the members gradually
drift away. Sometimes the leader rides, knowingly or
unknowingly, on the magical powers attributed to him
by the Child in his patients and makes little effort to
offer a progressive, well-planned therapeutic program.

A. THE DIAGNOSTIC INTERVIEW

Dr. Goedig came for consultation because his psychotherapy group was decaying. He had started with 8
members, but in a short time his average attendance
was reduced to 3. In order to clarify the situation, Figure 34 was drawn on the blackboard. Enquiry revealed
that the low attendance was not due to the usual "statistical" attrition, in which 50 per cent of the members
might be expected to withdraw during the first few
months, 50 per cent of their replacements during the
next few months, and so on. Indeed, the group cohesion was stronger than average in respect to with-
drawals; the weakness was of the type manifested by
irregular attendance. Only 2 of the 8 members had
permanently withdrawn, but the others attended spas-
modically. It was as though Dr. Goedig was holding out
some promise which was more attractive than usual but
was somehow delaying its fulfillment. Thus, the members were too intrigued to drop out for good but not
sufficiently interested to come regularly. From time to
time, one or another of them would come for a few
weeks, as if to see whether the group was any closer to
the end of the rainbow, and then stay away for a few
weeks hoping that things would advance meanwhile.
Hence, the average attendance of 3 seldom included the
same individuals for very long.

Dr. Goedig was an agreeable, kindhearted man with
some training in both psychoanalysis and transactional
analysis. He let his patients, selected from his private
practice on somewhat snobbish intellectual grounds,
proceed as they wished and occasionally threw in an in-

terpretation. If a patient spoke to him directly and he did not know what to say, he would fall back on a popular but erroneous idea of the canon of Freud (the euhemerus, as noted, of most psychotherapy groups) and "reflect the question" or exercise his "right" to maintain a poker-faced silence. He could not explain exactly how he acquired this "right." He felt that it was "good psychiatric practice" but was not sure what it was good for. On careful enquiry, it developed that he felt the right was conferred on him when he got his diploma.

This line of questioning was not what Dr. Goedig had expected, and it made him uncomfortable, but it impressed on him that the real purpose of the "psychiatric poker face" was to avoid becoming involved in games. Such immobility was not something to be exhibited arbitrarily to conceal the therapist's own ignorance or uneasiness or to convey a false impression of superiority; it was a rational procedure to be applied when rationally indicated, and not otherwise. His indiscriminate use of it was part of a game of Psychiatry on his side. Actually, he did it less for the patients' benefit than for his own.

This discussion revealed that he had no ongoing therapeutic plan and no well-defined program for conducting the group. His feeling was that somehow the patients would get "better" if they said whatever came into their heads and he said whatever came into his. In short, this was a flabby group. At no time did the patients understand clearly what was going on (culture soft), nor were his interventions consistent and well organized (culture lax). His analytic approach was too poorly defined and too lacking in direction to interest the Adult part of his patients. It was mostly the Child in each of them that brought him or her there to be mothered by Dr. Goedig and to see if the miraculous promise secretly held out by the therapist was nearer fulfillment.

B. Remedial Progress

After a few sessions, Dr. Goedig admitted that he was lazy, lacking in courage and not really committed to any system of therapy. He now decided to use transactional analysis and game analysis more systematically and vigorously, rather than maintaining his former eclectic approach. Dr. Q explained that there were two aspects to be considered: the first was the problem of ensuring more regular attendance and averting complete decay, and the second was the quality of the therapeutic results he hoped to obtain. For the first, it did not matter which approach he used, so long as he was committed to it. Such a commitment would result in a firmer, stricter, healthier group culture, which would give the Child in his patients increased confidence that he knew what he was doing; it would also give their Adults a feeling that he (and they) knew where they were going, how they were going to get there, and what could be done about it; in addition, it would offer an example of unswerving strength which they could apply to their own lives. These improvements would reinforce the group cohesion and increase the attendance. However, the quality of the therapeutic results did depend on which particular approach he selected. Dr. Goedig decided to give up "halfhearted psychoanalysis" in favor of a systematic and vigorous use of transactional and game analysis.

Again, it would have been an easy out for Dr. Q to suggest to a colleague who was lazy, lacking in courage and commitment and flabby in his approach, that he was in need of personal therapy. However, as it turned out, the situation improved without that. It took only a few weeks to establish increased vigor and confidence on Dr. Goedig's part, increased interest and zest on the patients' part and regular attendance.

During this period, Dr. Goedig continued to behave

in an apologetic, defensive, Child-Parent way to Dr. Q. But the gratifying responses of his patients soon encouraged him to be independent, so that his consultations became much more Adult-Adult and more and more focused on the details of the major and the minor group processes rather than on Dr. Goedig's capacities as a leader and therapist. After 6 months of weekly consultations attendance had risen from the previous rate of about 70 per cent to a new rate of about 95 per cent. After another 6 months, Dr. Goedig had become confident and skillful in his use of transactional analysis; his patients found this useful enough so that some of them wanted to bring their spouses for analysis of their marital games. The result was that after 18 months of consultation his group had grown so large that he had to split it in two. This attractiveness may have been due partly to the use of transactional analysis rather than some other approach, but it was also due partly to improvements in the firmness and the strictness of the group culture, as well as to the leader's increased understanding of group dynamics.*

A LITTLE BOY'S CLUB

Let us now return to the little boy Davy mentioned in Chapter 12, who always wanted to have meetings at his house and who later became a group therapist. When he was about 10 years old he tried to start a club, the Agamemnon Club, but somehow it never got off the ground. A consideration of the 6 basic diagrams soon makes some of its deficiencies clear. Since in this

* After 2 years Dr. Goedig had 3 groups springing from the original one, all 3 engaged in the most productive form of transactional analysis and with an aggregate 6-month attendance record of 96.5 per cent—the highest in Dr. Q's experience, exceeding the cohesion of his own therapy groups. This was an approximate 90 per cent reduction in absences. This is a gratifying example of the pupil excelling the teacher. "Dr. Goedig" is of course a pseudonym.

case the diagrams are relatively simple and easy to visualize, it will not be necessary to draw them.

1. The Location Diagram shows the basement of Davy's home. There are some things there to attract little boys: barred windows, places to hide, isolation from grownups and, since Davy's uncle was a physician, certain objects of scientific interest such as tapeworms in bottles, anatomic charts and a broken microscope. If Davy had wanted to start a junior Osler Society or Aesculapius Club, it might have sufficed. But there was nothing there for a group of Agamemnons: no swords, shields, guns, or lances. There were many other places available where courage could be shown and warlike games carried on to better advantage. The first deficiencies were improper equipment and poorly defined activity.

2. The Authority Diagram consists only of a euhemerus and a personal leader. The euhemerus, Agamemnon, was unknown to most of the candidates for membership and had no personal significance for the others. His canon—the infantry and the chivalry of the Trojan War —had been outdated for many centuries and was finished off during the recent hostilities of World War I. In existential reinforcement, Discobolos and Achilles had been replaced by Babe Ruth and Eddie Rickenbacker. The personal leader, Davy, had few of the magical or even the social attributes of leadership in the eyes of his contemporaries and had only one or two loyal followers.

The defects in the authority diagram extended to all aspects: historical (obscure euhemerus); cultural (meaningless canon, outdated culture); personal (naïve leadership); and organizational (no mother group). Actually, all the organizer had to offer in this area was a weak warrant: some cards headed "Agamemnon Club" which he had run off on a toy printing set.

3. The Structural Diagram was poorly defined. Eligibility was based on the autocratic provisional group

imago of one person, and that had a defect which is fatal in an autocrat: instability. The requirements for admission changed from day to day and from one recruitment speech to another—except for one item: the payment of one cent as an initiation fee, the proceeds to be spent on plums for the opening meeting. Unfortunately, due to differences in the tastes of various candidates, even this was threatened with erosion into a fruit-bowl which the organizer realized might be financially unattainable. Hence, the external group boundary soon blurred into vagueness. A proper internal structure might have offered some hope. If each candidate had been offered an office, there might have been some action; but Davy had no inkling of the principle of patronage. Under the guise of working zeal, he wanted to reserve for himself all offices except that of vice-president. Structurally, then, the Agamemnon Club was unstable, poorly defined and, in the circumstances, underorganized.

4. The Dynamics Diagram reveals weak cohesion and a profusion of active individual proclivities in the face of which survival becomes precarious. External disruptive forces, represented by Davy's parents, are only potential, but threatening enough to interfere with serious engagement in the internal group process. A vacant lot might have been better and would have allowed more freedom. The deficiencies here are a cohesion which is weak to begin with and is further weakened by continual agitation and a threatening external environment. This sets the stage for termination by decay.

5. The Group Imagoes are poorly differentiated; mainly, the leader is not clearly differentiated in their minds from the members. There is no place for him in their scripts; he is neither fatherly, big brotherly, nor rebellious; all he has to offer is idealism, and they are still too young for that. In fact, he does fit into the scripts of two of the bigger boys but not according to

his own provisional group imago. They cast him as an overambitious boy who is a prospective dupe; they help him recruit, with the idea of eventually running off with all the fruit at the first meeting. Of course, as members of the group apparatus, they excuse themselves from having to pay the initiation fee. Their absconding with the proceeds was the acutal occasion for the group breaking up. After that bad beginning, it never met again. But this only meant that it died by unexpected disorganization rather than by the oncoming decay. When the organ of survival itself, the group apparatus, is traitorous, the group is doomed.

6. The Transactional Diagrams were mostly commonplace. There was some organizational work, no time to establish rituals, and much participation in pastimes. The only game played was that which the absconders engaged in, with which the others became involved. There was no belonging or intimacy. Thus, nearly all the transactions were simple, complementary and Adult-Adult; only the two bigger boys carried on ulterior transactions.

TECHNICAL NOTES

The rule that joint management-labor consultations are superior to separate consultations for each class was introduced to me by Dr. Lester Tarnopol of San Francisco City College.

The problems of plantation labor as they arise in specific situations are recounted from time to time in *Pacific Islands Monthly* (Sydney, Pacific Publications Pty.).

The significance of attendance in psychotherapy groups, and the normal statistical expectations, are set forth in my paper on "Group Attendance" (*loc. cit.*).

The Agamemnon Club was started by one little boy, but only a few items would have to be changed for the analysis to apply equally well to such an important failure as the old League of Nations. That is why a consistent approach to ailing groups is so important. The careful study of any group, however trivial, may lead to conclusions which are of universal significance.

15

Management of Organizations

The same principles which are used in the therapy of small ailing groups can be applied to larger organizations with 1,000 or more members. It is only necessary to bear in mind that in a small group each member can be dealt with as an individual, while in a large outfit trends have to be taken into account before individual proclivities can be considered. The type of analysis given below is suitable for large hospitals and custodial institutions such as prisons, and with a few modifications can be adapted for business, political and military organizations.

GENERAL DESCRIPTION

The Elysium State Hospital was a modern, well-equipped, well-financed therapeutic community situated, like many of its kind, in a remote part of the state near a small town. There were more than 1,000 patients, and somewhat less than 1,000 employees. Dr. Q, as consultant in social dynamics and group therapy, had an opportunity to become acquainted with the administrative and the personal problems of the staff as well as with the psychiatric problems of the patients.

THE LOCATION DIAGRAM

The hospital had been built under the guidance of the best available architectural and psychiatric consultants, and the physical plant was satisfactory to the staff. Structurally, it was of the chordal form, with the Chief's office near the main entrance and the staff offices radiating out from there and penetrating into the wards and the clinical and the occupational departments. Stretching behind the buildings were large grounds for farming, construction projects, and recreation; these were open to patients who were eligible for extra-mural activities. Around the periphery were quarters for the junior staff members; the senior staff lived in town. Together they formed an important element in the social and the economic life of the area. Some of the patients' families also moved into the vicinity or visited frequently over the week-ends. Thus, the town of Elysium sociologically resembled an Army town, company town or college town in an agricultural area, with similar public relations problems to be dealt with by the external apparatus of the hospital.

THE AUTHORITY DIAGRAM

The authority diagram was relatively simple, as illustrated in Figure 35. Administratively, the Chief was responsible to the State Director of Mental Health, who was appointed by and responsible to the Governor, who in the final showdown was responsible to the voting public, the well-known "John Q. Citizen." The administrative manual was the State Welfare Code, which was subject to constitutional change by the State Legislature. All administrative acts of the Chief were constitutional and defensible if they obeyed this code. These were his personal and organizational responsibilities. Those aspects gave him little difficulty.

More troublesome was his cultural responsibility,

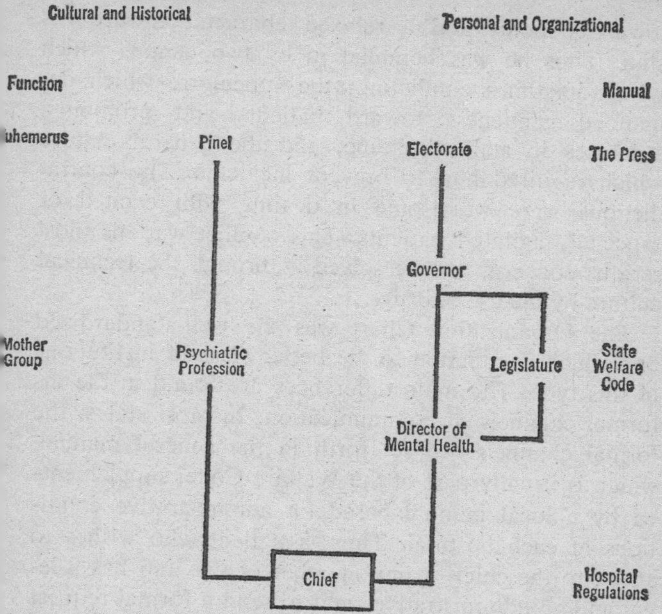

Cultural and Historical   Personal and Organizational

Function   Manual

uhemerus   Pinel   Electorate   The Press

Governor

Mother   Psychiatric   State
Group   Profession   Legislature   Welfare
                                                    Code

Director of
Mental Health

Chief   Hospital
                                            Regulations

Fig. 35. Authority diagram of a state hospital.

which was to the public through the press. In the general culture of the state it was considered bad form to have more than the barest minimum of absences without leave or other untoward incidents related to the hospital. The public had delegated to the Chief, as leader of an organ of the internal apparatus of their state, part of their imagined omniscience, omnipotence and invulnerability. An undue number of irregularities would mean that he had breached this imaginary contract, which was based on similarities in the group imagoes of a large number of plain citizens.

His historical responsibility was to his own subgroup, the psychiatric profession, under the euhemerus Pinel, the French doctor who had introduced gentleness into mental hospitals and whose picture hung on the Chief's wall. This required of him a scrupulous etiquette toward patients and a relaxed character toward his staff. Thus he was hemmed in by two canons which were sometimes conflicting: the subculture which demanded gentleness toward patients and prohibited strictness in staff discipline, and the general culture which required him to prevent incidents. The contradictions were worrisome in dealing with excited or especially agitated patients. This conflict was his most serious concern, and he solved it through the technical culture by the use of drugs.

The Organization Chart was the well-standardized one which is common to the better class of institutions of this type. The main differences are found in the informal channels of communication. In most states, the formal channels are set forth in the general manual, which is usually part of the Welfare Code, supplemented by a local manual based on administrative conditions at each hospital. Thus, a patient who wishes to speak to the chief or any member of the staff has a legal and an administrative right to send a formal request through formal channels. The informal channels depend on the persona and the personality of the chief in each locality. Within the limits set by the general manual, the chief of such an institution can make independent and usually final decisions regarding all internal matters and, to that extent, is an autocrat. The morale, or state of the group cohesion, depends largely on how he chooses to exercise this authority. In the Elysium State Hospital, the Chief was both accessible and available to the staff and the patients, and his example was followed by other members of the staff. Accessibility meant that informally, with proper eitquette, all channels of communication were open at appropriate times. A patient could stop the Chief or any other staff member without prior notice if they happened to meet in the corridor or on the ward and be assured of a courteous hearing. Availability meant that once a request was listened to, a firm decision or effective action would be forthcoming without undue delay.

The situation at Elysium was in contrast to that at two neighboring hospitals. In the first, the Chief chose to be inaccessible except through formal channels. This overfirmness spread through the lower echelons and became characteristic of the group culture. However, it was true that once the Chief was reached, decision or action would be prompt. In the second hospital, there was a high degree of accessibility, but very little came of it; the Chief would talk to anyone at any time, but it was almost impossible to get a firm commitment or reliable backing from him. In the first hospital, in spite of the availabilty, there was a high employee turnover which the staff attributed to the inaccessibility; in the second, even with the high degree of accessibility, there was a weak group cohesion which the staff attributed to the Chief's evasiveness and lack of availability or backing.

THE STRUCTURAL DIAGRAM

Despite the outstanding qualities of the Chief, there were certain chronic difficulties at the Elysium Hospital which were not peculiar to that institution, and which he was unable to eliminate, although he dealt with them as constructively as possible. These can be understood best by referring to the structural diagram shown in Figure 36. The major internal boundary separates two large general classes of membership: those for whom the hospital is a conditional voluntary group, called the staff; and those for whom it is an obligatory group, called the patients. These two classes can be distinguished by the fact that the staff can legitimately impose and can be observed imposing restrictions on the patients, while the patients cannot legitimately impose restrictions on the staff. But patients can discipline

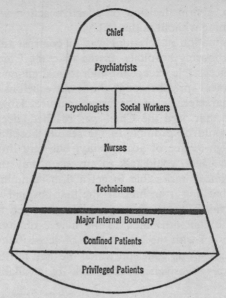

FIG. 36. Structural diagram of a state hospital.

other patients through the self-government provision of the therapeutic community.

These two classes correspond in many important ways to the classes found in an office or industrial plant, generally known as management and workers. Where the hospital has a chief, a professional staff, technicians (formerly called orderlies) and patients, the industrial plant has a chief, executives, foremen and workers. But there are also important differences. In industry, membership is voluntary throughout, although for the individual member the group may be psychologically constrained rather than personal. An Army unit has the same structure, with the major internal boundary between officers and enlisted men; and in wartime with a few exceptions membership is obligatory. In the hospital, the external boundary is open for staff and sealed for patients; in industry it is open for all members;

and in the wartime Army it is sealed for all members.

At the hospital, in contrast to industry (strikes) and the Army (griping), there was little difficulty at the major internal boundary. With a few exceptions, the patients and the staff got along well with each other. The main problems arose in the minor structure. The most troublesome agitation occurred at the minor boundaries of the leadership because it was there that the culture lacked firmness. It did not distinguish clearly between psychiatrists (medical personnel) on the one hand, and social workers and psychologists (para-medical personnel) on the other.

This difficulty arose because the principal activity of the hospital was psychiatric treatment, and both the medical and para-medical personnel acted as psychotherapists. The medical personnel felt that this lack of discrimination blurred the therapeutic distinction conferred on them by law and tradition and exposed the patients to therapists whose qualifications could not be judged clearly. The para-medical people resented the tradition that only medical personnel were properly qualified as therapists, and the more intelligent and sensitive ones felt that as individuals they might be better qualified by natural endowment than some of the less intelligent and less sensitive medical officers. In general, the medical people stood on their roles in the organizational structure, while the others spoke as personas in the individual structure; hence, they could not come to terms. Their local conflict was related to the same conflict in the general social culture of the state and of the country at large. At that time, constitutional (legislative) agitation was already quite intense over defining the boundary between the activities of the medical and the para-medical professions.

Dr. Q's solution was to side in general with the para-medical people in saying that therapeutic effectiveness depended more on persona than on organizational role, but to emphasize also that phyyicians were especially educated for diagnosis and treatment throughout their training, which was not strictly the case with the others. He meant to convey that physicians had a better start in this direction, but that gifted social workers and psychologists could become effective therapists with special training. The emphasis was shifted from therapy as part of the social culture of the hospital to therapy as a technical procedure which could be learned; and from therapeutic skill as something conferred by a constitutional diploma to therapeutic skill as something that resulted from the disciplined application of personal talents, knowledge and attitudes. There resulted murmurings among the psychiatrists which hinted that Dr. Q was a traitor to his class (the class of Constitutional Medical Therapists). But he was careful to speak and act at all time so Hippocratically among them that they could not find him lacking in devotion to the constitutional oath; since they could not find fault with his role or his persona, they had to look for defects in his personality; but their own Adult uprightness prevented them from staying at that level very long, as he knew it would.

THE DYNAMICS DIAGRAM

The next set of problems had to do with the relationships between the three forces of the group. (By a curious and unforeseen coincidence, the dynamics problem in a group, arising from the forces Pressure, Agitation and Cohesion [PAC], has the same abbreviation as the structural problem in the individual, arising from Parent, Adult and Child ego states [also PAC]).

While the external pressure in industry is represented by such factors as finance, labor unions and competition, in the case of the hospital it was represented chiefly by the press. Where the head of a corporation would give special attention to his sales staff to combat competition, the Chief of the hospital was particularly careful about the public relations branch of his external apparatus to combat a bad press, which could be the most powerful threat to the continued existence of the current organizational and individual structure of the hospital.

As already noted, conflicts between the group cohesion and the individual proclivities were influenced by interprofessional competition. This was complicated by the fact that even within the same profession each individual stubbornly insisted on doing things his own way. Each was engaged in his own private game with his patients—a fact which Dr. Q verified by sitting in on different therapy groups—so that there was little belonging or acceptance of others. The most promising weapon against this agitation was their professional training and pride.

Dr. Q's solution was to sharpen further the distinction between activity and process. He suggested a regular clinical seminar which would be compulsory for all staff members engaged in therapy, at which all organizational and personal distinctions would be resigned in favor of improving the effectiveness of treatment. This meant that during the seminar, the Parent and Child in each therapist would be kept in abeyance as far as possible in exchange for the privilege of complete Adult freedom to discuss the material presented. This seminar would be conducted by a senior administrative staff member who was not engaged in therapy and therefore would not have a competitive, dystonic proclivity. It would have to be someone who understood transactional analysis, so that he could conduct himself as an Adult with as little interference as possible from his own Parent and Child, in order to be able to deal effectively with outbursts of Parent or Child from the other staff members. The object was to increase their Adult thoughtfulness and prudence by making them give a public account of their activities and present their work for professional evaluation. There would be certain dangers in requiring adjustment from some of the more touchy staff members, and the skill of the moderator would have to be depended on to avoid this.

For such a procedure to be effective, it was advisable for the seminar to be held weekly at a fixed hour. If the hour were changed frequently, or the intervals between meetings were long or irregular, it would be too easy for rebellious members to forget to come or to make other appointments absent-mindedly. But if it was fixed in their minds that every Monday at 3 P.M., say, they were obliged to attend, it would be harder for them to find excuses to stay away. And Dr. Q knew from experience that it would be more difficult for them to change their individual proclivities if the intervals between meetings were longer than a week.

THE GROUP IMAGOES

The clearer it became to the staff members that their positions in the imago of the Chief would be influenced by their professional competence rather than by their personal operations (i.e., by their working effectiveness rather than by their skill at games), the more attention they would pay to the former. Of course, this made it difficult for the less competent workers, but tactful handling could soften any bad effects in this regard. However, even if the shift in emphasis from competence in and willingness to play games over to competence in and willingness to do good work resulted in resignations, no harm would be done. In the past forthright people had resigned because the organization was game-ridden; in the future, less competent people, who tried to get by on their games, would resign because of the high working standards. Where before the good people had been weeded out, with obvious disadvantages to the hospital, now the less desirable people would be weeded out, with obvious advantages. However, this would require the Chief to be more hard-boiled, since it is often easier for a leader to let a good worker resign than it is for him to let a good game-player go, which is why it is so easy for an organization to remain stagnant or go downhill, and so hard for it to improve. (Various governmental patronage organizations, versus the Bureau of Standards, a skill organization, come to mind.)

A special problem in relation to group imagoes was a tendency for some of the senior staff members to discuss the private structure of the group at staff conferences, doing a kind of diluted group therapy in the course of business or educational meetings. This is a frequent temptation in organizations engaged in group therapy. The idea is that if group therapy is good for the patients, it should be good for the staff members also. That may be true, but it requires more careful thought than it is usually given. If the staff needs such therapy, then there should be a special therapy group for them, but it should be quite distinctly separated from all other staff meetings and should be explicitly labeled. Otherwise, the following situation arises. A member who wants to say something to the point at a business meeting or training seminar feels that he never knows when he may be called upon to analyse his motives for saying it. He feels rightly that he is involved in a game of Psychiatry. Therefore, he has a tendency either to refrain from speaking, or to tailor what he says to the way the game has been going. In this way the activity of the meeting suffers, and the possible therapeutic benefit which can be derived from such a setup is not worth the sacrifice.

Furthermore, on general psychiatric and social dynamic principles, therapy for the staff of an organization is best done by an uninvolved, neutral outsider. The fewer games his patients have an opportunity to play

with him outside the therapy hours, the more straight-
forwardly a therapist can do his work. On the other
hand, adding a game of Psychiatry to those already
played between the staff members of an oganization
does not contribute to its working effectiveness. When
Dr. Q presented these considerations to the hospital administration, they appeared to receive them not only
with gratitude but also with relief and decided to eliminate "group dynamics" from their business and educational meetings.

THE TRANSACTIONAL DIAGRAMS

The staff of the hospital (at educational meetings),
and many of the patients in their therapy groups, received instruction in structural and transactional analysis. Thus, they learned to distinguish Parent, Adult and
Child in their relationships with people around them
and found that by giving some thought to what they
said, they could get more acceptable responses. Or, if
something went wrong, they might be able to find the
crossed transaction and avoid a future repetition of an
unpleasant or difficult situation.

The most important problem here was the therapeutic technic of those engaged in group therapy. As noted,
by sitting in at group meetings Dr. Q found that almost
every therapist in the hospital was indulging his Parent
or Child without realizing it. Many transactions which
they thought of as Adult therapeutic operations were
actually parts of their own games, usually games which
they would not play so openly with their wives or colleagues but were very likely playing with their actual
children at home and had apparently learned from their
own parents. In some cases it was safe to mention these
observations briefly, with possible constructive effects.

SPECIAL TERMS INTRODUCED IN PART IV

Flabby culture	Accessibility
Brittle culture	Availability

Appendix 1

Suggested Reading

Everything that has been written about man's relationship
to man belongs in a sense to the literature of social dynamics. According to Breasted, the earliest treatise on this
subject is the *Maxims of Ptah-Hotep* (3000 B.C.), and
what Breasted calls "the dawn of conscience" is also the
morning of group dynamics. It is exciting to speculate that
the first psychodynamic groups (groups involving the dis-
placement of feelings to substitute objects) were formed
by our ancestors when they put magic (apotropaic) paint-
ings on cave walls during the late glacial period; for this
making of magic and its delegation to a special individual,
the artist, is the oldest known possibility of a consciously
planned organization of living beings employing "psychological artifacts."

More specifically, however, there are older writings
which foreshadow, or even surpass, the findings and the
concepts of our present-day knowledge; and these, together with certain recent publications, should be part of
the intellectual equipment of those who wish to regard
themselves as literate and disciplined therapists of ailing
groups. The following is suggested as a minimum reading
list. The bibliographic references to the works mentioned
will be found on pages 298 to 301.

THE ANCIENT WORLD

There must have been just as large a proportion of per-
ceptive men and women in the population of the ancient
world as there is nowadays, but few of them had the opportunity to devote themselves to writing. Those who did
have bequeathed to us some provocative ideas about the

workings of organizations and groups, particularly concerning the qualities of leadership and the relationship between the leader and the members.

INDIA

The most pertinent of the Indian classics is the *Hitopadesa,* or *Book of Good Counsels,* in which a teacher imparts instruction in good leadership to the king's sons by means of fables, interlarded with quotations from the Vedas and the Mahabharata. These quotations are said to date from 1300 to 350 B.C.

CHINA

The classical literature of China is much more precise in this respect than many people realize. There are two philosophers in particular whose writings are interspersed with group dynamic principles: Confucius (551-479 B.C.); and Lao Tzu, a mythical figure representing a collection of writings from the 3rd century B.C. Even more specific is Sun Tzu (500 B.C.), whose *Art of War* is said to be the oldest military treatise in the world.

GREECE AND ROME

Of course, the best known classics in this field are the *Politics* of Aristotle and *The Republic* of Plato. Marcus Aurelius gives many hints about the qualifications, duties and especially the responsibilites of a leader. Less well known, but perhaps even more instructive in a practical way, is the *De Re Militari* of Vegetius, who flourished in the 4th century B.C. This was the most influential military treatise in the Western world from Roman times to the 19th century. Euhemerus belongs in this period (300 B.C.).

In general, the group dynamics of the ancients was chiefly concerned with political and military matters.

THE MIDDLE AGES

In the Western world the serious literature centered mainly around theology, although lawyers and political scientists were also active. Some provocative ideas are offered by such writers as St. Augustine and Thomas Aquinas.

THE RENAISSANCE

The most important writer of this period is Machiavelli. While he is notorious for his knowledge of the dynamics of intrigue, he is an equally profound student of the principles of good leadership and the correction of defects in this area.

A.D. 1500 TO 1800

During this period the relationship between the leader and the members was being subjected to more formal theoretical analysis, particularly by lawyers. The epoch is outstanding for its active observers and good thinkers. Their material was derived not from experiment, but from nature—i.e., from actual political situations, so that their principles could be tested against historical outcomes. Almost all the topics which have been dealt with in this book were discussed by the great philosophers of this era.

Their arguments are summarized by Otto Gierke in the fourth volume of his *Das deutsche Genossenschaftsrecht* (1913). The profundity of thought during these centuries was so great that it may be said that anyone who is not at least acquainted with it is a primitive in the field of group dynamics. Fortunately, the most pertinent material has been abstracted and translated from Gierke by Ernest Barker, Professor of Political Science in the University of Cambridge. Those who are not sufficiently motivated to read the text should at least read Professor Barker's stimulating introduction.

THE 19TH CENTURY

In the early years of this century the formal (structural and dynamic) approach was continued, and its value as an approach analyzed, by Auguste Comte (1798-1857), while the historical approach is represented by Hegel (1770-1831) in his *Philosophy of History*. The latter half of the century is marked by a distinct shift under the influence of two writers: Darwin and Marx. The evolutionist viewpoint quickly made itself felt and is presented in the works of Herbert Spencer and Walter Bagehot. As everyone is keenly aware nowadays, Karl Marx's writings gave rise to an enormous literature, whose influence on the study of group dynamics is most concisely illustrated by George

Plekhanov's short work *The Role of the Individual in History* and Frederick Engels' less well-known treatise *The Origin of the Family*. In the final decade, the psychological viewpoint emerged in Le Bon's celebrated treatise *Psychologie des foules*, which was almost immediately translated into English and was the principal stimulus for Freud's work on group psychology.

De Tocqueville (*Democracy in America*), J.S. Mill and Nietzsche represent other approaches which were influential during this period.

THE 20TH CENTURY

The modern scientific literature falls largely in three provinces: sociology, social psychology and group psychotherapy. Two of the notable early landmarks were Trotter's *Instincts of the Herd in Peace and War* (1916) and Freud's *Group Psychology and the Analysis of the Ego* (1921). Freud's *Totem and Taboo* (1912) is interesting collateral reading.

The sociologic literature has been ably reviewed many times. One of the most easily available surveys is that of Victor Branford, who favors "synthetic generality" rather than "biased particularism" for a genuine sociology.

Two viewpoints of social psychology are presented by Krech and Crutchfield, and J.F. Brown, respectively, the latter based on Lewin's topological and field theory. These are both college texts. A more technical consideration, including historical and theoretical background, an annotated bibliography and a selection of papers relating to current research is found in the recent symposium on small groups edited by Hare, Borgatta and Bales. A similar collection has been published by Cartwright and Zander.

Slavson and Scheidlinger have reviewed the literature of group psychotherapy, the latter with more inclusive and detailed discussion, particularly of Freud's theories.

From all these recent sources, it would appear that research in this field now follows one or other of the usual academic alternatives. The data is purposefully gathered and is then either subjected to statistical evaluation or fitted into a preconceived framework. These are both operations which can be performed by machines. As might be anticipated, the result is that in the whole of the vast "modern" literature there are few creative ideas as compared with the older writings. There is a conspicuous absence of what might be called "creative meditation about nature," that type of thinking which is characteristic of theoreticians such as Newton, Darwin and Freud, experimenters such as Galileo, Harvey and Fabre, and such dramatic problem-solvers as Archimedes, Kekulé and Poincaré.

Fortunately, creative thinking in the field of group dynamics does exist, but, because of its informal character, it is often neglected by reviewers and professional research workers. Some of the most interesting ideas have come from psychiatrists, possibly because they have more opportunity for "creative meditation" than most other groups of social scientists, who are more subject to academic pressures. Curiously enough, of the four who have (in the writer's opinion) made the most provocative observations, three are Englishmen; and the American, Burrow, worked in a small village. One is reminded of the epigram: "Penicillin could not have been discovered in America because the laboratories are too tidy." The work of these four writers—Bion, Burrow, Ezriel and Foulkes—is abstracted below. The reference numbers refer to articles by each author whose titles will be found in the bibliography.

BION

W. R. Bion, of the Tavistock Clinic (London), studied small groups in a naturalistic way by pushing aside preconceptions. He published his findings in a series of seven articles (1948-1951) in the periodical *Human Relations* and summarized them in an eighth article which appeared in the *International Journal of Psychoanalysis*. They have recently appeared in book form.[8] Few people claim to understand them completely, but some of the clearest and most instructive points can be simply stated as follows:

1. The group takes on a mature structure, the work group, to avoid certain kinds of groups which are feared: namely, the "basic assumption" groups.[3] The work group is concerned with reality and therefore has some of the characteristics of "the (Freudian) ego."[7]

2. The group demands a structure consisting of a leader and his followers and has a resentful (paranoid) attitude toward a leader who does not show the characteristics they think proper.[1-3]

3. The behavior of the members is influenced by a conscious or unconscious idea of how the group feels toward them, but they prefer to deny this.[2]

4. The "group mentality" expresses the will of the group, to which individuals contribute anonymously in very subtle ways. The group mentality makes it disagreeable for an individual who does not behave according to the basic assumptions.[3]

5. The "group culture" arises from the conflict between the individual's desires and the group mentality. It includes the structure of the group at any given moment, the occupations it pursues, and the organization it takes on.[3]

6. Whenever two people become involved with each other, both the group and the pair concerned make the "basic assumption" that the relationship is a sexual one.[3] This is the first basic assumption. Such a "pairing group" becomes anxious because of the feeling that they are dealing with an "unborn genius."[7] (It is hard to understand what Bion means by this).

7. When people meet in a group, the group assumes that their purpose is the preservation of the group. The second basic assumption is that the group will use the only two methods of self-preservation it knows, fight or flight. Pairing is allowed because it is an alternative way to preserve the group.[3]

8. A third basic assumption is that an external object exists which will provide security for the immature organism.[3] This gives rise to the dependent group, which is based on something like a religious system. Independent thought is stifled, heresy is righteously hunted, and the leader is criticized because he is not a magician who can be worshipped; a rational approach on his part is rejected.[4]

9. The dependent group opposes development on grounds of loyalty to its leader or to its traditional "bible," the word of the group god; or to somebody who has been made into the group god in order to resist change.[7] If left to itself, the dependent group will choose as its leader the least healthy member: a paranoid schizophrenic, a severe hysteric or a delinquent.[6] If the leader (e.g., Bion) does not interfere, the group tries to claim that he is both mad and dependable.[6] Since this is a contradiction, the group becomes uneasy. Then they try to bring in other groups to solve the problem.[6]

10. The basic assumptions which are not active at any given moment are stored in a "proto-mental" system in

which physical and mental are blended. There the relationships of the three basic assumptions become complicated.[5]

11. It is important to study what occurs when the group passes from one culture to another, as from the work group to one of the three basic assumption groups.[3]

12. The basic assumption groups attract the members because they give the illusion that a member can sink himself in a group without needing to develop.[4] Thus the group splits into an unsophisticated majority who oppose work, and a sophisticated minority which wants to develop.[7] The work group is constantly disturbed by influences which come from the basic assumptions[7]; nevertheless, the work group wins in the long run.[7]

13. The work group has to prevent the basic assumptions from interfering. Group organization steadies the work group; without organization, it might be submerged by the basic assumptions. Organization and structure are its weapons. They are the product of co-operation and their effect is to demand still further co-operation. A group acting on a basic assumption needs no organization or co-operation.[7]

14. In the basic assumption groups there is a spontaneous instinctive co-operation called "valency." Interpretations concerned with valency can and should replace psychoanalytic interpretations in group therapy. They may reduce the group to silence. It can then be shown that there is no way in which the individual in a group can "do nothing," even when he does "nothing."[6]

15. Psychoanalytic interpretations are justified by the therapist as attempts to overcome resistance but are really attempts to get rid of the "badness" of the group, its apparent unsuitability for therapeutic purposes. Such interpretations only strengthen the dependent tendencies of the group.[6]

16. The meeting of the group in a particular place at a particular time has "no significance whatsoever in the production of group phenomena." These exist anyway even before their existence is evident.[7]

17. The group brings out things which seem strange to an observer unaccustomed to using groups.[7]

18. Plato emphasized harmonious co-operation in the work of the group. Augustine postulated harmony through each individual's relationship with God. Nietzsche suggests that a group achieves vitality only by the release of aggressive impulses.[7]

At times Bion speaks modestly of these reactions as occurring "in every group of which I have been a member,"[1] and talks about what it means "to be in a group in which I was present."[1] However, at other times, he speaks of the things he observes as though they were universal to all groups, including historical groups. For example, when he says that "if left to itself, the dependent group will choose as its leader the most ill member,"[6] he does not make it clear whether he thinks that is due to his own very distinctive and interesting method of handling groups or is a universal occurrence. Lombroso's ill "men of genius," to take a large category, did not find it easy to be "chosen" as leaders, while R. Sears found that patient "leaders" showed more uniformity in kind than in degree of disturbance. In fact, Bion's concept of "basic assumption leaders" brings up the problem of whether there can be any true "leader" in a therapy group other than the therapist, no matter how strenuously a therapist tries to avoid active involvement. To use his own words, even a therapist who "does nothing" cannot do "nothing."

Bion has studied carefully certain important aspects of group psychology and has re-emphasized the value of observing groups in a naturalistic and unprejudiced way.

It remains to be seen whether the things Bion describes are always present in every group, or whether they only occur occasionally or in special kinds of groups: i.e., whether they are obligatory or incidental.

BURROW

Trigant Burrow, of the Lifwynn Foundation in Westport, Connecticut, was a prolific writer. The present summary is based on a study of eight papers, six written by him, and two by two of his followers, Hans Syz and William Galt. This was the material sent by Dr. Burrow when he was asked for a representative selection of his work. As with Bion, and for that matter with Freud, his ideas are easier to understand when they are in the making than after they have been elaborated as a result of further experience. Then the system may seem to an outsider too deep to follow clearly without personal instruction and interpretation from the originator or a well-trained disciple.

In the first paper, "The Basis of Group Analysis," published in 1928,[1] Burrow proposes a form of group therapy as "a valuable adjunct to our present endeavors in behalf of neurotic and insane patients." He states that "for several years I have . . . been daily occupied with the practical observation of these inter-reactions as they are found to occur under the experimental conditions of actual group setting." He already follows practices which many therapists came to prefer 15 or 20 years later on the basis of their own experience.

The number of persons composing a group session has come to be limited, empirically, to about ten. . . . The sessions are held once weekly and continue for one hour. The object of the group-analysis is to give the individual the opportunity to express himself in a social setting without the inhibitions of customary social images.

He makes clear that this is an attempt to uncover, through the application of psychoanalytic principles, the underlying meaning of social interchange.

Although in 1941 he stated that

the group method of analysis . . . bears no relation to the recently adopted measures of treatment now conducted under the name of group-therapy,[2]

it is clear from the foregoing that Burrow is the originator of what is now called group analysis or analytic group psychotherapy. On these grounds it can be claimed that, in addition to his later firsts in the study of group dynamics, Burrow was the first rational, systematic psychiatric group therapist. In fact, in many ways he may be regarded as the outstanding pioneer in the whole science of the study of small groups. Because he held some unorthodox views and stated them in a specialized way, his work is generally ignored or is given only the briefest passing mention, except among his own disciples. In his 1928 paper, he anticipated Bion to some extent in discovering what Bion calls basic assumptions, especially in regard to flight, fight and dependency; he anticipated Ezriel in analyzing "the here and now" or, as Burrow puts it, "the immediate group in the immediate moment"; and he anticipated Ackerman's discussion of "social roles." For that matter, in the last connection, Jung (1920) anticipated Burrow.

Burrow's work led him into a special consideration of the problem of attention, which had already interested him as early as 1909. He regards the behavior of people in groups as unnatural. Every member of a group, normal or neurotic, "appears to be acutely sensitive to the impression he creates upon others."[1] He is so preoccupied with this problem that he is actually unable to become a member of a group. Instead of being co-operative in the real sense of the word, he is at all times hostile and competitive. In fact, his whole participation in the group is clouded by a superstitious outlook.

Beneath the outer expressions of so-called normal communities there are the same fears, the same repression, insecurity, and evasion—the same emotional substitutions and guilt, the same unilateral secrecy and self-defense; the same superstitions, anxieties and suspicions; the same elations and depressions, whether transient or prolonged; in short, the same neurotic reactions that characterize the isolated patient.[6]

This attitude of hostile, superstitious, competitive self-consciousness is connected with a special kind of befogged attention which Burrow terms "ditention." But through experience, he found a technic for inducing another kind of attention, which he calls "cotention," in which the individual functions as a whole in co-operative harmony with his environment. The state of cotention is associated with physiologic changes. In his subjects, the respiratory rate dropped from an average of about 10 per minute in ditention to about 3 per minute in cotention; the oxygen absorbed per minute remained about the same, but oxygen was utilized much more efficiently in the cotentive state.[2] There were also changes in the eye movements and the electroencephalograms.[3]

It is Burrow's idea of cotention which is somehow difficult for outsiders to understand clearly, and this is probably the reason why his work has not been influential in a wider circle of group psychologists and group therapists. However, there is no doubt that in many groups there is at times a cessation of the normal attitude of self-conscious rivalry, and that sometimes under these conditions there is a rather profound change in the atmosphere of the group, an almost religious attitude which is quite different from any other experience in a group. Because this atmosphere is so impressive and meaningful and has apparently been overlooked by most "scientific" group workers (perhaps just because they are "scientific"), Burrow's work with cotention deserves careful consideration.*

Because his sentences are often hard to sort out, it is not easy to extract his ideas, but some of the principal ones, in somewhat simplified form, are as follows:

1. Group or social analysis is the analysis of the immediate group in the immediate moment.[1]

2. A social group consists of persons each of whom is represented by the symbol he calls "I" or "I, myself,"[1] the I-persona.[6]

3. This symbol is accepted by the other individuals in the group. It is the basis for their intercommunication;[1] they connive with each other in accepting each other's distortions of self.[6]

4. The social image shifts the individual's interest to his awareness of himself in respect to others' awareness of him. By virtue of this image each one of us tends to enact a given role, to portray a certain character or part in the social scheme of things.[1]

5. The individual is continually matching his impression or image of himself with the image or impression which others have of him.[1]

6. There is no difference between the social image of the neurotic and social images as they occur in normal individuals. Neither can attain a rational attitude toward these private images.[1]

7. The social image is tied up with early anthropomorphic ideas and is linked with hints of the supernatural.[4]

8. Feelings are persistently distorted in the reactions of the social community, so that private opinions with personal interpretations constantly override the evidence of the senses.[4]

9. As a result, man sees in outer objects a meaning not belonging to the object itself; therefore, man's world comes to be tinged with fanciful attributes of his own making.[4]

10. We fail to recognize the dictatorial influence of the father-image in our current social relationships.[4]

11. Man must recognize that he uses purely emotional symbols at the expense of his integrity as a species.[4]

12. There are two aspects of attention in the social proc-

* Recent experiments at the San Francisco Social Psychiatry Seminars indicate that cotention is probably closely related to game-free intimacy.

ess. In ditention, the affecto-symbolic image is dominant and distracting due to the intrusion of the self-image. In cotention the affective element is eliminated, and the organism's total relation to the environment resumes its primary unconditioned supremacy.[4]

13. Projection has become a universal reaction in man. It clutters his brain and impairs his natural channels of social contact and communication.[4]

14. Personalistic concepts are deviations from the natural growth processes; they are in the nature of conditioned responses which are imposed by the child's contact with the world of adults. Co-operative behavior among children is more primary than the competitive response. (Galt)

15. Man's behavior is at present guided by a dream state, as it were, by the image of an egocentric universe, due to a false stress on his capacity to form and employ the symbol or image. A breach is thus created between human beings through the exercise of their own adaptive assets. He tries to compensate for this uncertainty by further manipulations of this very same adaptive configuration. (Syz)

Ezriel

Henry Ezriel, of the Tavistock Clinic in London, has published three communications about group dynamics and the technic of group therapy which are of special interest. His conclusions may be summarized in part as follows:

1. One individual meeting another will try to establish the kind of relationship between them which will ultimately diminish the tension arising out of relations which he entertains with unconscious fantasy objects.[1,2]

2. Each member brings to the group meeting some unconscious relationships with "fantasy objects" which he unconsciously wishes to act out by manipulating the other members of the group.[1,2]

3. The behavior of fellow patients in the group acts like the stimulus of a projection test such as the Rorschach, provoking reactions born out of unconscious fantasies. Certain actions on the part of the analyst have a similar effect.[1,2]

4. The common denominator of the unconscious fantasies of all the members is represented by a common

group tension or common group problem, of which the group is not aware but which determines its behavior.[1,2]

5. In dealing with this common group tension, every member takes up a role which is characteristic for his personality structure because of the particular unconscious fantasy he entertains, and which he tries to solve through appropriate behavior in the group.[1]

6. The role which each member takes in the "drama" performed in the session demonstrates his particular defense mechanism in dealing with his own unconscious tension.[1]

7. The "transference situation" is not something peculiar to treatment but occurs whenever one individual meets another. Manifest behavior then contains, besides any consciously motivated pattern, an attempt to solve relations with unconscious fantasy-objects, the residues of unresolved infantile conflicts.[1,2]

8. Each member projects his unconscious fantasy-objects to various other members and tries to manipulate them accordingly. Each stays in a role assigned to him by another only if it happens to coincide with his own fantasy and if it allows him to manipulate others into appropriate roles. Otherwise, he will try to twist the discussion until the real group does correspond to his fantasy-group.[1]

9. The individual tries to diminish tensions either in activities which serve only this purpose or by activities superimposed on his conscious needs or the demands which the environment makes on him.[1]

10. Everything a patient says or does during a session gives expression to his need in that session for a specific relationship with his therapist; he attempts to involve the analyst in the relations which he entertains with his fantasy objects and with their representatives in external reality.[3]

11. There are three kinds of object relations; the required relationship which the patients try to establish within the group and in particular with the therapist; another, which they feel they have to avoid in external reality, however much they may desire it; and the calamitous one which they feel would follow inevitably if they entered into the secretly desired avoided relationship. For example, a group of patients require an intimate Christian name relationship among themselves in order to avoid a nickname relationship with the therapist which might, they feared, result in a calamitous rejection.[3]

12. Strachey emphasized that only the analysis of the "here and now" relationship represents a "mutative" interpretation, i.e., one which can permanently change the patient's personality (which means his unconscious needs). Rickman and others hold that none other than transference interpretations need be used.[2]

13. In the group, "here and now" interpretations get around the difficulty that the therapeutic group is an artifact which has no common infantile history. They also enable us to deal effectively with the patient's persecutory feelings which are prominent when extra observers are present.[3]

14. At times all the members of the group may be driven by forces beyond their control into what they themselves consider to be a useless discussion. For example, they may criticize a member who intellectualizes by themselves intellectualizing.[3]

15. The therapeutic group has the advantage that its preformed structure is of comparatively small influence as compared with the unconscious forces in each member. In a task group, real clashes of interest are hopelessly intermingled with unconsciously determined conflicts.[3]

16. The detailed examination of every remark made by patient and analyst in the group and the development of a set of dynamic concepts seem to be promising approaches for the formulation and the testing of hypotheses about the dynamics of human behavior.[3]

Ezriel's view that the therapeutic group is an artifact that has no common infantile history[3] tests his implication that what occurs in groups is essentially based on transference.[1-3] He recognizes the feared calamity as a projection[3] while linking the paranoid attitude of the group to the presence of outside observers.[3] He belittles the importance of the preformed structure of the therapy group and considers it hopeless to try to separate the task phenomena from the "unconscious conflict phenomena" in task groups.[3] These are all matters which seem to invite further study. The mutual manipulations of the members have been considered in more detail by G. Bach under the heading of "set-up operations."

FOULKES

Among the writings of S. H. Foulkes, of the London Institute of Psycho-Analysis, is a particularly striking article on leadership. Foulkes supports Bion's position that the therapist must avoid approaching the problems of group dynamics with a preconceived frame of reference:

The observer [should] avoid the fallacy of transferring concepts gained from the psychology of the individual, in particular psychoanalytic concepts, too readily to this new field of observation. . . . He will find all these, to be sure, in operation; but he will not learn much that is new.

By merely observing what happens before him, he will learn more about the dynamics of the group and,

indeed, new light will be thrown upon the mechanisms in individual psychoanalysis. . . . Group psychology must develop its own concepts in its own rights and not borrow them from individual psychology.

Foulkes' conclusions regarding leadership may be summarized as follows:

1. The group-analytic group is a caricature of a group, and its leader does not lead.

2. There are two basic problems in the group. The manifest level concerns the relationship to other people in adult life and contemporary reality. The other concerns the relationship to parental authority, as represented in the primordial image of the leader, and corresponds to past infantile and primordial reality.

3. The leader activates both analytic and integrative processes. Anxiety caused by the uncovering of hitherto unconscious material is balanced by the increasing strength of the group. The group can balance the impact of ever-new sources of disturbances through its own growing strength.

4. The first basic problem of social life is the clash between the individual's own egotistic needs and impulses and the restrictions imposed by the group. The individual learns that he needs the group's authority for his own security and for protection against the encroachment of others' impulses.

5. Therefore, he has to create and maintain the group's authority by necessary modifications of his own impulses. In return for this sacrifice he receives the support of the group for his own particular individuality. He must tolerate others if his own claims are to be tolerated and must restrict in himself what he cannot tolerate in others. That

this happens on a manifest level is only possible because the conductor does not play the part of a leader.

6. In the unconscious fantasy of the group, the therapist is put in the position of a primordial leader image; he is omniscient and omnipotent, and the group expects magic help from him. But while it is true that the family is a group, it is not true that the group is a family.

7. The group can reanimate directly the archaic inheritance of the "primal horde" psychology, as described by Freud (and, one may add, as stressed by Klapman).

8. As a result, the group shows a need and a craving for a leader in the image of an omnipotent, godlike father figure, an absolute leader, a position which the therapist cannot lose, although he may spoil it. (This craving was the clearest phenomenon noted by Bion[1] and has been further studied by Berne, Starrels and Trinchero.)

9. "The paramount need is to create a scientific view of group dynamics and such concepts that will enable us to understand and exchange each other's experiences and problems by expressing them in a language that is commonly understood."

10. There is a nucleus to the leader's personality, not at present further reducible by science, more by art and religion, a primary rapport, without which he cannot awaken or bind the spell of "the old enchantment."

There is some contradiction in Foulkes' concept of the therapist as a conductor who does not really lead, and the fact that no matter what the therapist does, he cannot lose his position as an absolute leader in the unconscious fantasies of the members. In addition, the group craves a "father-figure"; this rather contradicts the idea that the group is not a family. In many ways, it might be more consistent to reverse the dictum that "the family is a group, but the group is not a family," and say instead: "The family is not a group but the group is a family." Some aspects of this problem have been discussed by Beukenkamp and by Grotjahn.

MORENO

In addition to these four, the student should also familiarize himself with the sociometric concepts of J. L. Moreno.

METHODOLOGY

Those students of group dynamics who are not already familiar with psychoanalytic theory, or who have not taken it seriously enough, will enrich their powers of observation and evaluation, as well as discover a large body of important literature in the field, by remedying this deficiency. Many of Freud's works are now available in widely distributed paperback books. Those who wish an easily digestible résumé are referred to the writer's popular exposition of the subject (Berne).

As to the general methodology, J. Bronowski's review of R. B. Braithwaite's "Scientific Explanation" may be quoted. Braithwaite, who is Professor of Moral Philosophy at Cambridge, does not entirely agree with Bertrand Russell's maxim that: "Wherever possible, logical constructions are to be substituted for inferred entities." Bronowski states:

We must look for the evidence for the laws in the cross-connections between them. What we must adduce, I think, is the amount of simplification or order the laws bring into the wilderness of natural facts.

Other modern methodologic approaches which are easily available and can be understood to some extent by the nonspecialist are those of Bohr, Cantril, Erikson, Planck, Richter, Ruderfer, Stewart, von Bertalanffy, Weaver and Wiener.

SUMMARY

In this survey of the literature, from India and China, the ancient Oriental capitals of civilization, through Athens, Vienna, London, and New York to San Francisco, one principle of group dynamics has been recognized throughout. This was as aptly and concisely stated by Confucius as by any of his successors in the field:

The people are pleased with their ruler because he is like a parent to the people. If the deportment of the Prince is correct, he sets the country in order.

This is an attempt to answer the question which is fundamental to all theories of group dynamics: Why does any-one ever do what someone else tells him to?

BIBLIOGRAPHY

Ackerman, Nathan: "Social Role" and Total Personality, Manuscript, 1950.

————: The Psychodynamics of Family Life, New York, Basic Books, 1958.

Aristotle: Politics, translated by Jowett and Twining, New York, Viking Press, 1957.

————: Poetics, translated by Jowett and Twining, New York, Viking Press, 1957.

Aurelius, Marcus: Meditations, Mount Vernon, New York, Peter Pauper Press, 1957.

Bach, G. R.: Intensive Group Psychotherapy, New York, Ronald, 1954.

Berne, Eric: A Layman's Guide to Psychiatry and Psychoanalysis, New York, Simon & Schuster, 1957. (Also Grove Press, 1962.)

————: Games People Play, New York, Grove Press, 1964.

————: Transactional Analysis in Psychotherapy, New York, Grove Press, 1961.

————: Principles of Group Treatment, New York, Oxford, 1966.

Beukenkamp, C.: Further developments of the transference life concept in therapeutic groups, J. Hillside Hospital *5:*441-448, 1956.

Bion, W. R.: Experience in groups, Human Relations *1:*314-320, 1948 (1).

————: *Ibid., 1:*487-496, 1948 (2).

————: *Ibid., 2:*12-22, 1949 (3).

————: *Ibid., 2:*295-303, 1949 (4).

————: *Ibid., 3:*3-14, 1950 (5).

————: *Ibid., 3:*395-402, 1950 (6).

————: *Ibid., 4:*221-227, 1951 (7).

————: Group dynamics: a re-review, Int. J. Psycho-Anal. *33:*235-247, 1952 (8).

————: Experiences in Groups, New York, Basic Books, 1961 (9).

Bohr, Niels: On the notions of causality and complementarity, Science *3:*51-54, 1950.

Branford, V.: Sociology *in* Encyclopedia Britannica, 1946.

Breasted, James: The Dawn of Conscience, New York, Charles Scribner's Sons, 1939.

Brillouin, L.: Thermodynamics and information theory, Am. Sci. *38:*594-599, 1950.

Bronowski, J.: Sci. Amer. *189:*140-142, September 1953.

Brown, J. F.: Psychology and the Social Order, New York, McGraw-Hill, 1936.

Burrow, Trigant: The basis of group analysis, Brit. J. Med. Psychol. *8:*198-206, 1928 (1).

———: Kymographic records of neuromuscular patterns in relation to behavior disorders, Psychosom. Med. *3:*174-186, 1941 (2).

———: Neurosis and war, J. Psychol. *12:*235-249, 1941 (3).

———: The neurodynamics of behavior, Philosophy Sci. *10:*271-288, 1943, (4).

———: Phylobiology, Rev. Gen. Semantics *3:*265-278, 1946 (5).

———: The social neurosis, Philosophy Sci. *16:*25-40, 1949 (6).

Cantril, Hadley: The transactional view in psychological research, Science *110:*517-522, 1949.

Cartwright, D., and Zander, A.: Group Dynamics, Research and Theory, Evanston, Ill., Row, Peterson & Co., 1953.

Confucius: Wisdom of Confucius, edited by Lin Yutang, New York, Random, 1938.

de Montesquieu, C. L.: The Spirit of Laws *in* World's Great Classics, New York, Colonial Press, 1900.

de Tocqueville, Alexis: Democracy in America *in* World's Great Classics, New York, Colonial Press, 1900.

Engels, Frederick: The Origin of the Family, Chicago, Charles H. Kerr & Co., 1902.

Erikson, E. H.: Childhood and Society, New York, Norton, 1950.

Ezriel, Henry: A psycho-analytic approach to group treatment, Brit. J. Med. Psychol. *23:*59-74, 1950 (1).

———: Some principles of a psycho-analytic method of group treatment, Proc. First World Cong. Psychiatry, Paris, 1950, *5:*239-247, 1952 (2).

———: Note on psychoanalytic group therapy: interpretation and research, Psychiatry *51:*119-126, 1952 (3).

Fabre, J. H.: The Life of the Caterpillar, New York, Modern Library, 1925.

Foulkes, S. H.: Concerning leadership in group-analytic

psychotherapy, Int. J. Group Psychotherapy *1:*319-329, 1951.

Foulkes, S. H., and Anthony, E.: Group Psychotherapy, Middlesex, Penguin Books, 1957.

Freud, S.: Group Psychology and the Analysis of the Ego, London, Hogarth Press, 1940.

————: Totem and Taboo *in* Basic Writings of Sigmund Freud, New York; Modern Library, 1938.

Galt, William: The principles of cooperation in behavior, Quart. Rev. Biol. *15:*401-410, 1940.

Gierke, Otto: Natural Law and the Theory of Society, translated by E. Barker, Boston, Beacon Press, 1957.

Grotjahn, Martin: Psychoanalysis and the Family Neurosis, New York, Norton, 1960.

Hare, P., Borgotta, E., and Bales, R. (eds.): Small Groups, New York, Knopf, 1955.

Hegel, Georg: The Philosophy of History *in* World's Great Classics, New York, Colonial Press, 1900.

Hitopadesa: Translated by Epiphanius Wilson *in* World's Great Classics, New York, Colonial Press, 1900.

Jung, C. G.: Psychological Types, New York, Harcourt Brace & Co., 1946.

Klapman, J. W.: Group Psychotherapy, New York, Grune, 1946.

Krech, D., and Crutchfield, R. S.: Theory and Problems of Social Psychology, New York, McGraw-Hill, 1948.

Lao Tzu: The Way of Life, translated by R. B. Blakney, New York, New American Library, 1955.

Le Bon, Gustav: The Crowd, London, Ernest Benn, 1952.

Lombroso, Cesare: The Man of Genius, New York, Charles Scribner's Sons, 1910.

Machiavelli, Niccolò: The Prince and The Discourses, New York, Random, 1940.

Moreno, J. L.: Foundations of Sociometry, Sociometry *4:*15-35, 1941.

Nietzsche, F.: The Philosophy of Nietzsche, New York, Random, 1937.

Planck, Max: The meaning and limits of exact science, Science *110:*319-327, 1949.

Plato: The Republic, translated by B. Jowett, New York, Random, 1941.

Plekhanov, George: The Role of the Individual in History, New York, International Publishers, 1940.

Richter, Curt: Free research versus design research, Science *118:*91-93, 1953.

Ruderfer, Martin: Action as a measure of living phenomena, Science *110:*245-252, 1949.

Scheidlinger, Saul: Psychoanalysis and Group Behavior, New York, Norton, 1952.

Sears, Richard, Leadership among patients in group therapy, Int. J. Group Psychotherapy, *3:*191-197, 1953.

Slavson, S. R.: Analytic Group Psychotherapy, New York, Columbia, 1950.

Stewart, J. Q.: The natural sciences applied to social theory, Science *111:*500, 1950.

Sun Tzu: The Art of War, translated by Lionel Giles *in* Phillips, T. R., (ed.): Roots of Strategy, Harrisburg, Pa., Military Service Publishing Co., 1940.

Syz, Hans: Burrow's differentiation of tensional patterns in relation to behavior disorders, J. Psychol. *9:*153-163, 1940.

Trotter, W.: Instincts of the Herd in Peace and War, London, T. F. Unwin, 1916.

Vegetius Renatus, Flavius: De Re Militari, translated by Clarke, J. *in* Phillips, T. R., (ed.): Roots of Strategy, Harrisburg, Pa., Military Services Publishing Co., 1940.

von Bertalanffy, L.: The theory of open systems in physics and biology, Science *111:*23-29, 1950.

Weaver, Warren: Fundamental questions in science, Sci. Amer. *189:*47-51, September 1953.

Weiner, N.: Cybernetics, New York, Wiley, 1948.

Appendix 2

A Proposed Classification
for Social Aggregations

Any attempt to evolve a fruitful and comprehensive theory of group dynamics requires a careful definition of the term "group." The first essential is that it distinguish between "groups" and "nongroups." This distinction is rarely made in the literature. In addition, there are almost as many definitions as there are authors in the vast and ever-growing bibliography of the social sciences, which makes it difficult for people to understand each other precisely.*

A concrete example may make it clearer that there are important differences between various kinds of social aggregations. The number of people who may be found on the beach each day between 3 and 4 P.M. in Carmel, California, varies enormously (from fewer than 10 to many hundreds). This variation is strongly influenced by external factors, such as the weather and the season of the year, but has no known connection with the internal social situation in the community, partly because on sunny holidays in the summer by far the majority of beach visitors are from out of town. However, the number of people who attend parties in the same village is influenced only a little by external factors such as the weather and is heavily in-

---

* Anything that would improve communication between social scientists should be welcomed. There are not only semantic difficulties, which may be excusable up to a point, but in some cases, studied indifference. For example, there are two major journals devoted to group psychotherapy: (a) The *International Journal of Group Psychotherapy* and (b) *Group Psychotherapy*. In the whole volume of (a) for 1953, there are only four references to papers that appeared in (b).

fluenced by the internal social situation. For some years, the writer was "at home" every Sunday evening. No specific invitations were issued, but it was "generally known" that anyone who wished to come was welcome. The attendance at these gatherings corresponded rather closely to a series of appropriate random numbers; one week there would be 2 guests, the next 58, the next 23, and so on.

On the other hand, the writer also conducted three psychotherapy groups over a considerable period in the same village. In these organized groups, it was observed that the attendance was not at all influenced by the weather, nor by the social situation in the village, but mostly by two other factors: unavoidable external accidents and the internal situation of the group itself as perceived by certain individual members. The result was that in spite of considerable differences in the demographies of the groups, there was an almost incredible uniformity in the attendance records. When these three groups were compared with two similar ones held in San Francisco, the uniformities persisted. First, in each of the five groups, the attendance over the life span of the group (8 to 33 months) was 86 per cent plus or minus 3 per cent; secondly, absences due to psychological conflicts involving certain members of each group was 21 per cent plus or minus 3 per cent; thirdly, there was a modal attendance of 100 per cent in each group at 50 per cent plus or minus 8 per cent of meetings; and there were other uniformities.

When the mean attendance of the whole group-series, 88 per cent, was compared with the mean attendance over a period of other organized group-series, an even more surprisingly uniformity emerged. The aggregate attendance records of Kiwanis Clubs in California, Nevada and Hawaii for April, May and June, 1953, was 89.7 per cent; of Rotary Clubs in the United States for October 1952, 87.8 per cent; and of the two public elementary schools and the one high school in Carmel, together with the figures for the neighboring junior college, 89.6 per cent. Thus, the range in all of these group series was only 1.9 per cent and the maximal deviation from the 88.8 per cent mean of these four figures was only 1.0 per cent. These figures have been more fully discussed elsewhere, with some detailed tabulations.*

* Berne, E.: Group attendance: clinical and theoretical considerations, *Internat. J. Group Psychotherapy* 5:392-403, 1955.

Whether or not these uniformities will persist within such a small range when a larger set of group-series is studied remains to be seen. Nevertheless, the fact is that attendance at these organized groups had a different quality from attendance at parties and other unorganized meetings. Since the "existence" of all these aggregations depends on the physical presence of the members, the quality of the attendance records cannot be overlooked and is more important than many other factors in determining the dynamics of these congeries.

It is evident that there must be important differences in the alignment of the forces which determine attendance at these three types of social aggregations—the beach, the parties and the organized groups. These differences are of considerable practical import to the traffic officers in the village, to the host who must buy and prepare refreshments and to the leadership of the organized groups (schoolteachers, therapists, etc.) who are trying to accomplish some objective. Experience soon reveals that there are also differences in the atmospheres of these three types of congeries and in the relationships of the people who make them up. Therefore, there are good grounds for questioning the advisability of including them all under the same label (such as "group"). A more discriminating approach, like that used in other sciences, yields a classification of social aggregations that has proved to be of considerable practical and theoretical interest.

The use of such a method distinguishes five types of gatherings as they are found *in situ:* masses, crowds, parties, groups and organizations. Before these are systematically defined, they will be illustrated by some "dried specimens" whose living counterparts can be found in many communities.

Let each individual in the world be given the simplest possible distinction by assigning him a number. It is convenient to have the numbering begin in Carmel, California, which will be given a fictitious population of 40. The villagers will be assigned numbers from 01 to 39, the fortieth number, 00, being reserved for the observer. Presumably, there would be no number anywhere greater than 4,000,-000,000.

In the first situation, a large number of people, villagers and visitors, are wandering at random (from 00's point of view) on the beach. At any given moment, chosen at random, 00 finds himself lost in this *mass* of people. It is evident that he will have no way of predicting what company he will find around him, since all meetings take place by chance, at least as far as he is concerned. Under these conditions, he might find that one minute his neighbors consist of 6 visitors and 2 villagers, and a few minutes later it might be just the reverse. At any moment he might find himself standing next to any number whatsoever. This happens to be literally as well as hypothetically true in Carmel because the cosmopolitan Army Language School is situated nearby. The only thing 00 can be certain of is that he is not going to encounter a number over 4,000,-000,000.

In the second situation, 00 goes for his mail to the post office at the same hour as many of the other villagers. Since the majority of transients get their mail elsewhere, they do not join this particular *crowd,* but a few may stray into it due to various circumstances. 00 knows from experience that his neighbors at any given moment on the street leading to the post office at that time of day are more likely to have numbers between 01 and 39 than between 40 and 4,000,000,000. But he does not know how much more likely; because of continually changing circumstances, there is no sure way of predicting how many visitors will be in town and how many villagers will be out of town on any particular day. Here again, all meetings presumably (says 00) take place by chance, but it can be predicted with a degree of confidence based on past experience that there will be more encounters with people of one class (villagers) than with people of all other classes. By actual count, this prediction holds good quite regularly the year round in Carmel between 10:50 and 11:10 A.M. on the block leading to the post office.

In the third situation, 00 goes to a *party* to which only even-numbered villagers have been invited; that is, he finds himself for the first time in a congeries with an external boundary. Providing everyone obeys the rules, 00 can now for the first time predict something with complete certainty: namely, that no matter where he finds himself in this aggregation, all his neighbors (if anyone comes besides himself) will be even numbers between 02 and 38 inclusive. But he cannot tell which particular members will be next to him and which will not at any given moment. (The cases in which people do not all obey the rules belong to another chapter in the theory of group dynamics and will not be discussed here.)

In the fourth situation, 00 goes to a concert given only for and by even-numbered villagers. The musicians who perform at the meeting of this *group* are all squares (4, 16 or 36), and every square is a musician. In this situation, not only is there an external boundary, but there is an internal boundary (the footlights) which separates the musicians from the audience. 00 can here predict with complete certainty that all his neighbors (if any) will be even numbers between 02 and 38, inclusive; that any squares who come will be on the stage; that all others who attend will be in the audience; and that he himself will be in a different region from the squares. He is thus able to predict with certainty which people will not be sitting next to him but is still unable to predict which individuals will be sitting next to him.

SITUATION 5: AN ORGANIZATION

123456				
00	02	04	06	08
10	12	14	16	18
20	22	24	26	28
30	32	34	36	38

In the fifth situation, 00 attends a meeting of the political *organization* of the even-numbered villagers. Those from the first ward have numbers ending in 0 and sit on the left; those from the second ward have numbers ending in 2 and sit next right; and so on, up to those from the fifth ward, the 8's, who sit on the far right. Presidents of the ward committees sit in the first row, vice-presidents in the second row, secretaries in the third row, and treasurers in the fourth row. They are distinguished by their first digits, which are 0, 1, 2 and 3, respectively. As happened at about half the meetings of this organization, everyone attended, and the situation looked like this, including the out-of-town speaker, whose number happened to be 123456.

Now 00 could predict not only everything he had been able to predict before, but many other things. He knew that the chances were even that everyone would be there; and that if this happened he would know precisely the number of each of his neighbors in every direction. For example, he knew that in such a case, the one sitting farthest from him would be 38. And whether or not everyone came, he knew such things as: no member of the second ward would be sitting next to a member of the fourth ward; no president would be sitting next to a secretary; and so on. But more than that: he could predict with certainty that if he came to a meeting of the *same* organization 50 years later, he would know the first and last digits, that is, the function and the precinct, of every one of his neighbors, and in fact of everyone in the room; and that if there were some empty chairs, he would even be able to state the distinguishing digits, the roles and the precincts of the absent incumbents. But he could not predict the intermediate digits, that is, the personal identity of each individual who might be at that meeting in the distant future when most of the serial numbers would be larger than 4,000,-000,000. This kind of predictability about people yet unborn is a special quality of organizations which is shared only in part by parties and groups.

This set of typical gatherings (with the single condition that everyone obey the rules, since the theory of infractions must be considered separately) illustrates a scheme of classification which in the writer's belief includes and distinguishes every known form of human social aggregation. The usefulness of this scheme is increased by the fact that it somewhat parallels the usual colloquial distinctions. One interesting criticism which has been offered states that being able or not being able to predict who one's neighbors will be is a trivial basis for such an important classification and indicates a straining for the exactness of physical theory at the expense of good psychological thinking. This is a curious objection, since it appears that in most cases knowing who one's neighbors will be is quite the most important factor in determining voluntary group membership, or attendance at a party, and may even be decisive in regard to choosing which beach to go to in order to wander at random or which business organization to become associated with.

* * *

In constructing definitions for mass, crowd, party, group and organization, any aggregation of people will be called a congeries, providing it contains more than two individuals. (This limitation will avoid difficulties which it is unnecessary to deal with at this time.) Any individual who appears to the observer to differ from the rest of the congeries in some meaningful respect will be spoken of as differentiated. Any congeries within which individuals appear to the observer to be undifferentiated will be spoken of as structureless. A boundary is any factor or set of factors which appears to the observer to order the congeries by delimiting a significant region. Any set of individuals surrounded by a boundary will be called an enclave. Thus, membership in an enclave is one form of differentiation. An enclave which is ordered by internal boundaries into two or more regions will be spoken of as structured. Any congeries which is neither structureless nor structured will be called unstructured.

A mass is an undifferentiated, structureless congeries. The formal characteristic of a mass is that the observer cannot predict anything about who will be neighbors at any given moment. A mass is an apparently random assortment of people with no information about each other's probable whereabouts at any future time. This is the sort of thing politicians sometimes mean when they speak of "the masses," large numbers of interchangeable individuals living all over the place. The psychological meaning of "randomness" is distinguished from other meanings of randomness. Psychologically, whatever appears to be random is treated as random; the same set of phenomena might appear to be quite orderly to another observer.

A class is a set of individuals differentiated from the mass by an apparent tendency to respond in a similar way to certain events. The members of a class may be distributed at random in the mass, and in such a case again the observer cannot predict anything about who will be neighbors at any given moment. Therefore, a class is differentiated but may be scattered through a structureless, unordered congeries. Classes are not necessarily aggregations, but aggregations are formed out of classes. "The working class" is not necessarily a social aggregation in this country, but organizations, such as unions, may be formed out of it.

A crowd is a concentration of a class. The formal characteristic of a crowd is that the observer can predict that neighbors are more likely to belong to one certain class than to all other classes. A member of a crowd headed toward a football stadium may safely assume that most of his neighbors are responding in the same interested way to the impending event; that is, they too are headed for the stadium. Thus, a crowd is a differentiated, unstructured congeries. At times, however, a crowd may take on a temporary structure, as when people who respond with interest to accidents get together on the spur of the moment to attempt a rescue; at such times, there may arise a makeshift group structure consisting of leaders, workers and spectators, until an organized rescue squad arrives.

A party is an unstructured enclave. Its characteristic is that the observer can predict with complete certainty that within its boundary all neighbors will belong to the same class, but he cannot predict which particular members will or will not be neighbors. The members of a party are differentiated by being surrounded by a boundary. Therefore, the class includes only those members of the mass who can legitimately cross that boundary. But a party is distinguished from a group or organization by the fact that it has no significant internal boundaries; that is, there is no significant differentiation within the enclave.*

A group is a structured enclave. Its characteristic is that the observer can predict that within its boundaries all neighbors will be members of the same class, and, furthermore, he can predict which of those members will be in one region of the group and which will be in another. At a certain chosen point, a group may be said to become an organization; for example, when there are more than two, three or four regions, as the observer wishes. A group may be spoken of as completely organized when there are as many regions as members and the boundaries are fully stated. In a completely organized group the observer can predict the exact position of each individual in relation to his neighbors. This is the opposite pole from the unordered mass.

In applying this system of classification, some commonly discussed congeries may be approached most profitably by breaking them up into components which it is often useful, for practical reasons, to consider separately. A group consisting of an organization plus a party or crowd may be called a performance; one person may be responsible for the organization or players and another for the crowd or audience. This applies, for example, to football games and theatrical or musical performances and even to the extempore performances of a fire brigade.

---

*At an ordinary social party the host is merely an apparatus and not a leader; he is not "significantly" differentiated from his guests.

In practice, the definition of boundaries, especially internal boundaries, is rarely accomplished by a single act but is subject to repeated clarification and ratification; that is, it takes time. Nearly every known leadership seems to act on the principle that periodic physical meetings are necessary to ensure the definition, the vitality and the survival of a group, and that it is best given a physical site such as a hall or square where it "exists." In the present theoretical classification, boundaries are not defined in a material sense. In the real world, people and enclaves of people tend to buy, rent, appropriate, enclose or delineate footage or acreage for themselves. As far as the writer's knowledge goes, no enclave exists which does not have some kind of permanent or temporary "quarters." Thus, congeries might be considered in their physical locations, so that boundaries could be defined as actual architectural or territorial limits, with at least as much reality as the "territorial" boundaries of animals.* This occasionally raises difficulties, particularly in defining the internal boundaries of small, intimate groups, but these are not insoluble.

*   *   *

This system of classification leads directly into the major problems of group structure and group dynamics.

1. The organizational structure of a group may be defined as the relationships of its regions. The simplest structure to be considered is that with only one internal boundary. This may be represented in two forms: the chord and circle and the ameboid, respectively. Each delimits three regions. In Figures 37A and 37B, E represents the external environment, and L and M two regions within the group, typically, the leadership and the membership. This basic structure of an external boundary and a single paramount internal boundary occurs regularly and may be called the major structure of any group. Any elaboration of the organization through subdivision of L and M may be called the minor structure of the group, whether L and M represent leadership and membership, company and customers, performers and audience, officers and enlisted

---

* Noble, R. C.: *The Nature of the Beast,* Garden City, N.Y., Doubleday Doran & Company, 1945.
 Grant, W. C., Jr.: *Science 121*:137, 1955.

men, doctors and patients, instructors and students or whatever is applicable to the group under consideration.

2. Group dynamics may be defined as the study of the influences acting on and through the boundaries (or boundary zones) which are the basis of the group structure. Figure 37C, in which the ameboid form is used for the sake of clarity, represents the simplest possible alignment of such influences.

E represents disorganizing influences from the external environment, which may at a given moment threaten to disrupt the external boundary. This boundary represents a certain degree of order, and, therefore, the disruptive influence E represents disorder. The integrity of the external boundary is maintained by an opposing influence labelled M_1, derived in the case illustrated from the membership. The internal boundary is likewise in a state of dynamic equilibrium under the two opposing influences L and M_2. This boundary represents significance within significance, a still higher degree of information or order. This particular diagram, Figure 37C, may be translated as follows: "The energies of the membership are divided into two components. One is devoted to maintaining the integrity of the group in the face of physical and social disruptive forces from the outside. The other is devoted to transactions with the leadership.* The energies of the leadership are devoted to transactions with the membership."

Usually, L is also divided into two components, L_1 and L_2. L_1, like M_1, is engaged with E, while L_2 is engaged with M_2. If L and M are subdivided by a minor group structure, then forces collectively called L_3 would be diverted to the boundaries of the minor structure in L, and components collectively labelled M_3 would be diverted to the boundaries of the minor structure in M. This can be easily worked out if the simple basic alignment represented in Figure 37C is clearly understood.

---

* There are certain anomalies which have to be accounted for; for example: (a) where the group objective seems to be to provoke the environment; (b) where the environment appears to strengthen the external boundary. These cases can be incorporated without damaging the principle, but this will not be attempted here.

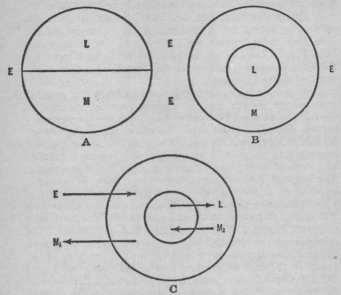

Fig. 37. Theoretical schemata.

The dynamic relationship between M_1 and E at the external boundary may be spoken of as the external group process. That between M_2 and L at the major internal boundary may be spoken of as the major internal group process. Engagements between components of L_3 or M_3 at the minor internal boundaries are part of the minor internal group process.

Glossary

This glossary contains brief definitions, for quick reference, of words used in a technical sense. Most of these refer either to structural features (components), dynamic influences (variables) or processes (functions). To locate further information about any of these terms, the general index should be consulted.

absence, accidental. An absence due to external pressure.

absence, resistance. One due to an active individual proclivity.

acceptance. Recognition by others that a member has given up some individual proclivities in favor of the group cohesion.

accessibility. Facility of communication between components, especially between lower and higher echelons.

accession. Occupation of a vacated leadership slot by predetermined rule, typically by succession.

activation. A group is activated when the constitutional sanctions become effective.

activity. The purposeful work done by a group on its material. A **constructive activity** increases order. A **destructive activity** increases disorder.

adaptability. The ability to adapt social techniques to the confronting reality.

adjustment. The process by which a member adapts his techniques and compromises his needs to the actual social possibilities.

adjustment, secondary. The final stage in the adjustment of a group imago or script.

313

Adult. A type of ego state. An aspect of the personality which is primarily engaged in objective data-processing and computing probabilities.

advantage. The gain or profit obtained from a transaction or a series of transactions. The net gain to the internal equilibrium is the **psychological advantage.** The profit in timestructuring and stimulation is the **internal social advantage** of a game, and the profit from the related pastime is the **external social advantage.**

agency. An organ or component of a group.

agent. One who exhibits some form of behavior with the intention of eliciting a response.

aggregation. Any collection of more than two people occupying a stated space. A **social aggregation** is one in which transactional stimuli evoke transactional responses. A **dissocial aggregation** is one in which no transactions or only the most trivial ones are taking place.

agitation. The collective strength of active individual proclivities.

agitator. A member who makes a direct attack on the group structure.

analysis, game. Analysis of the ulterior transactions which constitute a game.

analysis, structural. Investigation of the properties and relationships of the ego states available to a given individual.

analysis, transactional. Diagnoses of the ego states active in each individual engaged in a given transaction or set of transactions.

apparatus. The organs which ensure the survival of a group.

apparatus, external. The organ which deals with the external environment so as to minimize the threat of external pressure. Typically, it comprises procurement, preventive and combat branches.

apparatus, internal. The organ which deals with individual proclivities so as to maintain the structure of the group and the strength of the group cohesion. Typically it comprises a police branch and a morale branch.

arbitrary. Of an individual who does not adapt.

archaeopsyche. The organ of the mind that deals with Child ego states.

attitude. The predominant ego state with which the group or the individual carries on work.

attrition. Gradual destruction of the equipment and the personnel of a group by physical force.

availability. Promptness in dealing decisively with a communication.

belonging. A member belongs when he is eligible, adjusted and accepted.

boundary. A constitutional, psychological or spatial distinction between different classes of membership—an **internal boundary**—or between members and nonmembers—the **external boundary.**

boundary, closed. One which it is almost impossible to cross inwardly after the group is activated.

boundary, major internal. The constitutional, psychological or spatial distinction between the leadership and the membership.

boundary, minor internal. The constitutional, psychological or spatial distinction between different classes or individuals within the membership or leadership.

boundary, open. One that can be crossed freely in either direction.

boundary, sealed. One which it is almost impossible to cross outwardly after the group is activated.

build-up. Preparation of a group by the warrant and the group apparatus for an official act of the leader.

candidate. One who is attracted to a conditional group.

canon. The provisions which give form to the group cohesion. A regulating force consisting of the Constitution, the laws and the culture.

canon maker. A primal leader who institutes or changes canonical provisions.

canon, democratic. One with a fluid leadership, a flexible constitution and a permissive culture.

canon, primal. The original canon as instituted by the Primal Leader.

ceremonial, ceremony. A formal canonical ritual.

character, group. The abrogations of the social contract which are legitimate in a given group.

Child. A type of ego state. An aspect of the personality which functions in an archaic way.

Child, adapted. Childlike behavior which is under the dominance of Parental influence.

Child, natural. Childlike behavior which is not dominated by Parental influence.

class. A congeries or a number of individuals differentiated from a mass or from other classes by special characteristics.

cohesion. An operative force derived from the need of the members to maintain the orderly existence of a group.

congeries. Same as aggregation: **open congeries,** a mass or crowd; **structureless congeries,** a mass: **unstructured congeries,** a crowd.

constitution. A formal statement of the group canon.

contract, constitutional. The contract entered into by a member to respect the roles of the organizational structure on the terms stated in the constitution.

contract, social. An unspoken contract of etiquette which requires the members to respect each other's personas as presented in the individual structure.

crowd. An aggregation with no external boundary but with a certain degree of predictability.

culture. The material, intellectual and social influences which regulate the group work, including the technical culture, the group etiquette and the group character. Some of the most important qualities are as follows:

> **brittleness.** An unhealthy state in which the culture is overly firm and overly severe in relation to the strength of the group cohesion.
>
> **firmness-softness.** The degree of clarity with which the group culture is stated.
>
> **flabbiness.** An unhealthy state in which the culture is so soft and lax that the group cohesion is weakened in favor of individual proclivities, encouraging decay.
>
> **formality.** The degree of emphasis on etiquette; **informality,** the degree of tolerance toward character.
>
> **severity-laxity.** The degree to which sanctions are exercised: **prohibitive,** forbidding all initiative; **restrictive,** discouraging initiative; **permissive,** allowing initiative; **retributive,** with emphasis on punishment; **remunerative,** with emphasis on reward; **harsh,** with severe punishments for small transgressions; **mild,** with a minimum of punishment for large transgressions; **strict,** punishing every possible infraction; **tolerant,** overlooking infractions.

culture, technical. The economic, intellectual and technological resources available for the group work.

decay. The drifting away of members due to weak cohesion, encouraged by ideological erosion.

decomposition. The fragmentation of a group in the final stage of attrition, disruption, disorganization or decay.

delegation. An agency of the leadership which is accountable for its actions.

demeanor. The seriousness or casualness of a group.

deprivation, emotional. Lack of handling or stroking.

deprivation, sensory. Lack of sensory stimulation over a long period, giving an effect of profound monotony.

deprivation, social. Lack of opportunity for social transactions.

description. An Adult account of the Child's reactions or fantasies.

destruction. Destruction of personnel and equipment by physical force.

diagnosis. Referring to the diagnosis of an individual's ego state at a given moment. **Behavioral,** by observing the behavior of his mind and body. **Historical,** by tracing historically the prototype of the ego state. **Social,** by observing his transactions with other people. **Subjective,** by re-experiencing the prototype of the ego state.

diagrams. The 6 basic diagrams of group dynamics are:

authority, giving personal, organizational, cultural and historical influences bearing on the leadership.

dynamics, showing the state and the relationships of the group forces.

imagoes, showing the private structure of the group as it pertains to the problem.

location, showing the whereabouts and the characteristics of the personnel. If it incorporates a schedule as well, it makes a handy **discussion diagram.**

structural, showing the internal structure of the group.

transactional, giving an analysis of the pertinent transactions.

The 2 basic diagrams of social psychiatry are:

personality or structural, showing the 3 types of ego states for each personality.

transactional, showing the ego states active in each person engaged in a transaction.

differentiation. (1) The distinction of one class from another, or (2) the distinction of one individual from another in a group imago.

differentiation, degrees of. A group is **fully differentiated** when there is a one to one ratio between the number of members and the number of active slots in a given group imago. It is **overdifferentiated** when there are fewer members than there are active slots. It is **underdifferentiated** when there are more members than there are active slots.

discussion. A series of highly diluted transactions concerned with material—a pastime.

disorganization. Overpowering of the group cohesion by individual proclivities. It may result from erosion.

disruption. Overpowering of the group cohesion by external pressure. It may be gradual, by infiltration. If sudden, it may lead to decomposition through panic.

dynamics, group. The science which treats of the forces acting on the boundaries of the group structure.

dynamics, social. The science which treats of the forces acting on or within any social aggregation or between social aggregations.

dystonic. Of an individual proclivity which conflicts with the group cohesion or the group culture.

effectiveness. The capacity for getting a given amount of work done.

efficiency. The capacity for working economically.

ego state. A coherent system of feelings with its related set of behavior patterns.

enclave. An aggregation with an external boundary. It is **structured** if it has internal boundaries as well, like a group or organization, and **unstructured** if it has none, like a party.

engagement. (1) In general, any form of social action. (2) A member is engaged when he takes the initiative in his own or someone else's game.

environment, external. The universe outside the group space.

environment, internal. All contents of the group space which are not directly related to the structure of a group, including certain aspects of the members' persons.

erosion. An ideologic attack to encourage decay.

etiquette, group. Special rules, peculiar to a given group, for reinforcing the social contract.

etiquette, social. The etiquette of the community at large.

euhemerus. A dead primal leader or hero.

euhemerization. The traditional exaggeration of certain

qualities attributed to a primal leader or hero after his death.

executive. A leader or delegate who represents the canonical status quo.

existential reinforcement. The effect on the group cohesion of carrying out syntonic irreversible decisions such as those involving death.

external disruptive forces. Forces from the environment which threaten the structure of a group.

external pressure. The collective strength of external disruptive forces.

exteropsyche. The organ of the mind that deals with borrowed ego states.

extraneous fantasies. Fantasies not connected with what is going on in the group space.

extrusion. A forced movement across a boundary, usually outward.

firmness. The clarity with which the group culture is stated.

flexibility. (1) The ease with which the canon can be changed. (2) The ability of a member to modify or compromise the aims and objects of his individual proclivities in the process of adjustment.

fluidity. The degree to which the leadership depends on the will of the membership; if it tends to be self-perpetuating, it is **viscid** or **frozen.**

functions. Phases of the group process. **Incidental functions** may or may not occur in the life of a given group. **Obligatory functions** appear universally in a certain order.

gains. Synonymous with advantages.

game. A series of ulterior transactions leading progressively to a well-defined climax; a set of operations with a gimmick.

gimmick. The hidden or overlooked advantage derived from a game.

group. A social aggregation that has an external boundary and at least one internal boundary. From various viewpoints, groups fall into the following classes:

accidental. In which membership depends on an accident such as birth.

activity. One which is engaged in its activity.

ailing. One whose efficiency or effectiveness is impaired.

brittle. One which is too firm and too severe.

closed. In which membership depends on a historical condition.

— **combat.** One which is engaged in the external group process.

complex or **segmented.** An assembly of subgroups, each with its own internal organization.

complicated. One in which the authority is split between different canons: commercial and artistic in a theatre, for example.

compound or **graded.** One whose structure consists of a simple hierarchy.

conditional. In which membership depends on achievement.

constrained. One which the individual joins because he needs the perquisities that go with membership.

constructive. One whose activity is to increase order.

democratic. One with a fluid leadership, a flexible constitution and a permissive culture.

destructive. One whose activity is to increase disorder.

flabby. One which is too soft and too lax.

intense. In which the active individual proclivities are strong.

mild. In which the active individual proclivities are weak.

mother. One whose canonical authority is recognized.

obligatory. In which membership is compulsory for a certain class of people.

open. In which both membership and withdrawal are available to almost everyone at any time.

. . **optional.** In which membership depends on an invitation that can be refused.

personal. One which the individual joins so as to be with a certain class of people.

process. One which is principally engaged in the internal group process.

relaxed. In which the members feel that they are not overly threatened or frustrated.

sealed. From which it is not possible to withdraw.

simple. One which has a single leader and only one class in the membership.

strong. One whose cohesion is strong.

superstitious. One which is attempting to invoke miraculous intervention.

tense. In which the members feel frustrated or threatened.

totalitarian. One with a frozen leadership, a rigid constitution and a prohibitive culture.

Turgot. A theoretical group that devotes all its energy to one kind of work and has none left over for any other kind.

voluntary. One which can be joined by application.

weak. One whose cohesion is weak.

work. One which is principally engaged in its activity.

group imago. Any mental picture, conscious, preconscious or unconscious, of what a group is or should be like. In the course of the group process a group imago may go through the following phases:

provisional. Before entering the group or before the group is activated, based on fantasies and previous experiences with groups.

adapted. Superficially modified in accordance with the member's estimate of the confronting reality.

operative. Further modified in accordance with the member's perception of how he fits into the leader's imago.

secondarily adjusted. The final phase, in which the member relinquishes some of his own proclivities in favor of the group cohesion.

group forces. The three forces involved in the group process: pressure, agitation and cohesion.

group process. The conflicts of forces resulting from attempts to disrupt, disorganize or modify the structure of a group. The **external group process** results from conflicts between external pressure and the group cohesion and takes place at the external boundary. The **major internal group process** results from conflicts between individual proclivities and the group cohesion as represented by the leadership and takes place at the major internal boundary. The **minor group process** results from conflicts between individual proclivities and takes place at the minor internal boundaries.

group space. The psychological or spatial region enclosed by the external boundary.

group work. All work done by the members of a group in the course of the group activity and the group process. The **external group work** consists of the group activity and the external group process. The **internal group**

work consists of the major and the minor internal group processes.

harsh. A culture which imposes severe penalties for small transgressions.

hero. An individual who preserves the structure or the canon of the group in the face of strong opposition.

history. A journalistic account of past events, especially concerning the adventures of group apparatuses. Opposed to tradition.

impact. The quality in a leader which results in his image being highly charged in the group imagoes of the members or in the group tradition, usually related to his capacity for existential reinforcement of the group cohesion.

individual proclivity. The tendency of each member to behave in his own characteristic way; his need to express himself at the risk of or for the purpose of disorganizing the group.

initiative. The manifestation of an active individual proclivity. The vigor with which a member tries to change some aspect of a group in accordance with his provisional group imago.

insult. An illegitimate attack on a personality. **Rudeness** is an illegitimate attack on a persona.

intensity. (1) In group dynamics—the strength of the active individual proclivities. (2) In transactional analysis—the emotional strength of a transaction.

intimacy. The direct expression of meaningful emotions between individuals, without ulterior motives or reservations. A game-free relationship, usually between 2 people.

intrigue. A conflict involving only the minor structure of the group.

intrusion. Penetration of the major group structure by external pressure.

involvement. Participation without initiative in the games of other members.

laws. A body of formal statements confirming the constitutional details of the group etiquette, usually in strict, retributive terms.

laxity. Neglect of discipline.

leader. The leader of a group or organization is the individual who assumes or is granted by the membership a unilateral right to take the initiative and to impose sanctions and the power to enforce them. Leaders may be classified from various points of view as follows:

delegate. One who is accountable to higher authority for all his decisions.

effective. The individual whose decisions are most likely to take effect. In a small group, he can be picked out as the individual whose questions are most likely to be answered. The effective leadership lies in the individual structure.

executive. One who follows in the footsteps of the primal leader or of higher authority in reinforcing the canon.

personal. The actual living person who functions as the leader at any given moment.

primal. One who either establishes or radically changes the structure and the canon of a group in the face of strong opposition.

psychological. The individual whose image is most highly charged in the leadership slot of the private structure and to whom absolute or magical qualities may be attributed.

responsible. The individual who fills the leadership slot in the organizational structure and is constitutionally held responsible for his decisions.

sub. One who has certain independent powers but is accountable to higher authority for other decisions.

leadership hunger. The desire for someone to structure the work of the group.

manning ratio. Members (in the roster)/Slots (in the manning table). An organization or organ is **fully-manned** if this ratio is unity, **overmanned** if it is greater, and **undermanned** if it is less.

manning table. A table stating the kinds of roles in an organization and the number of slots for each.

manual. The most recent statement of the canon, particularly as it applies to the current state of the group.

mass. A structureless congeries in which no member can predict with any degree of certainty to what class of people his neighbors at any given moment will belong.

material. Anything which serves as an object for the group activity.

member. Sometimes used as a general term to denote any

individual from either the membership or the leadership.

membership. Sometimes used as a general term to include both the membership and the leadership.

membership, classes of. Membership in relation to the volition of the candidates: accidental, obligatory, optional or voluntary.

morale. Observed manifestations of a strong group cohesion.

mystique. Metaphysical doctrines included in the canon.

negotiation. The process of mutual compromise in adjusting provisional group imagoes to a projected reality. This depends on adaptation and requires flexibility.

neopsyche. The organ of the mind that deals with Adult ego states.

operative principle. The principle that an adaptable member does not take the initiative until he thinks he knows how he stands in the group imago of the leader.

organ. Structurally, a component of an organization. Dynamically, an arm of the leadership.

organization. An enclave with a relatively large number of internal boundaries.

organization, degree of. Roles (in the organizational chart)/Slots (in the manning table). An organization or organ is **completely organized** if this ratio is unity; **overorganized** if it is greater; and **underorganized** if it is less.

organization chart. A chart showing the roles provided for in the constitution and their functional relationships.

organizational identity. The functional relationships which remain constant regardless of changes in the individual structure.

palimpsest. A stage in the development of a script; an early childhood adjustment of the protocol in the natural course of growth.

Parent. A type of ego state. An aspect of the personality which reproduces the behavior and the state of mind of a parental figure.

Parental attitude. An active Parental ego state. There are two common forms. The **nurturing Parent** manifests a mothering or protective attitude. The **prejudiced Parent**

manifests a set of seemingly nonrational attitudes with a dogmatic or prohibitive tendency.

Parental influence. The restrictive influence of a latent Parent on an active Child ego state, so that the natural Child is inhibited and gives way to the adapted Child.

participation. The giving of any kind of transactional stimulus or transactional response.

party. An enclave without internal boundaries, although there may be an apparatus appropriate to the occasion.

pastime. A series of simple complementary transactions dealing with the environment and basically irrelevant to the group activity.

performance. A group activity in the presence of a party or crowd, the two taken together having special dynamic characteristics.

permeability. The degree to which the external boundary is open to crossings, giving rise to open, closed and sealed groups.

person. The individual viewed esthetically as a body and mind supplemented by cultural artifacts.

persona. The way a member chooses to present himself to the group. The way he wants to be seen.

personality. (1) The way a member is actually perceived in the private structures of the other members, regardless of how he wants to be seen or is supposed to be seen. (2) The structure represented in a personality diagram.

personnel chart. A chart showing the relationship between the organizational structure and the individual structure.

phantom. A member, and particularly a leader, whose slot is still actively charged in the private structure even though he is not actually present. Only autistic transactions are possible with a phantom.

primary components. Components whose relative or absolute strength cannot be changed without a constitutional amendment.

protocol. The original early childhood events from which palimpsests and scripts develop.

provisions, constitutional. Those statements, explicit or implicit, which seem to be essential for the activation and the survival of a group and which are found in the constitutions of all durable and effective organizations. They include the following provisions:

    autotelic. Providing machinery for changing the constitution itself.

existential. Giving the group formal existence by stating its name, duties, privileges and responsibilities.

regulatory. Providing sanctions for enforcing discipline and order in the course of the group work.

structural. Stating the boundaries and the eligibilities, particularly the major group structure.

teleologic. Stating or implying the purpose or activity.

pseudo-intimacy. Direct expression of emotions between individuals but with ulterior motives or reservations, as part of a ritual, pastime or game.

psychological level. The ulterior level of an ulterior transaction.

psychological situation. The factor which determines whether a group is personal, constrained or obligatory.

regions. The psychological or spatial areas differentiated by boundaries.

remunerative. Emphasizing rewards.

reorganization. Changing the organizational structure without necessarily altering the individual structure.

respondent. One who responds to the transactional stimulus of an agent.

retributive. Emphasizing punishments.

rigidity. (1) The degree of difficulty encountered in attempting to change the canon. (2) Excessive firmness and severity of a culture. (3) The inability of a member to resign or compromise the aims and the objects of his individual proclivities in the process of adjustment.

ritual. A predictable series of simple transactions not directly related to the group activity except in ceremonials and ceremonies.

role. (1) An element of the organizational structure. (2) The way an individual is canonically supposed to be seen and behave as part of the organizational structure; opposed to persona (individual structure) and personality (private structure). (3) An element of the script. (4) A pattern of behavior on the part of a member which meets or is designed to meet certain expectations of the other members, especially in a game or script.

schedule. A statement of the physical arrangements pertaining to the activities of an organization or group: space, time, equipment, and volume of people.

script. An unconscious life plan based on the protocol. The **script proper** is a pre-conscious derivative. The script proper goes through the same phases as the group imago in the course of the group process, yielding an **adapted script** or **adaptation,** an **operative script** and, finally, a **secondarily adjusted script.**

secondary components. Those whose strength can be changed at the discretion of the leader without a constitutional amendment.

slots. (1) An element of a group imago. (2) An element of a manning table or personnel chart.

social level. The superficial level of an ulterior transaction.

social psychiatry. The science which treats of the inner forces motivating specific transactional stimuli and responses. Distinguished from social dynamics, which treats of their outward effects.

social rituals. Those which are interspersed with the group activity as part of the group etiquette.

softness. Lack of clarity in stating the group culture.

stroke. The unit of ritualistic transactions.

stroking. Physical or symbolic stimulation as a form of recognition.

structure. The boundaries and the relationships between the components of an enclave. The structure of a group can be classified from various points of view as follows:

ameboid. In which the leadership is insulated from the external environment.

chordal. In which the leadership is in direct contact with the external environment.

individual. The specific individuals, represented by their personas, who make up the membership at a given moment.

organizational. The structure as shown in the organization chart.

private. The group imago of each member.

public. The individual and the organizational structures, which are open to public observation.

structure hunger. The need of the individual to have his time structured.

survival, effective. The ability to do organized work.

survival, ideologic. Survival of the private structure after the group ceases to exist as an effective force.

survival, physical. Survival of the personnel and the equipment of a group.

syntonic. Of an individual proclivity which reinforces the group cohesion.

tolerant. Overlooking infractions.

tradition. The selective distortion of history, especially of existential reinforcements.

transaction. The unit of social action. Transactions may be classified from various points of view, as follows:

autistic. A transaction with another member engaged in or elaborated only mentally due to inhibiting or prohibiting factors. It may be **adapted** or **unadapted** (arbitrary).

complementary. One in which the vectors are parallel.

conjunctive. Complementary or friendly.

crossed. One in which the vectors are not parallel.

diluted. One which is embedded in the group activity.

direct. One which is neither diluted nor indirect.

disjunctive. Crossed or hostile.

indirect. One in which the stimulus is directed to a third party in the hope of eliciting a response from the second party.

pure. One undiluted by irrelevancies.

simple. One which involves only a single active ego state in each of the parties concerned.

ulterior. One which involves major activity from more than one ego state in one or all of the individuals concerned. One with an ulterior motive.

work. Adult-to-Adult transactions concerning the group activity.

transactional response. The behavior of an individual who is reacting to a transactional stimulus.

transactional stimulus. Behavior, verbal or otherwise, exhibited by an individual hoping to elicit a response.

vector. A directional arrow in a transactional diagram.

warrant. The member of the group apparatus in charge of the build-up.

withdrawal. (1) Temporary or permanent physical withdrawal from a group. (2) A state in which a member is physically present but is in effect mentally absent from a gathering.

Author Index

If the same publication is mentioned repeatedly in the text, only the principal references are noted below.

329

Index of Subjects

333